WALK WITH GOD

Walk With God

25 TRUE STORIES

Rebekah Brewster

Quietbeauty Publishing

Contents

This book is dedicated to YOU,
as you dare to dream
that your future will be better than your past.

Photo Credits

The front cover photo is the Wright Brothers getting their airplane ready for the U.S. Military.

The back cover photo is Tommy Ratzlaff. We hope that this will help his memory never be forgotten. Thank you to Tommy Ratzlaff's family for allowing us to use his photo.

There are so many silent warriors out there who sacrifice for our freedoms. Many have given their lives. Tommy's photo is on the back cover to honor the memory of these silent warriors.

All photos in this book are courtesy of the Library of Congress and believed to be in the public domain unless otherwise stated. Photos have been presented in their original condition to show the history.

**Photo of the Wright Brothers learning
how to fly**

Legal Disclaimer

This book is the author's personal opinion and Christian faith.

The author does not speak for any other person or organization.

This book is history and entertainment. Stories of real people finding their way in life.

This book was written to help Christians and Bible study groups study the Bible. This book is designed to help Bible study groups start discussions about their faith.

This book is NOT legal, tax, investment or medical advice.

Any description in this book of violence or bad behavior is so we can learn from history. Please don't use anything in this book to make a bad decision or commit violence.

Throughout this book, each historical figure speaks for themselves. The opinions they express in this book do not reflect the opinions of the companies that they launched. This book is the author's personal opinion and does not reflect the opinions of the companies or people mentioned. The author does not speak for any company or person mentioned in this book.

Any use of people's names, trademarks or company names is believed to be allowed under the Fair Use of the U.S. Copyright Act and is for historical purposes because we need to know our history.

Since technology has changed over the last hundred years, please don't consider anything Henry Ford or Thomas Edison said in this book when buying your next car.

Quotes in this book are either in the public domain, used with permission, or used under Fair Use of the U.S. Copyright Act.

Even historians still disagree on what happened in history. This book has been researched by the author and believed to be true, however there are no guarantees. The author does not claim to be a historian.

Some grammar rules were broken for emphasis in writing this book. Also, since the English language has evolved considerably over the last several hundred years, some quotes have been edited to reflect modern English as well as for clarity and brevity. Now let's dive in.

1

How the Bible Changed the World

"The truth will set you free."
John 8:32b (CEV)

William Tyndale
Born about 1494
Died in 1536
From Gloucestershire, England

Long ago, in the year 1523, William Tyndale was running for his life. He had left a comfortable teaching career for a life of crime. If captured, he would face the death penalty for trying to translate the Bible into English.

Throughout the Middle Ages, most people had no opportunity to receive a formal education. Few people could afford to attend college. Tyndale was one of those few, whose family's affluent status enabled him to study at Oxford University. He graduated with a Bachelor's Degree in 1512 and then completed a Master's Degree in 1515.

According to his friend, Herman Buschius, Tyndale was *"So skilled in seven languages: Hebrew, Greek, Latin, Italian, Spanish, English, and French, that whichever one he spoke to you sounded like his native language."*[1]

No one knew that the whole reason Tyndale had studied all those languages was just to get the chance to read the Bible for himself. This was a time in history when most people had no access to the Bible. While the printing press had already been invented and the very first book printed was the Gutenberg Bible—it was printed in Latin—which most people couldn't read—or even afford to purchase.

At that time, Latin was the official language used in government proceedings, court records and official documents. It was the language of scientists, doctors, college professors and the most educated.

As Tyndale had once described, even most church services were conducted fully in Latin. *"They pray, bless, and give absolution in Latin. They only curse in English."*[2]

Latin had been the standard language of government ever since the reign of the ancient Roman Empire. By 405 A.D., the entire Bible had been translated into Latin and published by the scholar St. Jerome. This had been a long project for him, involving the consultation of various language experts and ancient Bible manuscripts.

For the next one thousand years of history, Jerome's Latin version was the only Bible available to the few who could afford a copy. When the printing press was invented in Germany, the very first book printed was that edition.

Translating the Bible into English had been declared a crime in 1408, almost one hundred years before Tyndale was born.

Two years later, in 1410, an even harsher law was passed in England. *"Anyone who should read the Scriptures in English would forfeit lands, cattle, possessions, and their life."*[3]

Why was the Bible being hidden from people? That question had haunted Tyndale for years as he studied at Oxford.

He had immersed himself in studying as much Latin, Greek and Hebrew as possible hoping that someday he could teach the Bible to the poor people. The whole reason he had completed his Bachelor's and Master's was to get access to the seminary.

In those days, you were required to complete several years of formal education in philosophy before you could even study the Bible. Tyndale described, *"In the Universities, they have ordained that no man shall look at the Bible until after he has completed eight or nine years of heathen learning, and is armed with false principles which shut out the understanding of Scripture."*[4]

After graduating from Oxford, Tyndale transferred to Cambridge University to enter seminary and become formally ordained to the ministry. But even in the seminary, Tyndale found no one wanted to read the Bible.

The apathy was astounding. Many future pastors had little interest in reading the Bible.

Tyndale tried to change that by starting a campus Bible study. While he succeeded in getting several friends to study the Bible with him, he grieved to watch too many others graduate and get appointed to lead local churches even while they lived scandalous lives. They spent more time in the local taverns than their own churches. The spiritual needs of the congregations were being neglected. With a true pastor's heart, Tyndale knew he had to do something about it.

After finishing his education, he moved back home and accepted the job of tutoring the children of Sir John Walsh, Knight of Gloucester. Meanwhile, his free time was devoted to going to the local towns and ministering to the people. Night after night, crowds gathered around him for hours as he stood on the street corner and opened his Bible to read to them.

That quickly got him in trouble with local authorities. For breaking the law, Tyndale was summoned before the Chancellor.

"He threatened me harshly, insulting me as though I was a dog,"[5] Tyndale described. But to everyone's surprise he was promptly released.

He could not be put on trial because the whole town had refused to testify against him. Tyndale returned home and continued teaching but couldn't stay out of trouble.

Living in the home of Sir John Walsh, Tyndale was invited to eat at the Knight's table. Sir Walsh enjoyed entertaining, often throwing big dinner parties.

Many wealthy and powerful leaders came from far and wide to enjoy these parties. The conversations around the dinner table were sometimes intense as they discussed the issues of the day.

One day the conversation at the table exploded when Tyndale asked the visiting guest, a distinguished religious leader, what he thought about the Bible. The guest replied that the Bible really didn't matter because, *"We would be better without God's law than the Pope's."*[6]

That was the last straw for Tyndale. Years of helplessly watching the people getting blocked from hearing the Bible made Tyndale explode in anger.

Glaring at that religious leader he thundered back, *"I defy the Pope and all his laws. If God spares my life long enough, I will make the boy who drives the plow, know more of the Bible than you do."*[7]

The other people at the table gasped in horror. Tyndale had just signed his own death warrant. Didn't he know what the Inquisition did to heretics?

Tyndale's life was quickly turned upside down. Never again would he enjoy the peace and quiet of a private life. Now he had to get out of town before his defiance was reported to the authorities. To protect his friends, the Walsh family, Tyndale left right away before they could get in trouble for what he had said. Fortunately, he had the right people helping him.

From his time preaching in the streets, Tyndale had gotten to know the local merchants. On the surface, these merchants specialized in selling the finest wool used for making expensive clothes. On the sly, they were smuggling forbidden books into the country.

Organizing themselves into a powerful group known as the Christian Brethren, they were hungry to learn as much as they could about God.

They had even persuaded Tyndale to teach a special Bible study just for them. When Tyndale decided to get out of town quickly, they had the right connections to help him escape. In a time when most people never traveled far from their birthplace, these merchants knew all the trade routes out of the area.

With some help from Sir Walsh, they got Tyndale safely to London. There a very powerful merchant, Sir Humphrey Monmouth, took Tyndale into his home. For the next year, under the protection of Sir Monmouth, Tyndale was able to start fulfilling his lifelong dream of translating the Bible into the language that the common people could understand—English.

The timing was perfect.

Just a few years earlier, in 1520, Pope Leo X had given his blessing to the printing of the Bible in its original languages.

This special edition, known as the Polygot, had been a labor of love by a Catholic Cardinal in Spain. Cherishing the Bible so much that he wanted people to be able to study the Bible in its original texts, he reached into his own pockets to publish it. This was a side by side edition, showing the Bible text in Hebrew, Greek, Latin and even the ancient Aramaic. Included were grammar dictionaries so readers could better understand the ancient text.

Also published just in time to help Tyndale was the Greek New Testament by Erasmus.

Erasmus had been born from a relationship between a priest and his housekeeper. Growing up hungry to know God, he had gone to college and specialized in studying Greek so he could better understand the Bible. He had become a well known college professor, teaching Greek at Cambridge University and writing several textbooks which Tyndale had studied. After years of studying ancient manuscripts of the Bible, in 1516, he published a groundbreaking New Testament in Greek that presented the Bible as it had been written.

What made both of these editions so remarkable was that after one thousand years of having one Latin version of the Bible available to scholars, now they could read the Bible in its original languages. Without these books, Tyndale would have had great difficulty trying to access ancient Bible manuscripts locked away in monasteries. Now with these scholarly books, Tyndale had everything he needed to bring the Bible to life. As he poured each day and night into this project, little did he know the massive influence he would have on the English Language.

At the time, English was a very rough language. There was no English dictionary. There wasn't even proper spellings for the raw words spoken on the street. So drawing upon his years of studying languages, Tyndale invented the English words that we speak today. Words like seashore, wave, network, scapegoat, brokenhearted, viper, intercession, uproar, longed and Thanksgiving.[8]

Putting these words together, Tyndale created what would become some of the most well known phrases of the Bible including:

"Let there be light."

"Ask and it shall be given."

"Signs of the times."

"Eat, drink and be merry."

"Fight the good fight."

"God is love."

"Be strong in the Lord"

"Behold, I stand at the door and knock."

"The just shall live by faith."

"I am the light of the world."[9]

Tyndale's wording would stand the test of time, with many future editions of the Bible keeping his work. Years later when the King James version was produced—eighty-three percent had been directly copied from Tyndale.[10]

Yet Tyndale himself never knew the difference he would make. He just wanted to put the Bible into the hands of the people.

In his own words he would later describe how the time he had spent preaching in the streets had inspired him.

"What drove me to translate the New Testament was the experience of realizing it was impossible to establish the people in truth, unless they had a chance to read the Bible for themselves."[11]

As Tyndale worked day and night, Sir Monmouth watched him and was impressed at how focused he was on his work, hardly even taking a break to eat.

Just as Tyndale was making major progress, the authorities heard about what he was doing.

Fortunately, Sir Monmouth would be warned in time to smuggle Tyndale out of England, sending him to Germany where he could get help from friends of Martin Luther.

In 1517, Luther had sent shock waves across Europe with his Ninety-Five Thesis. After years of trying to be good enough as a monk to earn his salvation, reading the Bible changed his life. Discovering Romans 1:17 made him realize that salvation was the free gift of God. He published explosive books challenging the major church theology of that time and declaring that the Bible was the final authority for all believers.

That got him in trouble. Luther was dragged before the authorities of Germany where he defended himself by saying, *"Unless I am convinced by Scripture or by clear reason, I will not recant. Here I stand, I can do no other. My conscience is captive to the Word of God."*[12]

To everyone's surprise, Luther's defense converted several powerful leaders of Germany who had watched the proceedings. They protected Luther, enabling him to continue publishing books. Those books quickly spread around the world. As more people began to discover the grace of God, the authorities moved quickly to crush that idea.

In 1521, King Henry VIII of England wrote a long rebuke to Luther, labeling him as the *"common enemy."* Then King Henry gave orders to, *"Extinguish the cursed sect of Luther,"* saying, *"Shed no blood if it can be avoided; but if this heretical doctrine lasts, shed it without hesitation."*[13]

When the Pope heard of this loyalty, he rewarded King Henry with the royal title of *"Defender of the Faith."*[14]

This was happening just as Tyndale was realizing *"There was no place in all England"*[15] for him to work on the Bible. Yet he knew exactly where to go.

The merchants got Tyndale safely to Germany. They kept him moving from place to place, always trying to stay one step ahead of the authorities. Along the way he visited and was greatly encouraged by Martin Luther.

Eventually Tyndale settled in the city of Cologne, Germany. There he finished translating the New Testament in 1525.

Two years after running for his life, Tyndale had finally completed his lifelong dream to give the common people the chance to read the Bible. But where would he find a printer willing to take the risk when many printers were closely watched by the authorities? Even with many leaders of Germany protecting Luther, the eyes and ears of other authorities were still watching. Tyndale had to proceed carefully. With some more help from the merchants, Tyndale found Peter Quentell who felt it was an honor to print six thousand copies of the Bible in English.

As the work began, Quentell's employees were thrilled that they were about to turn the world upside down. Unfortunately they did their bragging at the local tavern. Someone overheard and notified authorities. The authorities moved quickly. Just when the printing reached the halfway point, the presses were shut down.

Tyndale had gotten away. Fortunately he had been warned just in time to escape by ship to the city of Worms, Germany where many followers of Luther lived. There, another printer published three thousand copies of Tyndale's New Testament. This time Tyndale made the copies much smaller and easier to hide.

His merchant friends smuggled these Bibles into England by ship, hidden in bales of cloth. Those copies sold out in record time.

People were so hungry for the Bible that copies of it were literally getting torn apart.

Pages would get ripped out of the Bible and sold for exorbitant amounts to people desperate to read a few verses of Scripture. Other printers saw this massive demand only growing and began printing bootleg copies of Tyndale's Bible.

More smugglers got involved. Within months a massive wave of Bibles was flooding London.

The authorities were furious. Every effort was made to find these Bibles and destroy all copies. Anyone caught in possession of one was considered automatically guilty of the death penalty.

Cracking down on the smugglers, law enforcement was sent to raid various locations and find these Bibles. Ships entering England were thoroughly searched. Still many Bibles got through with the merchants finding better methods of concealment.

Something had to be done. As the Bible spread across England, the Bishop of London took matters into his own hands.

On October 24, 1526, he issued a public notice warning against the *"two thousand errors"* in this new Bible. He ordered everyone to turn over their copy for destruction to prevent the spread of this *"poison."*[16]

This poison was really serious. To counter Tyndale's influence, Sir Thomas More was commissioned to write the rebuttal. Examining Tyndale's Bible, More found lots of *"errors"* such as translating *"repent"* instead of *"do penance"* and *"knowledge"* instead of *"confession."*[17]

Tyndale had translated the Greek word *"ekklesia"* as *"congregation"* instead of *"church,"* implying that local groups of believers could gather to worship the Lord.

Even worse, he had also completely changed the meaning of the love chapter in 1Corinthians 13 by translating *"love"* instead of *"charity"* causing church authorities to worry that donations might plummet.[18]

This was a huge threat to hundreds of years of church tradition. Sir More wrote extensively, trying to make the people believe that Tyndale was a heretic.

When Tyndale heard about it, he replied, *"God is my witness, one day I will stand before our Lord Jesus and say that I never altered even one syllable of the Bible. Nor would I ever, even if every bit of money, fame, and pleasure in the world were offered to me."*[19]

Then Tyndale carefully studied Sir More's arguments and wrote hundreds of pages in reply. What bothered him the most was the idea that the common people couldn't understand the Bible for themselves.

Answering that argument, he wrote, *"Will you resist God? Will you forbid God from giving His Spirit to the laymen as well as you? Didn't God make the English language? Why do you forbid God to speak in English as well as Latin?"*[20]

By this time Tyndale had settled in Antwerp (present day Belgium). This was a safe place for him. Antwerp had a law that residents couldn't be arrested in their own homes. Here Tyndale was able to continue his work in peace while also mingling freely with the people.

The merchants continued helping him. Once again he was able to teach a special Bible study for them.

News quickly spread to England that Tyndale was seen living openly in Antwerp. When the King of England heard, he sent people to persuade Tyndale to return to England under the protection of the King. It was a compelling offer. This was the first time in years that Tyndale could return home to a comfortable life.

He turned it down. Telling the messengers that he would only return to England if the Bible was legalized, he said, *"I don't feel the poverty, loneliness, hunger, cold, or danger I endure, because of the hope that this labor will honor God and serve my country."[21]*

The work continued with Tyndale focusing on translating the Old Testament.

Knowing that it was a massive project, he tried to focus on small parts he could finish faster and get into the people's hands. After completing Genesis to Deuteronomy, Tyndale arranged for publication with a printer in Holland, figuring he could finish the rest later.

But when Tyndale took his papers and sailed from Antwerp to Holland, there was a massive shipwreck. All of his papers were lost at sea, leaving him to start over from scratch. Devastated by this delay, Tyndale settled in Holland, living with a widow named Margaret Van Emmerson. She financially supported him while he rebuilt his translation of Genesis to Deuteronomy.

After publishing that edition in 1530, Tyndale moved back to Antwerp where he lived with Thomas Poyntz.

Poyntz was related to Lady Walsh, the wife of Sir John Walsh. He was also a merchant that supported Tyndale. His home became a safe place for Tyndale to continue on his work. Yet while Tyndale was safe, his friends were still risking their lives to continue the work.

John Frith had been one of Tyndale's closest friends ever since they had met while studying at Cambridge. Through the years they had stayed in touch. Frith did everything he could to help distribute Tyndale's Bibles. Frith also published several of his own pamphlets about the Bible. That would cost him dearly. Frith was caught, thrown in jail and put on trial for heresy.

Tyndale was devastated to learn of the news. Knowing that Frith was facing the death penalty, Tyndale wrote him this letter:

"Fear not men that threaten, nor trust men that flatter, but trust the God that keeps His Word. Your cause is Christ's Gospel, a light that must be fed with the blood of faith. God will carry you through thick and thin for His truth's sake, even in spite of all your enemies. Commit yourself wholly and only to your loving Father God, then shall His power make you strong."[22]

When Frith's trial began, he was pressured to betray the people helping him. Frith didn't flinch. Staring down the judges, he boldly replied, *"The Word of God boils in my body like a fervent fire. Tyndale and I will never stop until the Bible in English is being learned by the poor commoners."*[23]

That was all they needed to hear for conviction. Frith was sentenced to the death penalty and executed on July 4, 1533.

Meanwhile, the authorities were closing in on Tyndale. Large rewards were offered to anyone willing to betray him. This caught the attention of a bounty hunter named Henry Phillips.

Disguising himself as a good Christian, Phillips went to Antwerp and secretly infiltrated the merchants who supported Tyndale.

These merchants were still paying Tyndale's expenses. Tyndale was frequently the guest of honor at their dinners and parties. So Phillips got to know these merchants well, working his way into the group until he had become a fixture in their inner circle.

That opened the door for him to befriend Tyndale directly. Phillips even moved next door to where Tyndale lived. Soon he was coming over for dinner at the Poyntz house. To everyone, he seemed to be the life of the party.

Everyone was charmed by him, except Poyntz who kept getting a bad feeling. Something wasn't right. Finally, Poyntz told Tyndale to stay away from Phillips.

Several weeks later, while Poyntz was out of town on business, Phillips made his move. He invited Tyndale out to a nice dinner where law enforcement was lying in wait. Late that night, Tyndale showed up for dinner, only to be arrested and dragged away. The chase had finally ended.

For the next year and a half, Tyndale was locked away in prison. Even there he continued the work, writing to his friends to bring him warm clothes, candles and the books he needed to translate the Old Testament. He also kept sharing the Gospel with everyone he met, until the jailor and several others had given their lives to the Lord. But time was running out for him. Now he had to stand before church authorities to answer for his crimes.

A special religious court was convened to put Tyndale on trial for heresy. Everything was done in Latin.

Not a word of English was spoken at the trial, lest the servants hear what they were debating. For evidence, the books Tyndale had written to help people grow in their faith were translated from English to Latin and used against him.

Tyndale declined the court appointed attorney and represented himself.

He stood before the panel of judges, which had been selected from the most highly educated theologians. They hated everything about him. The one that hated him the most was Ruward Tapper, Chancellor of the University of Louvain.

Ruward was actually heard saying, *"It doesn't matter whether the people that die for religion are guilty or innocent. It only matters that we terrify the common people by making a public example of punishing some highly educated men."*[24]

The trial dragged on and on for months with countless hours being spent debating theology such as whether salvation could be earned with good deeds. Back and forth it went with Tyndale arguing, *"It is the grace of God that does good works through us. Without Him we can do nothing. We are tools in God's hands just like the stone and sword with which David killed Goliath."*[25]

It didn't matter what Tyndale said. When it was finally all said and done, the trial ended exactly the way everyone knew it would.

Tyndale was convicted of heresy, stripped of his ministry ordination and sentenced to death.

Remaining defiant to the end, Tyndale kept the same boldness that he had put into all his writings. He had once written, *"Do the worst you can unto me. Your unkindness is nothing compared to the kindness of Christ. As long as Christ is in my heart I will love you because He asks me to."*[26]

All this time the merchants had been desperately trying to save his life. They appealed to the King of England, begging him to intervene. Poyntz even contacted all his friends in high places, pleading with them to do something. *"The death of this man would be a great hindrance to the Gospel."*[27]

The end came way too quickly. Despite everyone's efforts to save him, Tyndale was put to death on October 6, 1536. His last words were *"Lord, open the King of England's eyes."*[28]

Yet even when they killed him, they could not kill Tyndale's dream. Within months, the Bible would be legalized in England.

It started with Tyndale's merchant friends who were still smuggling the Bible into England.

When some of them were caught and thrown in prison, Queen Anne Boleyn personally intervened, granting a royal pardon.

They thanked her by producing a very elaborate special edition of Tyndale's New Testament with her coat of arms inscribed on the cover.

She was delighted to receive it. In the weeks that followed, she boldly walked around the palace with the forbidden book. She also devoured Tyndale's other book, *The Obedience of a Christian Man.*

In this book, Tyndale had made the case for legalizing the Bible.

He wrote, *"Christ commands us to search the Scriptures (John 5:39)."*

"Yet they say that Scripture is too hard, that you would never understand it without first learning philosophy and Aristotle. If that's true, then why did Paul warn us in Colossians 2:8, 'Beware lest anyone spoil you through philosophy and the traditions of men and not after Christ?'"

"They say that Scripture is too hard to understand without the scholars. But these scholars contradict each other."

"When they meet together they argue and brawl. One follows St. Thomas, another Bonaventure, Brugot, Dorbel, etc."

"In such diversity of spirits, how do I know who lies and who says the truth? By God's Word. But how can I, when you won't let me see Scripture?"

"If I must first believe the scholar, then the scholar is always right and truth depends on him. That's like trying to measure the measuring stick with the cloth. Here's twenty pieces of cloth, all different sizes. How do I know what size they are without a measuring stick? How do we know that St. Augustine wrote many things amiss? By the Scriptures, as he himself later discovered."

Then he wrote about his years in college where the seminary students wasted time arguing over little things like whether wearing a gray or blue coat would please God more.

"Man's wisdom divides, scatters, and makes sects. One man says its best to wear a white coat to serve God in, another says gray, another blue and a hundred thousand like things. Man's wisdom is plain idolatry. Christ warned that false prophets could come. Without Scripture, how do I know if they are trying to teach or deceive?"

"How can they say that they are helping your soul by forbidding the Bible when they let you read all these other books which corrupt your mind and rob you of Christ?"[29]

The Queen loved this book, filling her copy with personal notes. Then wanting to share what she was learning with a close friend, she loaned it to her maid, the Lady Gaynsford. That Lady was being courted by Mr. Zouch who also became interested in reading Tyndale's book. When Mr. Zouch picked up the book, he couldn't put it down. But when he was caught reading the book by the palace Cardinal, the book was confiscated.

Lady Gaynsford was devastated to learn the book she had borrowed was gone. She begged the Queen for forgiveness. Queen Anne didn't get mad. She only replied, "That will be the dearest book that the Cardinal ever took away."[30]

Then Queen Anne marched straight to her husband, King Henry VIII. She implored him to command the return of her book. He did. Then she asked him to read it.

As King Henry VIII began to read Tyndale's book, the Cardinal came in to see the King to protest the spread of Tyndale's "heresy."

The King rolled his eyes. Why was he getting told what to do? Wasn't he the King? Besides he had never liked that Cardinal anyway. Ordering the Cardinal to leave, the King declared, *"This book is for me and all Kings to read."*[31] Then he borrowed the Queen's copy of Tyndale's New Testament.

That was the start of one of the most radical shifts in history. King Henry would do the right thing—legalize the Bible—for all the wrong reasons.

At the time, King Henry was desperate for a male heir to his throne. After his first wife, Catherine of Aragon, had suffered through unsuccessful pregnancies, he decided to abandon her. Blaming her for everything, he appealed to the Pope for an annulment to the marriage on the basis of no male heir.

The real reason was because he had his eye on another woman. When the Pope refused to grant the annulment, King Henry banished Catherine of Aragon and secretly married Anne Boleyn. Yet without having the Pope's blessing, King Henry faced the possibility that any children born from his second marriage would not be qualified to sit on the throne.

Tyndale had publicly challenged King Henry's unfaithfulness to Queen Catherine which had angered the King and might have been why the King failed to save Tyndale's life. Yet reading Tyndale's other book, *Obedience*, the King saw something that he could use to protect his royal power.

In the book, Tyndale had shown from Scripture how civil government was a lawful power ordained by God. Therefore the King could make decisions about his nation without asking permission from anyone. That was a radical idea in a time when people thought you had to earn your salvation by doing good works.

Tyndale had also challenged hundreds of years of tradition by writing: *"God has promised the merits of Christ to all those who repent."* So how could anyone else have the *"Power to sell that which God gives freely?"*[32]

Reading that book was part of a long sequence of events that resulted in King Henry cutting all ties with the Church.

Then King Henry started his own church denomination, declaring himself as the final authority of all churches in England and seizing control of all church property.

All of England was ordered to swear allegiance to *The Succession Act,* which protected the right of the King to choose his heir to the throne.

The King ordered new articles of faith written for the Church of England stating, *"Bishops and Pastors are commanded to inform the people that grace and remission of sin only comes from God through our Savior Jesus. There is no other mediator."*[33]

Then in order to consolidate his power over England, King Henry ordered the Bible to be printed in English, commissioning one of Tyndale's friends, Myles Coverdale, to do it.

The first ever authorized English copy of the Bible was printed in 1537. It relied heavily on Tyndale's work, including what he had been able to translate of the Old Testament before running out of time. A copy was placed in every church in England. Orders were given in the King's name that the common people were allowed to come to church and read the Bible so *"They may better know their duties to God, to their sovereign Lord the King, and to their neighbor."*[34]

The clergy was even warned by the King's orders, *"Not to discourage any man privately or publicly from hearing the Bible. But you shall motivate every person to read it."*[35]

Yet while promoting the Bible, King Henry would not follow it. He continued having affairs, marrying more wives, and ruthlessly disposing of them. After three years of marriage to Anne Boleyn, he accused her of treason. At her execution, she said only good things about her husband and told the executioner she forgave him. In the end, history would remember King Henry VIII for hurting his wives.

Yet history would forget how the Bible was rapidly spreading. By the time that King Henry VIII gave his final speech to Parliament in 1545, the Bible had become so widely circulated that the King noted it was being discussed, debated and even sung *"In every alehouse and tavern."*[36]

Tyndale's dream would come true way beyond anything he could have imagined. Within fifty years after his death, the Catholic Church would publish the Bible in English.

Generation after generation of children would grow up knowing far more of the Bible than those religious leaders who had once so bitterly opposed Tyndale.

History would prove what Tyndale had understood. That it was important for people to know the Bible for themselves because it sets them free. The entire course of history was changed as the common people began to read the Bible. Once they knew what God had actually said, they began to challenge every church tradition that didn't follow the Bible. This caused the world to move from the Dark Ages into the period of Enlightenment where humanity began to stand up for their civil rights. More than anything else, people began to challenge the ancient idea that any one person could hold absolute power.

In 1559, England passed a law making weekly church attendance mandatory at the official Church of England. Violators would be fined. No one could question it, because the monarchy was considered still the final authority of the church. People protested by publishing books like, *An Admonition to the Parliament*, which quoted from the Bible that only Jesus is the true head of the church.

When King James I came to power, he received a petition from one thousand British pastors requesting specific changes in the Church of England to purify it according to the Bible. He rejected their ideas but granted their request for an updated Bible translation.

King James felt that a new Bible translation was necessary because he was concerned about the rising popularity of the Geneva Bible translation. That translation had been produced by Protestants fleeing religious persecution in Europe. It disturbed King James because it used the word *"tyrant"* hundreds of times and had too many footnotes about the rights of the people.

King James wanted a Bible translation more supportive of his ideas. In a 1609 speech to Parliament, he explained no one could teach him anything or question his decisions because what he wanted to do was God's will. The people's duty was *"Not to interfere with such ancient rights of mine."*[37]

One British church congregation disagreed. In the early 1600's, they left the official Church of England to form their own congregation.

One of them, William Bradford described why. *"As the Lord's free people. They had entered into covenant to walk with God according to the Bible no matter what it would cost them."*[38]

Yet forming a new church congregation got them in trouble. Many of their members, including women and children, were thrown in jail. That sparked a massive public outcry which led to their release.

Still King James vowed, *"I will make them conform."*[39] Authorities continued harassing them until they had no choice but to flee the country. Or so they tried. Back then, no one could leave England without permission from the King. The ship captain they hired for transport betrayed them. Yet again they were thrown in prison. Weeks later when they were released, they tried again. And again. And again. Standing on 2Timothy 1:12 they persevered until making it safely to Holland.

There life was much harder than they had expected. The only jobs they could find were low paying with long hours. Harsh conditions aged everyone quickly. Their children suffered the most. Within a few years they had decided, *"Prison in England was better than freedom under these afflictions in Holland."*[40]

After fasting and praying for God's guidance, they decided to follow Hebrews 11:13-16 and move someplace they had never been before. Boarding the Mayflower, they entered history known as the Pilgrims.

When they reached America, on November 11, 1620, they signed the Mayflower Compact, creating self-government in America, *"For the glory of God and advancement of the Christian faith."*[41]

Their settlement would rapidly grow as more families moved to America, looking for freedom.

In 1647, Massachusetts launched the first public school system in America to teach the children to read so they could read the Bible.

The actual text of the law stated: *"The chief project of that old deceiver satan is to keep people from knowing the Bible, by keeping the Bible in an unknown language, and keeping people from learning to read so that religious sounding deceivers could cloud the true knowledge and meaning."*

"The Lord is assisting our efforts to prevent education from being buried in the graves of our ancestors. It is ordered by the authority of this court that every town that the Lord has increased to fifty households shall appoint a paid schoolteacher to teach all such children to read and write."[42]

By 1682, the city of Boston had gotten in trouble with England. American pastors taught directly from the Bible the seeds of a free spirit. News quickly spread back to England that the people of Boston were no longer swearing the oath of loyalty to the King. That was not what King Charles II wanted to hear. He sent orders back to Boston demanding that the Massachusetts colony, *"Make a full submission and entire resignation of their charter to his pleasure."[43]*

British soldiers were sent to Boston to enforce the King's wishes. When British Colonel Percy Kirk stood ready with five thousand soldiers to brutally crush any rebellion, the people of Boston met together to discuss their next move.

Standing on Psalm 118:8 and 2 Samuel 24:14, they decided,

"Blind obedience is sin and highly displeasing to the King of Kings. Better to suffer than to sin. Better to trust God than put confidence in princes. If we suffer because we dare not comply with the wills of men against the will of God, we suffer for a good cause and shall be remembered as martyrs by the next generation."[44]

Just as word of their defiance reached England, King Charles II suddenly died in 1685. No sooner had King James II come to power and tried to enforce his power over America, than he was overthrown by England's own Glorious Revolution in 1689. America would enjoy peace until the reign of King George III.

When America declared independence in 1776, Benjamin Franklin suggested to Thomas Jefferson that the new national motto should show the Bible story of Moses parting the Red Sea, while Pharaoh's chariot was overwhelmed by the water, and include the words *"Rebellion to tyrants is obedience to God."*

Thomas Jefferson thought the motto should reflect the Israelites being led through the wilderness with the cloud by day and pillar of fire by night.[45]

When the British Parliament debated how to deal with the American revolt they were surprised to hear this report from a British official: *"If you ask an American who is his master, he will tell you he has none but Jesus Christ."*[46]

When British troops came and punished Boston by blockading their port, William Prescott smuggled supplies across the enemy lines to keep the people from starving. Encouraging sinking hearts he reminded everyone, *"We must all sink or swim together. Let us all be of one heart and stand fast in the liberty wherewith Christ has made us free (Galatians 5:1)."*[47]

Thousands of men volunteered for America's first military after reading Thomas Paine's book, *Common Sense,* which explained why civil government could function without a king. That was a revolutionary idea in a time when most people thought that nations would collapse into anarchy without a king to maintain law and order.

In that book, Paine argued straight from the Bible that while nations needed to be governed by honest leaders, *"For all men being originally equals, no one by birth could have a right to set up his own family in perpetual preference to all others forever. Neither can it be defended on the authority of scripture. For the will of the Almighty as declared by Gideon (Judges 8:23), and the prophet Samuel (1Samuel 8:7-18), expressly disapproves of government by Kings."*[48]

Paine noted that even when Jesus said *"Render unto Caesar the things that are Caesar's"* that was teaching respect for civil authority without authorizing the idea of absolute power.

Common Sense became one of the most widely read books in America, selling over a hundred thousand copies. It was read aloud in many taverns and town hall meetings. George Washington himself had the entire book read aloud to the military so that they could understand why America had declared independence.

Thomas Paine wasn't the only one teaching political science from Bible verses. This radical theology of human rights spread like wildfire from pulpit to pulpit as American pastors shredded generations of theological tradition with the Bible.

Boston pastor Jonathan Mayhew taught from 2Corinthians 3:17, *"Where the Spirit of the Lord is, there is liberty."*

"Who knows but someday after our liberties are established we may have the honor to save Britain herself from ruin!"[49]

Founding Father John Adams wrote that copies of this colonial sermon *"Were read by everybody. This minister was well known in both Europe and America, but he threw all the weight of his fame into serving his country until his death."*[50]

As the war continued, more soldiers were needed. One Sunday morning, a Lutheran Pastor in Virginia, Peter Mulhenburg, figured out how to recruit soldiers from his own congregation.

Standing in his pulpit, he preached a powerful sermon about how according to Ecclesiastes 3:8, *"The Bible says that there's a time to preach and a time to pray, but those times have passed away. Now the time has come to fight."*[51]

At the end of the sermon, he ripped off his clergy robes to *"Reveal to the startled congregation the uniform of a Colonel in the Continental Army."*[52] He announced that this was his last sermon as he was leaving to report for military duty. Would anyone like to come with him?

Three hundred men from his congregation volunteered to follow him as he left that afternoon to join General Washington's troops. He would be promoted to Major General and commissioned to lead the 8th Virginia Regiment. After the war, he was elected to serve in the first U.S. Senate.

As America became a nation, more and more generations of children were raised reading the Bible for themselves. Many of those children would grow up to change the world.

President Abraham Lincoln, who grew up reading the Bible while working on the farm, declared it was *"The best gift God has given to man. But for it, we could not know right from wrong."*[53]

Through Genesis 3:19, Isaiah 10:1, and Luke 11:17, he explained to the nation why slavery had to be destroyed.

Lincoln referenced the Bible so often that during the famous Lincoln/Douglas debates, Douglas accused Lincoln of *"A proneness for quoting Scripture."*

Lincoln replied with the parable of the shepherd going after the lost sheep. Then he said that Douglas was the lost sheep who needed to *"repent"* for promoting slavery.

Here's how Lincoln made the Biblical case against slavery:

- Even if slavery was legal—it was still the type of wicked law God condemns in Isaiah 10:1.
- Lincoln: *"Can we afford to sin any more deeply against human liberty? It is written, 'Woe unto them that decree unrighteous decrees.'"*
- The evil had to be destroyed before it destroyed the nation.
- Lincoln: *"A House Divided against itself could not stand. (Luke 11:17) I believe this government cannot endure permanently half slave and half free. It will become all one thing or the other."*
- According to Genesis 3:19, slavery should not exist because slaves had the same right to profit from their own labor as everyone else.
- Lincoln: *"He is my equal and the equal of every man in the same right to eat the bread which his own hand earns. It may seem strange that any men should dare to ask a just God's assistance in wringing their bread from the sweat of other men's faces."*
- Society had a moral obligation to protect the rights of its people.
- Lincoln: *"Jesus said, 'Be perfect as your Father in Heaven is perfect.' (Matthew 5:48) Now I suppose that the Savior did not expect any human could be as perfect as God. But he set that up as a standard and he who did most towards reaching that standard attained the highest degree of moral perfection. So I say in relation to the principle that all men are created equal—let it be as nearly reached as we can."*
- That the injustice of slavery brought God's judgment.
- Lincoln: *"Those who deny freedom to others, don't deserve it for themselves and under a just God cannot long retain it."*

Later when the Civil War was ripping the nation apart, Lincoln again turned to Scripture to comfort the people. His second inaugural address referenced at least eight different verses. Here's the part that people remembered the most:

"Fervently we pray that the scourge of war would pass away. Yet if God wills that it continue, until all the wealth piled by the bondman's unpaid 250 years of toil be sunk, and every drop of blood drawn by the lash is paid by another drawn by the sword, then as it was said two thousand years ago, it still must be said, 'The judgments of God are true and righteous (Psalms 19:9)." [54]

The Emancipation Proclamation was signed by Secretary of State William Seward, who insisted, *"The whole hope of human progress is suspended on the ever growing influence of the Bible."* [55]

After the Civil War, Booker T. Washington saw classrooms flooded with eager students as newly freed slaves were finally able to attend school. *"As fast as any kind of teachers could be secured, not only were day schools filled but night schools as well. The great ambition of the older people was to try to learn to read the Bible before they died. With this goal, men and women who were fifty or seventy-five years old would often be found in the night school."* [56]

Many schools would use the famous dictionary written by Noah Webster who believed, *"Education is useless without the Bible."* [57] Webster also produced a modern translation of the Bible in 1833.

Many other famous Americans would cherish the Bible including people like the famous oil baron, Rockefeller.

Before he became the most financially successful person in American history, he had once been one of those boys working on the farm and reading the Bible.

He would grow up to launch one of the largest companies in the world yet still have time to teach an adult Sunday School class at his church for many years.

In one of those lessons, he taught the class why reading the Bible was so important. *"Christ is to be studied. We should learn more of His Word and learn of His love for us; the greatness of His loving sacrifice which led Him to the cross that we, His brothers, might live with Him forever."* [58]

Another famous American businessman, A. A. Hyde who pioneered the cold medicine industry, wrote about how the Bible had helped him. He said, *"Deep and intimate knowledge of the Bible tends to produce reason and judgment far beyond any other book. It also creates courage to motivate life."*[59]

One of the greatest scientific minds in American history, Dr. George Washington Carver quoted directly from the Bible when he testified before Congress. As the Congressmen asked him how he had been able to invent so many helpful products, Dr. Carver described how those answers were found in the Bible.[60]

Knowing the Bible would also inspire Rosa Parks when she sat down on a bus and brought a nation to its feet.

She wrote that reading the Bible *"Helped me in my day-to-day problems. From my upbringing and the Bible, I learned people should stand up for rights like the children of Israel stood up to the Pharaoh."*[61]

The rest is history.

Today very few original copies of Tyndale's New Testament remain. Queen Anne's copy now sits in a museum, reminding everyone of how precious the Bible was to her. Only three other copies are known to exist—two of which are missing pages.

In 1994, the British Museum paid one million pounds for the most complete one of those copies, because they believed it was *"The most important book printed in the English language."*[62]

1

Study

*"Study this Book of Instruction continually.
Meditate on it day and night so you will be sure to obey
everything written in it. Only then will you prosper and
succeed in all you do."*
Joshua 1:8 (NLT)

The most important book we could ever read is the Bible. As we journey through life, the Bible lights the darkness for us, showing us which way to go and giving us the chance to go far beyond what we thought we could do.

As busy as you are, there's still plenty of ways to absorb the Bible. Play it in your car while you drive. Listen to it on your smartphone while you workout. Or if you're more of a visual learner, try watching the Visual Bible. The entire Gospel of John and Book of Acts have been made into full length movies that you can enjoy with your family.

So where's the best part of the Bible to start reading?

The secret to understanding the whole Bible is to focus on Christ. Starting by reading in the New Testament helps us learn how to follow Jesus' example so that we can build our lives on the strong foundation of His words.

As Jesus described, *"So then, anyone who hears these words of Mine and obeys them is like a wise man who built his house on rock. The rain poured down, the rivers flooded over, and the wind blew hard against that house. But it did not fall, because it was built on rock."*[63]

Here's an easier way to read through the Bible. Start in the book of John where we can learn about the life of Christ. Each day read as much as you can absorb. For some people that is a whole chapter. Others might meditate on a few verses at a time until the verses are buried deep in their soul. Continue moving forward, reading through the whole New Testament while letting the Holy Spirit reveal new things to you. Once you complete the New Testament, then read Psalms and Proverbs. Next go back to Genesis and read through the whole Bible from start to finish.

Read the Bible through an understanding of Christ who is *"The visible image of the invisible God."*[64] If certain parts of the Bible don't make sense, dig deeper. Remember that the goal of all our Bible reading is learning how to become more like Christ.

Think About:

*"Your word is like a lamp that guides my steps,
a light that shows the path I should take."*
Psalms 119:105 (ERV)

*"A thorough knowledge of the Bible
is worth more than a college education."*[65]
-President Theodore Roosevelt

*"Scripture passages should be as familiar to our children as
their daily education at school. Who knows but that promise they
learned may prove to be the turning point in their lives."*[66]
-John D. Rockefeller Sr.

2

R. G. LeTourneau

"I know what I am planning for you," says the Lord. *"I have good plans for you, not plans to hurt you. I will give you hope and a good future."*
Jeremiah 29:11 (NCV)

R. G. LeTourneau
1888-1969
From Vermont

Construction is one of the toughest jobs. Yet the construction work done today is much easier than it was a hundred years ago, because of what was invented by a man who dropped out of school in the seventh grade.

Robert Letourneau was the child who couldn't sit still. He always struggled in school, finally dropping out in the seventh grade. When his parents pushed him to go back to school, he refused.

At fourteen years old he insisted he could work full time and take care of himself. So he moved to Portland and found a job doing heavy manual labor at an iron factory.

Working day after day, in a time when most work was done by hand instead of machine, was very hard.

The harder he worked, the more he thought that there must be a better way. Hour after hour of having to dig and move dirt by hand made him start thinking.

"I hadn't wheeled ten barrows of the stuff that had soaked up about two weeks of Portland's rain before I was hunting for an easier way of moving dirt."[86]

This was back in the time when many factories had unsafe conditions. When a fire broke out and the factory burned down, LeTourneau and the other men escaped. Now they were out of a job.

Hearing that there were lots of good jobs available in San Francisco, he moved there. He found a job just in time to experience the 1906 Earthquake.

Early one morning, he woke up as *"The shock dropped my room ten feet while my bed and bureau swapped places."*[87]

The people in his building survived the earthquake. Still there was tremendous damage. The earthquake had resulted in fire destroying much of the city.

Desperate for work, he began doing whatever odd jobs he could find. According to him, *"I was in many ways an iron molder, lead burner, brick layer, carpenter, gold miner, stump puller, irrigation ditch digger, farmer and oak chopper. Everything the hard way, by hand, or, with the exception of the oxyhydrogen torch, by tools that hadn't been improved in centuries."*[88]

What made the work so frustrating was the lack of machinery to help. Plus, safety was still lacking from many work environments of that time. Lighting was poor. Items were left on the floor that could easily trip people. Gloves were not used.

Industrial accidents were frequent but worker's compensation did not exist. LeTourneau would suffer from these bad conditions, losing several front teeth in an accident at work, when rigging collapsed on his face.

He still kept taking any job he could find. At one point, he was part of a team constructing the California Stanislaus River Bridge.

He later described, *"Accidents on the ground were frequent, even before the clumsy steam cranes began lifting the beams to the riggers waiting on the structure."*

"The best of crane operators, jerking at a confusing array of long handles, and tromping on foot pedals, was lucky to line up a beam within inches of where it was to be placed, after which the riggers, working with no safety devices or nets, had to use their own weight to get it into position. The steel hanger with three years' experience was greatly admired in those days. Not for his skill, for his survival."[89]

When World War I came, LeTourneau tried to enlist in the military. He was turned down due to the injuries he had sustained in his career. He still found a way to serve his country by working as an electrical mechanic in the Navy yard.

After the war, LeTourneau moved to Stockton, California and opened his own car repair shop. There he fixed whatever cars people brought to them, while his partner did the books.

Soon they had a thriving side business of rescuing stranded motorists. This was back in the time when if a car broke down by the side of the road there was no AAA to come and change a tire or provide a tow. LeTourneau became the mechanic who would go out at all hours of the day or night to rescue people.

By the side of the road, he would work on their car until it was running again. It was hard labor and brutal hours but it taught him more mechanics than he would have learned in the classroom. Soon they were making all kinds of money.

Yet no matter how much money came into the business they couldn't seem to get ahead. LeTourneau began to wonder where all the money was going.

When he took a look at their accounting records, he discovered that his partner was spending the money faster than it came in. They were deep in debt. LeTourneau would have to shut down his repair shop and try to find another job.

Hearing that the California Highway Department was about to spend lots of money building new highways, LeTourneau decided to bid on these contracts. To his surprise he received several contracts, only to realize that he had won the contracts because no one else wanted the work.

Building roads required moving an enormous amount of dirt. The only way to do it was with men and mules. As work began, everything went wrong. Rough soil loaded with hundreds of heavy rocks broke all his machinery. The work would stop while the expenses continued, eating away at his profits. Days would pass where he had to pay his men while he figured out how to move the dirt.

The only way he could make payroll was by inventing special dirt digging equipment. As he would later describe, *"On that rock-strewn, gully sliced, rattlesnake-infested job, I had to invent the first mechanical bull-dozer to break even."*[90]

Breaking even meant he wasn't making money. Things went from bad to worse with his business. He was losing so much money that his wife had to get a job as a maid just to keep a roof over their head. LeTourneau felt humiliated at having to depend on his wife's income. Praying to God for guidance, he began wondering if maybe he was in the wrong business. Maybe God would be pleased if he shut down his business and went into full time ministry. The more he thought about it the more it seemed like the right thing to do.

So he approached their pastor for advice. *"I had an idea that in order to serve God, I would have to be a preacher or a missionary. When I asked the Pastor he said, 'Let's pray about it.'"*

"So we both knelt down and prayed. When we arose from our knees, he said these words to me—they still ring in my ears as the voice of God speaking to my soul—'God needs business men as well as missionaries.'"

"I answered—I will do my best to be God's businessman."[91]

LeTourneau was relieved to know that he could please God by using the mechanical skills, which came so naturally to him.

He went back to work on building roads for the government, even though each contract seemed more difficult than the one before.

However, when he got stuck, he would remember something from his years of working with machinery. Trying new ideas that had never been tried before, he would have to make his own parts, because he couldn't buy any parts for the type of machinery he was inventing. Soon his new inventions were making things run smoothly. He was finishing projects faster than anyone could believe.

One day in 1926, he was building the Crow Canyon Highway. This road required cutting across several hills, moving massive amounts of dirt.

The work was hard and LeTourneau was sweating profusely when someone approached him.

Henry Kaiser had been watching him work. He was impressed that LeTourneau was completing a three year project in only six months! Realizing the potential of LeTourneau's inventions, Kaiser offered to buy all of his equipment and patents.

That money paid off all of LeTourneau's debt and enabled his wife to quit her job. LeTourneau was thrilled. For the first time in his life he had the freedom and finances to begin developing some of his other mechanical ideas.

Soon he had invented new machinery that was so advanced he had a very lucrative business selling revolutionary types of construction equipment.

In 1931, LeTourneau won another government contract. This time it was a million dollar project to build the Boulder Dam highway on the Colorado River in Nevada and another half million dollars to build the Orange County Dam.

New projects brought new problems. This time his engineers had seriously underestimated how many rocks were hidden in the soil. The soil was so difficult to work with, that it slowed down LeToureanu until all his profit was gone. Once again he was right back in financial trouble, with creditors threatening to take his business. LeTourneau had no idea what to do.

He recalls, *"It was the beginning of the business depression. I found myself in debt for several hundred thousand dollars."*

"Many firms in better shape than ours, went down, never to rise again. My payroll was about five weeks behind. We had stalled the materials men until we couldn't hold them off much longer."

"My attorney said to me, 'You can't go any farther. You must file for bankruptcy. The papers are made out and should be filed today.'"

"I said, 'Wait a few days longer.'"[92]

The next day LeTourneau went to church. While sitting in the pew listening to the sermon, he asked God what to do. He heard God respond to him, *"Put Me on your payroll and pay Me when you pay the others."*[93]

LeTourneau thought about it and realized he had nothing to lose. He went home and did just that only to be surprised by how *"From the minute I made God my business partner. Things started to go."*[94]

The answer was also waiting for him at home. When LeTourneau went back to work he received a call from a very angry customer. The customer complained that he couldn't get the machinery he had just bought from LeTourneau to move on sand. The tires just sank down into the sand, leaving the machinery stuck.

What type of tires could work on sand? Thinking about it, he remembered, *"About a year before I had purchased a set of the largest rubber tires then obtainable, thinking they would work better than steel tires on tractor-drawn machines, although I had never been able to convince any contractor to try, much less buy, a scraper thus equipped. I still had these rubber tires and they gave me an idea."*[95]

Trying something different, LeTourneau put the rubber tires on one of his machines and took it out to the customer's job site. To everyone's surprise, the rubber tires worked great on the soft sand. The customer was so happy he asked LeTourneau to make him another machine just like it.

When LeTourneau asked for a down payment, the customer paid him the full purchase price of twenty-five thousand dollars. It was exactly the money that LeTourneau needed to pay bills and escape bankruptcy.

This was also the simple idea that would transform the heavy machinery industry, making rubber tires the standard for new machinery.

As LeTourneau ordered thousands of those tires from Harvey Firestone, he thanked God for showing him the solution. *"What a wonderful God we have! Why don't we believe Him more?"*[96]

LeTourneau continued to trust God even when something horrible happened on May 30, 1937.

One day he was going on a road trip across Tennessee with his wife and three friends. Traveling in broad daylight on a sunny day, LeTourneau was riding in the back seat with his wife when he saw a car approaching from the other side of the road. Suddenly, the other driver took his eyes off the road to look down in the back seat. That car swerved across the road. They collided head on.

Five people died, including all three occupants of the other car and the driver and front passenger traveling with LeTourneau.

LeTourneau and his wife were seriously injured. *"Both of my hips were driven out of their sockets. My pelvis was broken, a piece of bone was broken off the side of the hip socket, my chest was crushed, a leg was broken and a foot crushed."* He described. Looking over at his wife he saw *"She was bruised and bleeding, cut from head to foot. I tried to talk to her but she was unconscious."*[97]

LeTourneau crawled out of the wreck, rescued his wife and then lay on the pavement to wait for help. Feeling the pain rip through his body, He prayed, *"Lord, I love You and I still believe that all things work together for good to them that love You. I'm not asking why. All I'm asking is that Your will be done."*[98]

When LeTourneau was taken to the hospital he was in such bad shape that not even the doctors thought he would make it.

Thinking that he was going to die anyway, they refused to operate on him. LeTourneau protested until they gave him some treatment and put him in a cast. He was ordered to stay in bed until his body healed.

Bedridden with nothing to do but think, LeTourneau invented a special stretcher that could be wheeled around, so he could get back to work. Eventually he would completely heal from his injuries while he would continue inventing new machinery for the rest of his life.

He would receive over three hundred patents on his creative ideas.

The federal government became his primary client, buying thousands of his machines.

When World War II came, thousands of pounds of dirt had to be moved. Bases had to be constructed in combat zones. New roads had to be dug and bridges built, all of which required moving enormous amounts of dirt.

All over the world, LeTourneau's equipment could be found getting the job done. When Japan attacked Pearl Harbor, his machinery was used to clear wreckage. When the Allies invaded on D-Day, they used his equipment to push through the Nazi defenses.

Somewhere around seventy percent of the dirt moved by Allies during the war, was done on LeTourneau's machines.[99]

He explained, *"They had to build roads from India across Burma to China, across every major island in the South Pacific, and through the wilderness of northern Canada to Alaska. This was the greatest dirt-moving project the world has ever seen."[100]*

That made LeTourneau a millionaire.

He gave back to the community in a big way, supporting many charitable projects and helping many people.

To pass his knowledge down to the next generation, he built a special college in Texas, to help train military veterans in mechanical skills. As his college grew to include a school for training missionaries, LeTourneau insisted on teaching mechanical skills to the missionaries.

They needed to know how to fix their vehicles should they break down in the middle of nowhere on the mission field. This trained a whole new generation to serve around the world.

LeTourneau continued serving the Lord for the rest of his life until he passed away with a stroke at age eighty. He was buried where his heart was on the campus of LeTourneau University. When his wife passed away a few years later, she was laid to rest beside him.

Their charitable foundation had grown to over forty million dollars by the time they died. Today it is still being invested where it can do what Jesus would do.

LeTourneau's words continue inspiring people to realize:

"You will never know what you can accomplish until you say a great big 'yes' to the Lord."[101]

2

God Is Not The Thief

Jesus said, "The thief comes only in order to steal, kill, and destroy. I have come in order that you might have life— life in all its fullness."
John 10:10 (GNT)

When LeTourneau suffered a severe car accident, he didn't blame God for it. He chose to trust in God, even when life was hard. Can we also trust God when life doesn't make sense?

More than you could ever dream, God loves you. He began planning good things for you even before you were born. He's already provided everything you need to accomplish those good things.

You are the most important thing to God.

He said, *"I have written your name on the palms of my hands."*[102]

You are worth far more to God than countless galaxies, stars, or planets. He pays so much attention to you that *"God even knows how many hairs you have on your head. Don't be afraid."*[103]

As far as God is concerned, *"Whoever touches you, hurts what is precious to Me."*[104]

God's promise to you is that *"I will never forget you."*[105]

Because you matter so much to God, the devil tries to hurt you because that's the only way he can hurt God.

Once upon a time, long ago before humans existed, the devil was one of the most powerful angelic beings in Heaven. He led worship before the throne of God.

Then God decided to create something more powerful than the angels. God decided to make people in His own image. Did the devil get jealous? Maybe the devil decided to rebel when he heard *"God did not choose angels to be the rulers of the new world that was coming."*[106] As Heaven watched, God created humans and focused all His attention on them. Angels were left wondering, *"Why are people so important to You? Why do you even think about them?"*[107]

Ever since the devil rebelled and was thrown out of Heaven, he has had to watch God show His love to us humans. God has held nothing back from us, even sending His own Son to die for us. *"God's divine power has given us everything we need for life and godliness."*[108]

God gives us EVERYTHING. The devil gives us NOTHING. The devil is only a thief trying to take away what God has given you. The devil's biggest weapon is trying to get us to hate God.

"Don't give the devil a way to defeat you."[109] Thus the Bible warns us, *"Keep your mind clear, and be alert. Your opponent the devil is prowling around like a roaring lion as he looks for someone to devour. Be firm in the faith and resist him, knowing that other believers throughout the world are going through the same kind of suffering."*[110]

Our job is to RESIST the devil—RESIST the thief's attempts to hurt us.

God is only good. There is no evil in Him. That's why the Bible tells us, *"Whatever is good and perfect comes to us from God."*[111]

The heart of God loves you and wants the best for you.

The more you read the Bible, the more you'll see God's heart trying to protect people. Trying to keep them from making a mistake.

In Genesis 4:6-7, God loved Cain enough to warn him before he made the biggest mistake of his life. God warned Cain that he would be tempted to hurt his brother but he could resist the temptation. Yet Cain still chose to go astray.

All of us will also be tempted to make bad decisions. We will be tempted to blame God for the bad things that happen.

No matter what happens in life, keep trusting in God's love for you. Yes, there will come a time when life seems unfair.

When it feels easy to get mad at God, remember how God warned His people in the Bible, *"It is your destruction, O Israel, that you have been against Me, for in Me is your help."*[112]

Think About:

"If your child asks for bread, do you trick him with sawdust? If he asks for fish, do you scare him with a live snake on his plate? As bad as you are, you wouldn't think of such a thing. You're at least decent to your own children. So don't you think the God who conceived you in love will be even better?"
Matthew 7:9-11 (MSG)

"I trust God to reward me, not people, wealth, or probabilities. God works with or without resources, as He pleases."[113]
-William Colgate

"Whatever successes have occurred were achieved when we were acting under the Guidance of His Spirit, and only failures have occurred when we were attempting to work by our own plans and abilities."[114]
-Merrell Vories

3

James Kraft

"Draw near to God and He will draw near to you."
James 4:8 (NASB)

James Kraft
1874-1953
From Ontario, Canada

What would you do if you were down to your last sixty-five dollars and stranded in a strange city? James Kraft turned this problem into the key to his future, opening the door to his success.

Kraft grew up in Canada near Lake Erie. His entire childhood was spent suffering from poor eye sight, but since he was born into a family with eleven children there was no money for glasses.

In his own words he described, *"Nearsightedness was so distressing that I assumed everyone on earth suffered continuously from furious headaches, and that all the earth had the blurry image of a boat seen from under water."*[67]

That changed when he was fourteen and an eye doctor vacationed in his little town.

As Kraft helped him, the doctor began to notice his poor eyesight. *"He watched me as I tended his horse and washed his buggy."*

"Then he said, 'You're going over to Buffalo tomorrow and get fitted for a pair of spectacles!'"

The kind doctor paid for what would enable Kraft to experience, "The wonder of a world in focus." For the first time in his life, "The look of the hills, the road, the streams, even of the people who, as they walked, took on definite lines instead of a blur."[68]

This whole new world opened to Kraft just in time to attend high school. Just as he began to really enjoy high school, he was faced with a major crisis. His parents had fallen behind on their mortgage. The family farm was facing foreclosure. What were they going to do? Where could a family with eleven children move?

Knowing that he had to do something, at sixteen years old, Kraft dropped out of high school to start his own business. He made money delivering the fresh eggs from their farm to local businesses. That one idea ended up not only saving the farm but also paying off his parent's mortgage. Then they didn't mind the fact he had dropped out of high school.

When new government regulations were passed making it too expensive for him to continue that business, he found a job at the local general store. He saved up as much as he could.

In 1902, he left home and moved to Buffalo, New York where he invested in a cheese business. Things were going great. Then his partners asked him to travel to Chicago, to see if they could expand the business by opening a new location there. Little did Kraft know that this was their plan to get him out of the way, so they could shut down operations and disappear with his investment.

Kraft traveled to Chicago, only to quickly find out that he was stranded in a strange city, swindled by his partners in New York, and surviving with just sixty-five dollars left.

This is where many people give up. Kraft considered it but figured there must be a way out. How could he start a new business with his last few dollars? After thinking long and hard, he purchased a horse and wagon to start delivering fresh cheese to local grocery stores.

The idea was to pick up large blocks of cheese early in the morning at the market then sell it to the local grocers, who might appreciate not having to go to the market at the crack of dawn themselves.

Once again things didn't work out. The more Kraft knocked on doors, the more doors slammed in his face. Pretty soon his money had run out. He had no idea what to do.

One night, as he drove home he felt so discouraged, he was ready to give up on the cheese business. Feeling like the only person he could talk to was his horse Paddy, Kraft began wondering what he was doing wrong.

As Kraft would later describe it, *"With a number of disastrously poor business days behind us, my small finances exhausted, my hopes for the morrow non-existent, we were a sorry pair, Paddy and I. Night after night, I had sat up trying to figure ways of making my hopes and dreams work. It was obvious to me—if not to Paddy—that nothing was going to work. I was a failure."*[69]

Kraft turned to his horse and wondered out loud, *"What's the matter with us, Paddy?"*

"I spoke to him for he was a companionable kind of partner, even in gloom."[70]

Then he felt God's voice respond to him as a deep inner knowing. *"You're trying to do this without Me."*

That hit him hard. Kraft thought about it all the way back home. Then he made a promise to God.

"I resolved to let God have direction in my life. And from that moment forward, my life began to change in every way."[71]

While Kraft had been raised in a Christian home and knew the Lord at a young age, that night he realized he had become too busy for God.

That changed immediately. Time alone with God became Kraft's priority, despite the distractions of everything else.

He continued to be a hard worker in his delivery business, putting in long hours and refusing to rest until the work was finished. Yet his focus stayed on listening to the guidance of the Holy Spirit.

One of his favorite Bible verses became Revelations 3:20, which in Kraft's own words made it as simple as: *"To dine with God—to have His nourishing counsel and His fellowship every day—it is necessary only to hear and to open the door."*[72]

Years later after his tiny cheese delivery service had become one of the largest companies in America, and a news reporter asked him for the secret to his remarkable business success, Kraft thought about that night.

He described the story of himself and Paddy and how since then *"There has never been a day so busy that I have not found the time to be quiet, to listen, to read the Bible which is always in my desk—to pray—to reflect. A man who cannot, with an effort of will, turn from whatever he is doing, to be quiet within himself is a slave to his environment. He has never learned to listen."[3]*

At the turn of the century, selling cheese was a hard business. Lack of electricity left lack of refrigeration, making it difficult for grocery stores to sell cheese before it spoiled. Being in the cheese business made Kraft start looking for ways to solve these problems.

He continued selling cheese to grocery stores during the day while beginning to experiment with it at night. He tried different ways to process cheese to improve its shelf life.

By 1916, he had patented his ideas for processing cheese. Four of his brothers moved down to Chicago to help him expand the business. Together they launched the J.L. Kraft and Brothers Company.

One way that Kraft figured out to preserve cheese was by canning it. This opened the door for him to approach the U. S. Military with a product they could purchase to feed troops. This could remain fresh in all types of environments with no refrigeration. Soon the military had become Kraft's biggest client.

Millions of pounds of Kraft's cheese kept the troops fed during World War I. By the time the war ended, Kraft controlled the cheese market.

Continuing to innovate with new ideas, Kraft began marketing inexpensive easy dinner options just as the Great Depression left people with very little money to feed their families. Macaroni and Cheese was one of his most popular products, keeping families fed when they couldn't afford very much.

Kraft continued making money throughout one of the worst economies in American history. While other companies went bankrupt, he expanded.

During World War II, millions more pounds of Kraft cheese were sent to battlefields across the globe. When the war ended and food rationing was no longer necessary, cheese consumption skyrocketed.

No matter how much money he made, it never changed Kraft's heart for God. He just made the money serve the Lord alongside him. Kraft was active in his local church, teaching Sunday school for forty years.[74] As he found many ways to help people both inside and outside the church, his dedication to Christ inspired those who knew him.

W.A. Criswell was a young preacher starting out in the ministry when he spoke at Kraft's church. Kraft invited him home for dinner. Criswell would later describe how impressed he was to hear Kraft describe his main focus in life. *"My first job is serving Jesus."*[75]

In his free time, Kraft had a hobby of collecting the precious stone of jade around the world. To honor the Lord, he took the best jade from his collection and developed a special jade glass window for Chicago's North Shore Baptist Church.

It took years to find just the right stones and months to carefully carve them. Once finished, the window, made completely from translucent jade, measured about six feet high by three feet long.

Kraft had personally cut each of the four hundred and sixty-six pieces of jade that focused the light on the name of Jesus written in the middle.

Kraft believed in the importance of having hobbies because

"The development of any good hobby can help a man to learn the quietness of spirit which is a condition of success in his life. In a workshop, a man can be very close to God."[76]

Although Kraft died in 1953, his inventions still dominate the food industry and his company remains one of the largest in the world. What Kraft wanted to be remembered about him was the one thing he had learned in life. *"The safest, surest and swiftest road to victory is prayer."*[77]

3

The Real Secret

"He rewards those who seek Him."
Hebrews 11:6(GW)

God wants to spend time with you just like Moses did in the Bible. *"The Lord would speak with Moses face-to-face, just as someone speaks with a friend."*[78]

When Jesus walked the Earth, He said, *"I call you friends, because I have told you everything I heard from my Father."*[79]

So what does it mean to be a friend of God? Take a moment and think about what you do with your friends. Aren't the best moments of your life spent with them? Together you relax and have fun. You tell them what's happening in your life and how you feel about it. They share their thoughts and feelings with you. That's what God wants from you.

Jesus said, *"Look! I stand at the door and knock. If you hear My voice and open the door, I will come in, and we will share a meal together as friends."*[80]

Yet God never forces Himself into our life. He waits for us to come to Him and it hurts His feelings when He has to say, *"My people have forgotten me days without number."*[81]

We try so many other things to solve our problems, while missing the easiest answer right in front of us. God describes this as:

"My people have done two things wrong. They have abandoned Me, the fountain of life-giving water. They have also dug their own cisterns, broken cisterns that can't hold water."[82]

God knows how to solve the problems that are bothering you right now. He is waiting for you to seek him. Take a little time every day to talk with God. Thank Him for everything. Worship Him. *"Join with us in the fellowship that we have with the Father and with his Son Jesus Christ."*[83]

Think About:

"When you pray, go to your room, close the door, and pray to your Father, who is unseen. And your Father, who sees what you do in private, will reward you."
Matthew 6:6 (GNT)

"I prayed all the time about my work. Everywhere, I was always talking to the Lord. I was a conductor of the Underground Railroad for eight years, and I can say what most conductors can't say: I never ran my train off the track and I never lost a passenger."[84]
-Harriett Tubman

"Let us dwell longer at the feet of Jesus that we may lead many souls to the Spring of Everlasting Life."[85]
-Henry Crowell

Harvey Firestone

L to R: Henry Ford, Thomas Edison, President Harding, Harvey Firestone

"What do you mean, 'If I can?' Jesus asked."
"Anything is possible if a person believes."
Mark 9:23 (NLT)

Harvey Firestone
1868-1938
From Ohio

In the days of horse and buggy transportation, Harvey Firestone worked in sales at the Columbus Buggy Company in Detroit. Until the day that everything changed. One day while he was at work, a customer walked in and wanted to buy some tires.

Tires? Why would he want tires? Normal customers wanted the full horse drawn carriage. Asking this customer why he would be interested in just one set of tires, Firestone never dreamed how the conversation they had that day would change America forever. That customer was Henry Ford.

Both Ford and Firestone had grown up in farming families. Firestone's father was a shrewd businessman who raised sheep to provide the highest quality wool. His father taught him many business skills but the one thing he always emphasized was *"Never rush in on a deal, let it come to you."*[115]

Watching his father, Firestone noticed that he would take the time to really study the market prices before making deals. *"If his research convinced him that the market was not a good one either to buy or to sell in, he simply went home again."*

"He often held his stock a year to get better prices, and he was so good a judge of conditions that I do not recall that he ever made a mistake by holding. If the market were high and seemed to be going higher, he would seldom wait long to sell, and he never held back in the hope that the prices would soar to some impossible figure."

"He never had to sell his sheep or wool because he was hard up, and hence he always got the top of the market." Firestone remembered.

"His reputation for getting a price became so widespread that the wool buyers came to my father first, for they knew that, unless he sold, the other farmers would not sell."[116]

There was something else about his father that Firestone admired. His deep faith in God.

Firestone described his father as *"The most considerate man I have ever known. He was a Christian, worshipping at the Grace Reformed Church."*[117]

While Firestone admired his father, he didn't want to be a farmer.

He dreamed of moving to the city, going to college and having a career in accounting. At eighteen, he left home to attend Spencerian College in Cleveland, Ohio.

After graduating, he found a job doing accounting for a mining company. When the company went under, he took a sales job for a company selling medicines. Even though Firestone quickly became the highest grossing salesman at the company, the company still went bankrupt because none of the other salesmen were selling anything.

Firestone found himself having to get a sales job at the Columbus Buggy Company. This was a hard job. The buggies he sold were luxury editions with something new called rubber tires.

Firestone showed customers how rubber tires gave a much smoother ride across the bumpy cobblestone streets of Detroit. Still it was a tough sell. Many locals would rather buy the cheaper buggies sold by competitors for only $35 instead of paying $115 for a luxury edition with rubber tires.

The buggy company was going bankrupt and Firestone was wondering how much longer he would have a job, when Henry Ford walked in the door.

Ford asked Firestone to recommend the best tires. When Firestone asked why he would need a set of tires, Ford told him about his dream.

Growing up on a farm, doing heavy physical labor had inspired Ford to invent machinery. Even at a young age, Ford was experimenting with inventing ways to make life easier for farmers.

In his own words he described, *"It was life on the farm that drove me into devising better transportation."*

"A farmer doing his chores will walk up and down a rickety ladder a dozen times. He will carry water for years instead of putting in a few lengths of pipe. His whole idea, when there is extra work to do, is to hire extra men. Yet it is the waste effort that makes farm prices high and profits low."[18]

Inventing all sorts of new machines to improve efficiency on the farm inspired Ford to become a mechanic. As soon as he could, he left home to start an apprenticeship in Detroit. That taught him about the leading technology of that time—steam engines. Upon finishing the apprenticeship he was hired by Westinghouse to repair their engines.

Ford really enjoyed this work because it taught him how engines worked. The more he worked on engines, the more he dreamed of building an engine that could power a car.

In the backyard shed at his home, Ford built a car from scratch that was powered completely by steam. Once he got it running, he tested it out on the street only to find out that it didn't work as well as he had envisioned. To drive the car, he had to sit on top of a boiling hot fire. Just how safe would that be for families? *"It had a kerosene heated boiler and it developed plenty of power and a neat control,"* he described, *"But the boiler was dangerous."*[119]

For two years he tried everything to make it work only to give up on steam technology *"But I did not give up the idea of a horseless carriage."*[120]

While keeping track of the news to see if any new technology would be invented that could make machine transportation work, Ford came across a scientific magazine article about a new gasoline powered generator in Europe.

The first practical internal combustion engine had been built in 1876 by German inventors Nikolaus Otto and Eugen Langen. This Otto Engine ran on one-cylinder and was marketed as a power source for factory equipment. When news of this new technology spread around the world, in 1885, the Eagle Iron Works Factory in Detroit purchased an Otto engine to power their machinery.

There was just one problem. When the engine broke down, no one knew how to fix it. How could they call a repair service? So they called a young mechanic with a good reputation named Henry Ford.

Ford described, *"No one in town knew anything about this engine. Rumor was that I did. Although I had never touched one before, I carried through the job. That gave me a chance to study the new engine."*[121]

Could this engine power a car? Ford worked on it until he realized the serious limitations. The fly-wheel necessary to power the engine was too big and heavy for practical use in a moving vehicle. Plus, reliable transportation would require a much more consistent power source.

Meanwhile, Ford's ability to fix engines had caught the attention of the Edison Power Company. They offered him a job at $45/month. Ford accepted their offer and took the night shift.

That gave him the money to pay his bills and buy equipment to make parts to continue working on his dream. Day after day at home in his garage, Ford kept trying to build a car. He spent every penny he had on parts. According to him, *"I read everything I could find, but the greatest knowledge came from the work. There is an immense amount to be learned simply by tinkering with things."*[122]

In 1886, Carl Benz of Germany patented a three-wheel car with a one-cylinder engine and Mercedes Benz was born.

Three wheel cars had never appealed to Ford. Believing that four wheels were safer and more stable, that's how he built all of his cars. He also refused to use a one-cylinder engine, trying to make his car more powerful and efficient for the harsh road conditions of that time. The other problem he had to solve was the cost. Cars being produced in Europe were so expensive that most people never thought they could afford one.

How could he make the car affordable for regular families?

Remembering how hard work on the farm had been, he dreamed of making the car affordable to make life easier for everyone.

That day when Ford walked into the Columbus Buggy Company, he had finally built the four-cylinder car in his home garage. Now he needed four tires to test drive his invention.

The first time Ford had built a car, he hadn't been able to find any tires so he had used bicycle ones.[123] This time he needed something better. He asked Firestone to recommend the best set of tires.

When Firestone asked what the tires were for, Ford explained his dream of making the car that regular families could afford. They talked for a long time about the future. Firestone recommended something new: air inflated rubber tires that gave a much smoother ride than the typical steel or solid rubber tires.

Ford bought a set and then promised that if things worked out, *"I may be back for more."*[124]

More tires? If Ford really could build that car for America, lots and lots of tires would be needed. Firestone started thinking about starting a tire company. This was the beginning of a lifelong friendship between Ford and Firestone.

But first, Ford went home and had to solve another problem. The car he had built in his garage was too big to fit through the door. How could he take it on a test drive? Ford had to knock out a wall to drive the car out of the garage.

For the next several months, everyone stared at him in amazement as he drove the car down the local streets.

According to Ford, *"My gasoline buggy was the first and for a long time, the only automobile in Detroit. It was considered to be a nuisance, for it made a lot of noise that scared horses. Also it blocked traffic. For if I stopped my machine anywhere in town, a crowd was around it before I could start up again. If I left it alone even for a minute, some curious person always tried to run it. Finally, I had to carry a chain and chain it to a lamp post whenever I left it anywhere."*

"And then there was trouble with the police. I don't know why. There were no speed limit laws in those days. Anyway, I had to get a special permit from the mayor and thus for a time enjoyed being the only licensed chauffeur in America."

"I ran that machine about one thousand miles through 1895 and 1896 and then sold it to Charles Ainsley of Detroit for $200. That was my first sale. I had built the car not to sell but only to experiment with."

"I wanted to start another car. I built three cars in my home shop and all of them ran for years in Detroit."[125]

All this time Ford was still working at the Edison Power Company. He had even worked his way up the corporate ladder to becoming the head engineer for the Detroit branch. That earned him an invitation to the annual Edison Convention in Manhattan Beach. In August of 1896, Ford attended the convention and found himself seated at the head table with Thomas Edison himself.

The convention discussed the future of electricity, predicting that soon electric cars would be driving on roads across America. Ford described, *"They predicted that carriages would soon be on the streets by the thousands and would require much attention in the way of recharged batteries and of course that meant enormous revenues."*

The discussion of electric cars continued even when the convention took a dinner break. While Ford was still sitting at the table with Edison, one of the other guests pointed at him and told Edison that Ford had built and been seen driving his own gas powered car around town.

That got Edison's attention immediately. Edison's first question was *"Is it a four-cylinder engine?"*

Ford nodded.

Then Edison asked if he was using spark plugs.

Ford described, *"That was before spark plugs had been invented. He wanted to know if I exploded the gas in the cylinder by electricity and whether I did it by a contact or by a spark. He said that a spark would give a much better ignition."*

"I had made what we today would call a spark plug. He asked me no end of details and I sketched everything for him, for I have always found that I could convey an idea quicker by sketching than by just describing it."

"When I had finished, he brought his fist down on the table with a bang and said, 'Young man, that's the thing—you have it. Keep at it. Electric cars must keep near to power stations. The storage battery is too heavy.'"

"'Steam cars won't do either, for they have to have a boiler and fire. Your car is self-contained—carries its own power plant—no fire, no boiler, no smoke and no steam. You have the thing. Keep at it.'"

Ford continued, *"That bang on the table was worth worlds to me. No man up to then had given me any encouragement. I had hoped that I was headed right—sometimes I knew that I was—sometimes I only wondered if I was—but here all at once and out of a clear sky, the man who knew the most about electricity had said that for the purpose, my gas motor was better."*[126]

After the convention ended, Ford went home and kept building more cars in his home garage. For the next few years he was the talk of Detroit. That caused him problems at work. Eventually his direct supervisor called him into the office to complain about that stupid idea of a car. They didn't want Ford developing gasoline powered machinery at home, while he worked at an electric business.

The company offered him a promotion and a raise *"But only on the condition that I would give up my gas engine and devote myself to something really useful. I had to choose between my job and my automobile,"* Ford later recalled.

So Ford quit his job to start his car company.

There was someone else who believed in his dream—his friend Harvey Firestone. While Ford built his car company, Firestone launched his tire company. Both of them faced a very uncertain future in an industry considered ludicrous.

Later describing the public opinion of that time, Ford would say, *"There was no demand for automobiles. The horseless carriage was considered merely a freak notion and many wise people explained why it could never be more than a toy."*[127]

A scientist of that time, Dr. George Washington Carver recalled, *"When the automobile first was being introduced, the people laughed and jeered and talked of how impossible it would be to get rid of horses."*[128]

That made it difficult for Firestone to raise the money to launch a new business.

He had to show potential investors how much more comfortable rubber tires would make driving. So he took potential investors for a ride in his horse drawn buggy across the bumpiest cobblestone streets.

When they commented on how smooth the ride was, Firestone replied, *"Millions of Americans will enjoy that riding comfort if they can buy tires easily."*[129]

That won him enough new investors that he was able to buy a tire shop which had just closed down.

Now Firestone had a business but not enough customers. The automobile was being introduced to the public and still too expensive for many people to afford. So Firestone had to make a living by selling rubber tires for horse drawn carriages. Just in time, news would spread across America that the White House had ordered rubber tires for President William McKinley's horse drawn carriage.

That sparked interest. Soon customers were coming to Firestone for tires. Yet very little was known about rubber tires. Most of them gave out in less than 4,000 miles.

How could Firestone build a tire that could last over 4,000 miles? Firestone had to learn by experimenting to see what worked.

Every time he drove somewhere it was another opportunity to learn something about tires. This was back in the time when most roads in America were dirt. Potholes were common. Firestone would later describe how the rough road conditions quickly destroyed most tires. On one trip, it took him over seven hours to drive sixty miles. He said, *"Most of that time we spent monkeying with the tires. Every few feet—it seemed—we had a blowout. The tires stayed on well enough. The trouble was with the shape of the rim."[130]*

As difficult as it was, Firestone kept trying until he figured it out. By the time that Henry Ford was ready to roll two thousand new cars off the assembly line in 1905, Firestone had developed long lasting good tires.

Firestone wasn't the only tire company that wanted the lucrative contract with Ford. Firestone had to compete for the contract by proving to Ford that his tires were better quality.

After two months of hard tests that involved driving those tires hundreds of miles across the worst possible roads, Ford was impressed with the quality. Firestone won the first of many contracts with Ford.

Yet even having guaranteed sales didn't guarantee profits. Back then, the raw materials needed to make rubber tires were hard to find. Inconsistent supplies caused the cost of rubber to fluctuate from dollars to pennies and back to dollars. That left tire retailers unable to clear out their inventory as consumers often waited for the price to fall before purchasing tires.

How could he stabilize the supply of raw materials? Firestone had been thinking, *"An automobile without a tire is useless; and so is a tire without an automobile. And yet these two great industries depend on rubber and no rubber is grown in the United States."[131]*

Could they invent synthetic rubber? Working with his friend Thomas Edison, they sent out a team across the country to study all sorts of plants. Yet none of them could figure it out. The answer would come in a different way.

One day some of Edison's workers were at the local state fair when they saw a display table with some very impressive inventions. At the table was Dr. George Washington Carver. Edison's team was stunned to realize that long before the car had been mass produced, Dr. Carver had already figured out how to make rubber from the sweet potato. When the team reported back to Edison, he was deeply impressed too. He offered Dr. Carver a massive salary to come join his research team. Dr. Carver turned the job down because he felt called by God to be a college professor at Tuskegee Institute.

When Edison introduced Dr. Carver to Henry Ford and Harvey Firestone, they were so impressed that they also asked him to come and work with them. Once again Dr. Carver declined but he did help them. Dr. Carver invented even more ways to make synthetic rubber from other sources including both the peanut and milkweed.[132]

Years later, this simple invention would turn the tide of World War II. When Japan cut off all access to all international rubber suppliers by invading the nations that produced it, America still had the supplies necessary to make thousands of tires for trucks, tanks, and airplanes.

But first Firestone would improve the way America shipped goods by pioneering the trucking industry.

In 1918, Firestone launched the *"Ship by Truck"* advertising campaign, which changed the way that goods were transported in America and rapidly increased the need for tires. Then Firestone lobbied the federal government to begin paving American roads.

In 1919, there were 2,300,000 miles of highways connecting America. Less than twelve percent were paved.[133] Rough dirt roads made cross country travel very difficult. To study the condition of American roads, that same year the U.S. Military sent a convoy of three hundred soldiers, in about seventy vehicles, to drive cross country from Washington D.C. to San Francisco, California. On that convoy was a young soldier named Dwight D. Eisenhower.

The convoy also had two trucks full of tires sent by Firestone. Through the next two thousand miles, the soldiers noticed how Firestone's tires survived better through mud and sand than the army's regular tires.

When they drove through Ohio, Eisenhower met Firestone and brainstormed ways to fund a national paved highway system.

(That dream came true years later when Eisenhower became president and passed the Federal Highway Act of 1956.)

When the Great Depression came, money was scarce. Tire sales plummeted. Firestone found himself struggling to keep his business afloat under the worst possible economic conditions.

Just as the demand for family car tires evaporated, a whole new market emerged.

R. G. LeTourneau was inventing new dirt digging equipment, which would revolutionize the construction industry. He needed all sorts of customized rubber tires for his large machinery. Firestone would win the contract to make tires for LeTourneau's machines.

In the years that followed, Firestone broke sales records even in a bad economy. He also realized, *"I would have accomplished less if I had lacked the prod of necessity. I feel that if I had had all the money I wanted when I founded my business, it would never have become as big as it is."[134]*

People were impressed by his success. They couldn't believe that he could make a nice profit while his three biggest competitors experienced major deficits. When Firestone sat down for a meeting with his bankers, New York banker Myron Taylor introduced Firestone as *"Here's a man who made five million dollars in the rubber business last year— enough to pay dividends on his capital stock!"*

The head of First National Bank, George Baker said, *"You must have had God for a partner."*

Firestone grinned and replied, *"I did."[135]*

All those years Firestone had also remained close with his friend Henry Ford. They vacationed together with their friend Thomas Edison. Together they went camping in the woods, looking for peace and quiet. Edison enjoyed figuring out how to get electricity to their camp, even in the middle of nowhere. Ford built custom cars to transport their baggage. One car he built was refrigerated to transport their food.

Sometimes special guests such as President Warren Harding and the Secret Service would join their outdoor adventures. They would gather around the campfire, discussing everything from science to business to the economy.

Those trips were taken across America in the days of dirt roads which took a heavy toll on their vehicles. Sometimes their cars would break down. That's when Ford would roll up his sleeves and tinker under the hood until the car was running smoothly again.

Other times, when they drove down the back roads of America and saw families stuck by the side of the road with broken cars, Ford would again roll up his sleeves and help them.

Then one time their own caravan broke down in a way that even Ford couldn't fix. While driving a Lincoln car on a dirt road, they found themselves stuck in the mud.

Nothing they did could free the tires.

Eventually they had to walk to the nearest farmhouse and knock on the door. The farmer graciously offered to bring his horses and pull their car out of the mud.

While the farmer was hitching the horses to the car, the farmer's little son turned to Ford and said, *"Mister, you have the wrong kind of car. My father drives a Ford and it never gets stuck in the mud."*[136]

He had no idea he was talking to the real Ford.

That made Henry Ford so happy, when he got home, he shipped a brand new car over to surprise the family.

Along the way Firestone also fell in love, married and raised seven children. He taught his children to know the Lord, taking them to church on a regular basis.

On February 7, 1938, after coming home from church, he didn't feel well. He laid down to rest and passed away at age sixty-nine.

Henry Ford grieved the loss of one of his closest friends saying, *"Firestone and I went through many of the same experiences. He was a fine man. During all those years we did business, I knew I could trust his word all the way."*[137]

Harvey Firestone & Henry Ford Photos

Henry Ford fishing with Thomas Edison

Ford with his first car and ten millionth car

Ford chopping wood while camping with Firestone and
Edison

Firestone and Ford peeling potatoes during the camping trip

L to R: Ford, Edison, President Harding, Firestone

Ford with Firestone

4

Try Something New

*"Businessmen go down with their businesses
because they like the old way so well they cannot bring
themselves to change."[138]*
-Henry Ford

*"But the Lord says, 'Do not cling to events of the past or
dwell on what happened long ago.
Watch for the new thing I am going to do. It is happening
already—you can see it now!'"*
Isaiah 43:18-19 (GNT)

What would have happened if Firestone and Ford had listened to their skeptics and abandoned their dreams?

Today cars are such a normal part of our lives that it's hard to visualize a time when they were laughed at.

However, no matter how far our modern technology advances, change never comes easy. The moment you start thinking outside the box, people will always tell you why it won't work.

Most people do things the way that everyone else is doing it. Or the way things have always been done. Few people do things differently. Yet success requires innovation. Invention is birthed by trying something new.

God has new innovative ideas to give you if you can accept them. If you can think outside the box, dream big and try something new, you can go beyond what you thought you could do.

What holds many people back from creativity is the status quo. What is familiar becomes comfortable and attached to us.

However, the danger of tradition is its potential to keep you locked into the failure of the past, because the way things are being done isn't always the best way.

"Where the Spirit of the Lord is, there is freedom."[139]

God wants us to enjoy the freedom He has given us, instead of being trapped in the manmade limitations that people teach us. In the Bible, the Apostle Paul taught us how to break free of generations of traditions.

He wrote, *"Christ made us free. Stay that way. Do not get chained all over again in the Law and its kind of religious worship."*[140]

The Holy Spirit will help you stay on the right track if you focus on following Him instead of the tradition. *"But if you let the Spirit lead you, you are not under the law."*[141]

It takes faith to walk down the pathway with God, since we can't see where it leads. But God is there with us all the way, carrying us through the difficulties.

"As parents carry their children, He carried you wherever you went until you came to this place."[142]

Think About:

*"The mind of a wise person will know
the right time and the right way to act."*
Ecclesiastes 8:5b (GW)

*"It is the small daily accomplishments
that lead to big orders and big sales."*[143]
-Harvey Firestone

*"There's no limit to what you can do to benefit mankind if you
will take what you've learned and put it together in new ways."*[144]
-Dr. George Washington Carver

Dr. George Washington Carver

Jesus said, *"Ask and you will receive, search and you will find,*
knock and the door will be opened for you."
Luke 11:9b (CEV)

Dr. George Washington Carver
1864-1943
From Missouri

On January 21, 1921, Congress held a hearing. Should a tariff on peanut imports be approved? Just how important was the peanut to American agriculture? With the financial future of countless farmers hanging in the balance, the U.S. House Ways and Means Committee needed more information. Leading scientists were asked to testify. Each one was given only ten minutes to make their case. One by one they presented good information.

The Congressmen listened politely. Then Dr. George Washington Carver walked in and captured their attention with his presentation. When his ten minutes ended, they asked him to continue.

For almost two hours, the Committee listened closely as Dr. Carver explained how much the South's economy depended on the peanut. The Civil War had devastated the economy, making it very difficult to earn a living. For many families, the only way to feed their family was growing cash crops like cotton. Yet year after year of constant cotton production had depleted the soil. Bugs like the boil weevil had attacked and destroyed the crops, hurting their income.

The solution was crop rotation. Dr. Carver had discovered that planting peanuts would replenish the soil's nutrients and repel the boil weevil. Yet solving one problem had created another. How could they sell the peanuts? At that time, peanuts were considered nothing more than food for farm animals.

Dr. Carver had been approached by farmers like Cora Varner who begged him to invent products that would use the peanut because *"We can't eat thousands of acres of the things and we can't sell that many either."*[45]

So Dr. Carver had locked himself in his laboratory and worked.

The Congressmen couldn't believe their eyes as Dr. Carver pulled out dozens of products he had invented from peanuts. Flour, dyes, nutrition bars, diabetic foods, milk, cream, buttermilk, instant coffee, Worcestershire sauce, oils, face cream, wood stains, candy and even ink. Inventing all these products, one man alone in a laboratory had created enough new demand for peanuts to save the southern economy.

Yet rising demand for peanuts had resulted in them being imported, which again hurt American farmers.

Asking the committee to pass the peanut tariff to protect the farmer's income, Dr. Carver emphasized, *"We cannot allow other countries to come in and take away our rights from us. America produces better peanuts than any other part of the world."*

Plus, growing peanuts provided a food source that could sustain the nation if there was a food shortage. He explained, *"If you go to the first chapter of Genesis, we can interpret very clearly what God intended when He said, 'I have given you every herb that bears seed upon the face of the Earth, to you it shall be meat.' That is what He means: there is everything there to strengthen and nourish and keep the body alive and healthy."*

Congressman Garner asked, *"You're saying that the properties of the peanut combined with the sweet potato are a balanced ration that could sustain the human race even if all other food sources were destroyed?"*

Dr. Carver, *"Yes, sir. From the sweet potato we get starches and carbohydrates and from the peanut we get all the muscle building properties. The peanut and sweet potato are two of the greatest products God has ever given us—a perfect nutritional balance."*

When Dr. Carver finished his testimony, the entire room applauded. Congressman Carew said, *"You have given the committee a great service."*[46]

Immediately Congress passed the *Emergency Tariff Act.*

Dr. Carver returned to his lab and continued inventing many of the products that we use today.

Today, history remembers him as one of the most brilliant, influential and successful scientists. His experiments produced many profound discoveries including helping extend the life of President Franklin Roosevelt with a special medicine he made.

Other U.S. Presidents such as Calvin Coolidge sought to learn from this humble man. World renowned inventors like Thomas Edison and Henry Ford pleaded with Dr. Carver to come and help them. World leaders including Gandhi in India and Stalin in Russia sought to learn from him.

Yet one of the most remarkable things about him is how he started.

Dr. Carver was born in a dangerous time in Missouri's history just as the Civil War began in 1861. At that time, there was very little law enforcement on the western frontier. Women and children were left home alone, as most able-bodied men went to fight the Civil War.

Criminals took advantage of the situation, resulting in a dramatic rise in violent crime. Ruthless outlaws rode freely, taking whatever they wanted and leaving behind a trail of destruction. Violence bled from Kansas to Missouri. Valuables were stolen, barns were burned down, homes were invaded and people brutally murdered.

One group of outlaws heard that farmers Moses and Susan Carver had hidden money on their property in Missouri. That was true. The Carvers had done well enough to save up some money. It was hidden on the farm, but they wouldn't let it go that easy.

When the outlaws came and tied up Moses Carver, he refused to talk. They beat him to a pulp, demanding to know where the money was hidden. Moses kept his mouth shut, never telling them that the money was hidden under a beehive. Finally the outlaws gave up, but left with something else they could sell. They took the mother and child that were owned by the Carver family.

Dr. Carver had been born under the horrific system of slavery to a teenage mother that had been purchased by Moses and Susan Carver.

His father had also been trapped under the evil system, a slave who passed away in a logging accident on a nearby plantation just before he was born. When the outlaws came, they kidnapped Mary and her baby with the plan to sell them further south.

Moses Carver had been badly injured by the outlaws. Knowing that he didn't have the strength to ride after the outlaws, he went to town for help. He found a retired military veteran with special forces type training, named Sergeant John Bentley. Moses asked Sgt. Bentley to go find Mary and her baby, offering him an expensive horse in return.

Sergeant Bentley accepted the offer and quickly rode off, looking all through Missouri and Arkansas for the mother and child. By the time he caught up to the outlaws, Mary had already been sold. She would never be seen again but the outlaws still had the baby. Being too sick with the whooping cough had saved the baby from being sold.

Sgt. Bentley rescued baby George Washington Carver and went home, never realizing that he had just saved the life of the one person who would rescue the entire South.

For the first ten years of his life, George Washington Carver was raised by Moses and Susan. Throughout his childhood, he struggled with constant illness which greatly limited his activities. What little energy he had he spent exploring the forest where every flower caught his attention. As he studied the plants and flowers deep in the woods, he talked with God and God answered his questions.

One day he asked God for a pocketknife. That night he dreamt of walking through the nearby cornfield and finding that just below a hill, a watermelon lay next to a pocketknife. Next morning, Carver went outside to the hill and found both the watermelon and the knife. That would be only the first of many answered prayers in his life.

Yet getting education was much harder to find. Carver went to the local grade school only to discover he wasn't welcome because of his skin color. But this student rejected by human teachers would receive a much better education directly from the Great Creator.

Still wanting to go to school, Carver kept looking for an opportunity. Eventually, he found a school in another town that he could attend.

Leaving home at age ten, he moved in with another childless couple, who raised him as their own son. Recognizing his genius mind, they encouraged him to continue exploring. When he graduated from school, they insisted that he attend college.

He applied to different colleges and was excited to receive an acceptance letter from Highland College. On the first day of classes he showed up, eagerly looking forward to continuing his education. They kicked him out because he hadn't mentioned the color of his skin in his application.

When they told him to leave, he had nowhere to go. Every penny he had was spent on the train ticket to get there. He decided to look for work and a place to live in the town.

He found both. A local church welcomed him with open arms. Once they found out how he had been treated by the college, they worked hard to make things right. Several members offered him a job.

One family took him into their home. He worked and saved every penney he could so he could try again to get into college.

In 1891, he became the first African American student accepted to Iowa State University. There he studied art, music, chemistry, painting, and plants. He also stayed busy with the Debate Club, Art Club, National Guard Student Battalion, as well as becoming the Chairman of the YMCA.[147]

He paid his own way by waiting tables and washing laundry. By 1896, he had graduated with both a Bachelor's and a Master's Degree in Agriculture. He was offered a teaching position at Iowa State as the first African American Professor there.

Then one day he received a letter that changed everything. Booker T. Washington wrote to him, pleading for him to come and help the Tuskegee Institute in Alabama.

Tuskegee was experimenting with the innovative concept of allowing students to attend who could not afford to pay tuition if they would work for the school in programs which taught valuable job skills.

Washington wanted to open an agricultural department to grow crops on campus, using student labor, to produce food for the cafeteria while also teaching students agriculture skills. He described, *"We began with a farm because we needed to eat."*[148]

Asking Dr. Carver to come and lead the Agriculture Department, Washington wrote, *"Our students are poor, often starving. They travel miles of torn roads, across years of poverty. We teach them to read and write, but words cannot fill stomachs. They need to learn how to plant and harvest crops."*[149]

Dr. Carver prayed about it and felt the Lord leading him to accept the position at Tuskegee. So he moved down to Alabama and built his laboratory from scratch, making science equipment from things he found in the trash.

Determined to make life easier for the families who struggled to scratch a living out of the stubborn ground, he described, *"As I worked on projects which fulfilled a real human need, forces were working through me which amazed me. I would often go to sleep with an apparently insolvable problem."*

"When I woke, the answer was there. Why, then, should we who believe in Christ be so surprised at what God can do with a willing man in a laboratory? Some things must be baffling to the critic who has never been born again."[150]

The people who worked with him noticed that something was different about him. Dr. Carver was very close to God—walking and talking with God like people talk to their human friends.

When asked about his walk with God, Dr. Carver replied, *"It's all very simple, if one knows how to talk with the Creator. You remember what He said in the Proverbs, 'Those that seek Me early shall find me.' So I just follow His advice and find Him. All my life I have risen regularly at four o'clock and have gone into the woods and talked with God. There He gives me my orders for the day."*

"Alone there with things I love most I gather specimens and study the great lessons Nature is so eager to teach us all. When people are still asleep I hear God best and learn my plan. I never grope for methods. The method is revealed the moment I am inspired to create something new."

"I live in the woods. I gather specimens and listen to what God has to say to me. After my morning's talk with God I go into my laboratory and begin to carry out His wishes for the day."[151]

Dr. Carver would also describe his relationship with God when he was invited to speak at a meeting in Minneapolis. When asked how he had invented so many things from the peanut, he told this story. *"Years ago I went into my laboratory and said, 'Dear Mr. Creator, please tell me what the universe was made for?'"*

"The Great Creator answered, 'You want to know too much for that little mind of yours. Ask for something more your size, little man.'"

"Then I asked, Please Mr. Creator, tell me what man was made for."

"Again the Great Creator replied, 'You are still asking too much. Cut down on the extent and improve the intent.'"

"So then I asked, Please Mr. Creator, will you tell me why the peanut was made?"

"That's better, but even then it's infinite. What do you want to know about the peanut?"

"Mr. Creator, can I make milk out of the peanut?"

"What kind of milk do you want? Good jersey milk or just plain boarding house milk?"

"Good jersey milk."

"And then the Great Creator taught me to take the peanut apart and put it together again. And out of the process have come all these products."[152]

Dr. Carver had brought samples with him of both the good jersey and plain boarding house milk. People tried them and were very impressed.

Pastor Jim Hardwick, who had attended the lecture, went home and told everyone, *"I went expecting to learn science and came away knowing more about prayer than I have ever learned in the theological schools."*[153]

When Dr. Carver taught students, he emphasized the need for studying science and the importance of a strong work ethic. *"God created these plants for man's use but without science you don't even know what they are."*

Then quoting from Psalms 121:1, he talked about how when the Bible tells us to look at the hills, *"God doesn't mean just looking at the hills without seeing anything. God wants us to <u>search</u> with everything we know: with chemistry and physics and botany."*

Speaking of the hills, Dr. Carver displayed paintings he had painted himself with colors he made from the clay soil of the Alabama hills. He described, *"God put that color into the hills of Alabama and it has stayed there unchanged for centuries. Why should it fade when I use it to paint a flower?"*[154]

In those speeches Dr. Carver also pointed out the importance of getting an education. He talked about how all the years he had spent studying nature and plants helped him as he talked with God in his lab. Describing how faith and knowledge mixed in the laboratory, he told the students how he conducted his experiments.

In a different speech, Dr. Carver went into further detail describing how God had taught him to work with the peanuts. Once again he told the story of the day when he asked the Lord, *"Mr. Creator, what is in the peanut?"*

Deep inside he heard the Holy Spirit respond to him, *"I have given you some brains. Take the peanuts into your laboratory and take them apart."*

Dr. Carver joked with the students that God didn't say how much brains he had.

Then he continued, *"With such knowledge as I had of chemistry and physics I set to work to take the peanut apart. I separated the water, the fats, the oils, the gums, the resins, sugars, starches, amino acids, etc."*

"There! I had the parts of the peanut all spread out before me. I still didn't know what to do with the parts. I looked at the Creator and He looked at me."

"The Creator said, 'I have given you three laws: compatibility, temperature, and pressure. All you have to do is take these elements and put them together, observing these laws, and I will show you why I made the peanut.'"

"I went on to try different combinations of the parts under different conditions of temperature and pressure, and the result was what you see."[155]

Dr. Carver showed samples of the various products he had produced from the peanut. The students were greatly impressed. Many of them would later describe how this motivated them to continue their education and work hard.

Yet even though many people were inspired by Dr. Carver, there were also some people who doubted him. Refusing to believe that he could invent all of these products by listening to God, skeptics tried to publicly discredit his research.

On November 20, 1924, an editorial was printed in the *New York Times* criticizing him for, *"A complete lack of the scientific spirit. Real chemists do not scorn books and they do not ascribe their successes, when they have any, to 'Inspiration.' Talk of that sort will merely bring ridicule."*[156]

Dr. Carver responded by writing a long letter to the newspaper.

The *New York Times* printed what he had written to the editor. *"I was very interested to read your editorial about myself. I regret exceedingly that there was such a gross misunderstanding over the meaning of 'Divine Inspiration.'"*

"Inspiration is never in conflict with information; in fact, the more information one has, the greater will be the inspiration."

"Paul, the great Scholar, says in 2Timothy 2:15, 'Study to show thyself approved unto God, a workman that needs not to be ashamed, rightly dividing the word of truth.'"

"Again he says in Galatians 1:12, 'For I neither received it of man, neither was I taught it, but by revelation of Jesus Christ.'"

"I have pursued developing products from the potato. I know of no one who has ever worked with these roots in this way. I know of no book from which I can get this information, yet I will have no trouble in doing it. If this is not inspiration and information from a source greater than myself then tell me what it is."[157]

His inventions went way beyond the peanut. He developed new products that increased the demand for soybeans, pecans, and sweet potatoes, enabling even more crop rotation and soil replenishment. And his peanut research continued to build America's economy.

By World War II, five hundred million dollars worth of peanuts were selling each year.[158] Listening to the Lord, one man alone in a laboratory had transformed American agriculture.

For forty years at Tuskegee, Dr. Carver taught practical ways to apply science and continued to invent more helpful products.

According to Jim Hardwick, one of Dr. Carver's friends, *"Once someone asked him to make something for diabetics. He went into his laboratory and prayed and almost immediately there came to him a method of producing a flour that was sweet and yet entirely devoid of all sugar content, a real treat for diabetics."*

"During World War I, when the soldiers needed most of our wheat supply and we had our meatless, wheatless and sweetless days, the government tried to find a substitute for wheat. Meanwhile, at Tuskegee Institute, they were saving two hundred pounds of wheat flour a day by using sweet potato flour with wheat flour and even making a better loaf than before."

"Again the U.S. Government sent for Carver to come to Washington, this time not with peanuts, but with a sweet potato exhibit. He simply amazed the experts who had gathered to confer with him."

"It was after the conference that Dr. David Fairchild, agricultural explorer in charge of the United States Dept of Agriculture, spoke of Dr. Carver as 'One of the most remarkable and extraordinary minds I have ever met.'"[159]

That wasn't the only way he had served his country. Dr. Carver was often asked for help by the U.S. Military.

While Dr. Carver never talked about what he did for them, years later someone who had worked in intelligence with him told *The Jackson Daily News* that *"His specialty was solving the mysteries of the secret inks used by German agents in transmitting news to Berlin, and he never failed to find the original formula or develop the re-agent that brought out the writing."*[160]

Dr. Carver's inventions also included creating some of the most beautiful things out of the ugliest.

Harvey Hill was a Christian leader traveling across America to lead prayer meetings. While he met lots of people, the one person he wanted to meet the most was Dr. Carver. When he visited Carver at Tuskegee, he was stunned to see the remarkable museum display of Carver's work including:

- *"Paints, stains and varnishes made from the clays of Alabama;"*
- *"Artificial marble made from wood shavings;"*
- *"Beautiful wall hangings made from feed sacks and wrapping strings;"*
- *"Rugs and mats made from okra and iron weed fiber;"*
- *"Charming watercolor landscapes from coffee grounds and orange peel;"*
- *"Fruits and vegetables that Dr. Carver had canned some thirty-five years before, to encourage farmers to grow vegetables;"*
- *"Paving blocks, insulating boards, cordage, paper and rugs, made from cotton;"*
- *"Over one hundred products just from the sweet potato; and"*
- *"Three hundred different products made from the peanut."*

The one thing that Hill couldn't take his eyes off was the display of weeds.

He described, "*Normally weeds are gathered and burned; but here were dozens of useful products the great scientist had made from the waste materials of nature's wild plants.*"

That evening at dinner, Hill told Dr. Carver, "*Your exhibit is the most outstanding thing I have ever seen!*"

Dr. Carver replied, "*Were you able to grasp the spiritual significance of our little museum?*"

Hill opened and closed his mouth. No, he hadn't thought about it.

Dr Carver continued, "*The Lord directed you here to receive His message. What that message is, you will have to find out for yourself.*"

Hill went to bed that night still wondering what he was missing. He wouldn't have to wait very long.

He described, "*During the night I had a dream in which I found myself in the museum, standing before the exhibit of products developed from the weeds. Reverently I stood there admiring what the Creator had accomplished with the assistance of one who was working in humble obedience and cooperation with Him.*"

"*In my dream I said, 'Lord, what is the meaning of all this?'*"

God's still small voice replied, "*Harvey, if Dr. Carver can produce the useful and beautiful from the old, ugly, discarded weeds, then you, with God's help, can produce useful and beautiful souls from ugly discarded lives.*"

Then he woke up. It was very early in the morning. Birds were singing. Sunlight was spreading across his window. Excited about his dream, he jumped out of bed, quickly dressed and rushed over to tell Dr. Carver about it.

Dr. Carver was surprised to see him up that early in the morning. Hill wrote, "*I exclaimed with considerable excitement, 'Dr. Carver, God has revealed the message.'*"

"*I told him of my dream. Smiling, he said, 'I knew our museum would speak to you, if you gave it an opportunity.'*"[161]

Dr. Carver's biggest admirer was Henry Ford. He loved to visit Dr. Carver at Tuskegee and learn from him.

As Dr. Carver described, *"When Henry Ford visited Tuskegee, he seemed quite upset that I walked up a flight of stairs to my apartment. He told Tuskegee's President Patterson that if I wouldn't move to the ground floor, he would pay to install an elevator right by my floor for my exclusive use."*

"After my elevator was in operation for a week, I could feel the difference in my strength. My heart operated better. Mr. Ford is always so thoughtful. He really is a dear soul."[62]

Henry Ford became one of Dr. Carver's closest friends. Whenever they were together, if anyone said anything disrespectful to Dr. Carver, Ford would make it very clear he didn't want to be anywhere that Dr. Carver wasn't welcome.

In Detroit, Ford built a special tribute in his museum to honor Dr. Carver's work.

When Ford held a scientific convention he invited Dr. Carver to come and give the keynote address. In a time when parts of America were still segregated, Ford and Dr. Carver worked to break down many barriers in the scientific community.

By the time Dr. Carver died in 1943, he was one of the most admired men in America. His remarkable achievements had won many awards.

The U.S. Navy named a ship for him. President Franklin Roosevelt dedicated the first ever federally funded memorial (honoring someone who had not been a U.S. President) to remind future generations the brilliance of this humble man.

Today his words continue to inspire people to realize *"God is going to reveal to us things He never revealed before if we put our hands in His."*[63]

Dr. Carver with his Tuskegee staff

5

Ask and You Shall Receive

Jesus said, *"Stay joined together with me, and follow My teachings. If you do this, you can ask for anything you want, and it will be given to you."*
John 15:7 (ERV)

As we walk through life, there will be many times when we don't know what to do. That's the time to ask God for help. *"Do any of you need wisdom? Ask God for it. He is generous and enjoys giving to everyone. So he will give you wisdom."*[164]

Have you ever hesitated to ask God for what you really want? Religious tradition has trained us to feel guilty for praying for anything beyond our basic needs. Yet God wants to do much more for us than just providing our daily needs. He wants to *"Daily load us with benefits."*[165]

"The Lord will withhold no good thing from those who do what is right."[166] The desire of your heart matters to God.

"Seek your happiness in the Lord, and he will give you your heart's desire."[167]

God never asked you to suffer in silence. While you're waiting on Him, He's waiting on you. He wants you to take the initiative and come to Him. The way Jesus described it was *"So far you haven't asked for anything in My name. Ask and you will receive so that you can be completely happy."*[168]

Before you go to anybody else, go to God for help. He can show you how to fulfill your destiny. *"Just ask, and I will give you whatever you need."*[169]

Think About:

"Don't worry about anything, but pray and ask God for every-thing you need, always giving thanks for what you have."
Philippians 4:6 (ERV)

"Our problems, whatever they are, have a way of diminishing when we take them to God."[170]
-Wallace Johnson

"God gave us success beyond men's expectations, after we rejected human wisdom to follow God's plan by experimenting and adapting to changing conditions."[171]
-Merrell Vories

6

William Colgate

"The Lord will protect you as you come and go, both now and forever!"
Psalm 121:8 (ERV)

William Colgate
1783-1857
From England

William Colgate was the oldest of eleven children born to Robert and Sarah Colgate. Robert's grandfather was a pastor. His father was a church deacon. They served in a local gathering of believers, who were devoted to the Bible.

Trouble was brewing for them. It was a difficult time to raise a family in England. The Revolutionary War was drawing to a close, leaving bitter feelings on both sides. Furious over the results of the war, King George III was cracking down on free speech in England. Anyone criticizing the government was ruthlessly punished.

Robert Colgate was one of those people speaking his mind. Throughout the war, he had been closely following the news, hoping America would gain its freedom. But living in England, that wasn't what people wanted to hear. Soon expressing his opinions had gotten him into big trouble.

Robert had powerful friends in government who tried to protect him. Yet even his friend William Pitt, the Prime Minister of England, couldn't save him from the King's wrath. Pitt could only warn Robert to leave England before he was arrested.

Jail didn't scare Robert. Nor the fact that he could be held indefinitely without trial. But what about his family? They would suffer the most if he was locked away. So Robert made the difficult choice to leave everything and sail with his family to America.

There things didn't work out so well. First he bought a farm close to Baltimore, Maryland and tried to cultivate it. After plowing the land and planting his crops, Robert discovered that the person who sold him the farm didn't actually own it. By the time he realized he had been scammed, it was too late. The real owner showed up to reclaim the property, leaving Robert with nothing.

Broke and discouraged, Robert moved to upstate New York and found a job working for a farmer. Once again things went sideways. Robert was accused of stealing and sued by the farmer. When he couldn't pay the court judgment, he was sent to debtor's prison.

Yet while he suffered in prison, he was grateful to be in America. By then he had become an American citizen. He wrote letters home to encourage his wife and children that someday things would be better. *"My dear children, rejoice with me and be thankful. I trust God."*[180]

Meanwhile, his family scrambled to make a living. As the oldest of eleven children, young William Colgate had to figure out a way to help.

Thinking that maybe if he moved to New York City, he might find a job and be able to support his mother and siblings, William decided to leave home at age twenty.

While walking to the city, he met a neighbor who worked as a boat captain. He told the neighbor he didn't know what to do, his only job skill was making soap. The neighbor offered to pray for William and encouraged him to dream big. *"Someone will soon be the leading soap maker in New York. It can be you as well as anyone. I hope it may. Make an honest soap, give a full pound. Be a good man, give your heart to Christ and give the Lord all that belongs to Him of every dollar you earn."*[181]

When he got to New York City, he was able to find a job at a soap company, Slidell & Co. After three years of working for them, William decided to start his own business. He launched the Colgate Company in 1806. Little did he know how his business would forever change the lives of American ladies.

At that time, most women had to make their own soap. It was a smelly, dirty, ugly process involving separating and boiling animal fats. While many families were used to living off the land and making whatever they needed, no housewife really enjoyed the chore of having to make their own soap.

William figured that if he could make sweet smelling, pretty bars of soap, the ladies would want to buy his products. Plus moving to New York City gave him access to many more customers. About 75,000 potential customers lived within walking distance of his shop. That was how he could solve the problem of distribution in a time when railroads hadn't yet been built across America.

William opened his little store in NYC, focusing on quality products and good customer service. He also pioneered the idea of a delivery service. Upon making his very first sale, he volunteered to personally deliver the purchase to his customer.

That cost him money. As the only worker in his shop, he had to close the shop and miss sales to make the delivery, but his idea worked. *"The delivery of this cake of soap may have cost me double my profit on that first sale, but I won a good customer and have kept him ever since."*[182]

His first customer told all their friends about the really good soap at a decent price with free delivery at the Colgate Company. Soon William had so many customers that he was able to hire help and purchase delivery carts. Several of his brothers moved there to help him.

Word continued spreading about the quality soap he produced. One of his frequent customers, a cloth merchant who used lots of soap at his factory, raved about how this soap was *"Superior to any soap I ever used."*[183]

More sales came. As the business grew, he continued helping his family. Then one day his dream came true, he had made enough money to buy his parents a farm.

By this time his father had been released from jail. Finally owning his own farm, Robert was able to help William by producing some of the soap ingredients.

Robert wrote to William that there weren't any local churches for several miles. So when the people of his town heard that he had experience preaching, they asked him to start a church.

Robert wrote, "*We meet in a schoolhouse, my listeners being from various different denominations. I think it better to teach the principles of Christianity than to dwell on doctrinal issues that have caused so many divisions and been so destructive to that love which ought to reign among all sincere Christians.*"[184]

Meanwhile, the animosity still brewing between England and America boiled over into the War of 1812. The battle began on the high seas as British ships harassed American ships headed to trade with Europe. Tempers flared. Cargos were seized. American crews were captured and forced into involuntary servitude on British ships.

There were so many Americans being kidnapped and forced to work on British ships that President Thomas Jefferson shut down the entire American shipping industry. That brought international trade to a standstill. American manufacturers couldn't sell their products abroad and European products couldn't be imported.

The U.S. Embargo Act of 1807 hurt America's economy but helped William Colgate. Once no more soap could be imported from Europe, demand for American soap skyrocketed. During the two years that the Embargo lasted, William sold more soap than he had ever dreamed.

The Embargo ended just before James Madison became President in 1809. Yet as soon as American ships began traveling overseas again, trouble on the high seas continued.

By 1812, six thousand American citizens had been kidnapped by the British. President Madison declared war.

During the War of 1812, William Colgate was the main supplier of soap to the American military, making his little company became a major force. Still even with more demands on his time than ever, he made time to serve as a deacon in his local Baptist church.

William would change American churches forever. When he joined the church, music was not a part of the service. William figured out how to change their minds, by volunteering to pay for an organ to be brought to the church for a concert on a week night. Everyone at the church was invited to attend, enjoy the music and then decide if the organ should stay or leave. The idea worked. The organ stayed, bringing beautiful music to the worship services.

At the time, churches didn't take offerings. To pay their bills, they rented pews. Each pew went for a different price. Since church had become the place where local businessmen mingled, networked, and developed deals, pews had become status symbols.

Wealthy families paid large sums to rent the best pews while poor people felt too embarrassed to attend church, not wanting to ask anyone for permission to sit in their pew.

In the earliest days of America, George and Martha Washington paid five pounds to rent their pew at the Protestant Episcopal Church of Fairfax, Virginia.

Years later, Abraham and Mary Todd Lincoln paid $200/year for their pew at the First Presbyterian Church of Springfield, Illinois from 1841 until 1861, when they left home to move to the White House.[185]

Pew rentals bothered William. What was the point of having church if the doors were closed to those who needed it the most?

Approaching the church leadership, William said, *"Churches charge for pews because they feel they cannot otherwise pay the bills. Yet Christ gave us the duty, 'To preach the gospel to all nations.'"*

"Our city has many people who are not attending church, because of the cost of the reserved seat system. Although parents and their children should come to church, they won't, when they feel like intruders upon the supposed rights of others. No one wants to feel beholden to someone else. Now if the seats are free, we lay no stumbling block in their way, and remain faithful to the characteristic of our gospel—it is preached to the poor."[186]

The church leadership responded that offering free seats was too risky. Several other churches had tried to offer free seats only to run out of money and close their doors. They didn't have any choice.

William wouldn't give in. He kept protesting the pew rental system and asking them to rely on free will offerings. He even volunteered to cover any potential budget shortfalls. Finally, they agreed.

When the pastor announced the new free seat system, the wealthy families in the church were deeply offended. They wanted to know their pew was waiting for them, even if they showed up late and distracted the whole congregation so they could walk up and sit down in the front rows.

Now that latecomers were seated in the back and anyone who showed up early could sit in the front, the wealthy members stopped coming to the church.

The church finances dropped rapidly. Members kept complaining. As the church treasurer, William Colgate could see the growing budget deficit. As the offerings declined, he kept reaching into his own pocket to keep the church afloat. But the church leadership couldn't stand the possibility of failure and decided to end their experiment. Once again they announced that pews would be rented.

That made William Colgate leave.

The church leadership panicked. They had just lost their biggest giver! The pastor visited William, begging him to stay. William refused, saying the church had lost its true calling.

William researched his idea of buying a church building, finding a pastor and offering free seats. When a good building became available, he purchased it and organized a church planting team. To find a good pastor, William asked around for someone with a big heart for people. He found a young seminary student named W. W. Everts.

Once the church building was ready and Everts had graduated from seminary, William invited Everts to come and pastor. Then William volunteered as an usher, seating people in the church.

The doors were opened, services began and word soon spread across New York City. People came by the multitudes.

One of the new people who came was Professor Harvey. He described, *"At that time I was a student at New York University, but not a Christian. My earliest memory of Deacon Colgate was at the Baptist Tabernacle on Mulberry Street."*

"The church building was large and surrounded by a dense population. It focused on inviting in the non-churched masses. When I walked in, there were two ushers greeting people at the door: Deacon William Winterton and Deacon William Colgate."

"I can never forget the warm, friendly greeting from Colgate, which quickly made you feel comfortable. Soon as the service ended, he was positioned back at the door, inviting people to return again."

"No wonder the church was soon crowded with a congregation enthusiastic in their love for Christ and people. It didn't take long for church membership to double to over one thousand people. William Colgate excelled best in influencing people."[187]

What happened next was described by another eyewitness named C. A. Buckbee. *"People kept saying that churches allowing free seats would fail. Few ministers were willing to come pastor a new and small congregation in a big city that had no income from rented pews.*

"Yet Deacon Colgate's free-church began to look like a success. Baptisms were frequent and when the time came for Evangelist Knapp to begin his meetings he found the people in a revival spirit.

"For nine weeks the church was crowded every evening and frequently thousands were unable to get inside the large building, in which more than two thousand persons sat or stood for hours listening to Jesus' words. All this time Deacon Colgate was at his post—helping in winning and caring for souls. Leaving all his business to others, he might be seen daily going to the homes of converts or inquirers to encourage them."

"The effect of the great revival in 1839-1840 was far-reaching. It made the Tabernacle one of the most influential churches in New York. One thing that surprised me, and I did not know how to explain it for years—how it was that such a large number of converts kept steadily on in their Christian life."

"I learned years after that Deacon Colgate had been watching them. He had suggested a system of neighborhood prayer meetings for young converts. The result was that very few fell away from their love of the Savior."[188]

As the church grew, more pastors were hired who also appreciated the help that William Colgate provided.

Another pastor who worked with him was Dr. Edward Lathrop. He described, *"When I was called to the church in New York, it was my first experience as a young pastor. In many ways I was not ready for the difficult work ahead. Many things that I should have known, I had not yet learned."*

"Deacon William Colgate never scolded me for my ignorance or mistakes. He never tried to boss or threaten me, but would gently take me by the arm and ask if I could teach him which of two ways would be better, as though he himself didn't know and needed my guidance. Thus, without embarrassing me, he was guiding and correcting me in love."

"Plus, he always took upon himself the blame for whatever the people had complained about in church."[189]

Just when things were going well, a scandal developed in the church. There was a lady who had been despised in the community for having an affair with a prominent businessman. Even years after marrying the businessman, she was still considered too scandalous to be accepted by polite society. When she came to the church and got saved, the church board was displeased.

As the church leadership met in private to discuss her membership application, William said, *"We have been praying to God for the conversion of sinners. But we have not told Him what kind of sinners we wanted. After He saves this lady we don't know whether to receive her or not."*

"Perhaps if we should be a little more careful hereafter to tell the Lord just what kind of sinners to convert, we may not have to be troubled."[190]

The other deacons chuckled then voted unanimously to welcome her. She became, *"One of the most respected and helpful members of the church."*[191]

William continued serving in the church for the rest of his life. One of his friends, the Reverend George Hatt described, *"As a Christian he was known as a fearless defender of the truth, no human reasoning could turn him aside from a 'Thus says the Lord.' As a deacon he was true to his office as a peacemaker."*

"If anything occurred to disturb the harmony of the group, he would rise with his pleasant smile, and say 'Brethren, let us remember we are in God's presence who taught us to love one another.'"[192]

While William loved serving in the church and was frequently there, he also loved the Bible. His favorite copy was the one given to him by his father. One day William left his Bible in his church seat. It disappeared.

William looked everywhere, but never found it. He thought, "What a pity any should so need a Bible as to steal it!"[193]

Thinking about how people may not be able to afford a Bible, William launched the American Bible Society. Board members would include many prestigious members of the community including former President John Quincy Adams. The new organization distributed many Bibles and accomplished a lot, until the members began to focus on minor doctrinal differences.

When Baptist missionaries in India requested a Bible in Bengalese, their request was denied. The Bible Society was too busy fighting over whether to translate the word "baptize" as "sprinkle" or "immerse."

When this dispute brought everything to a screeching halt, William knew he had to intervene. Telling them to stay focused on the main priority of getting the Bible into the hands of the people, he told them to get the job done. They didn't listen. The fighting continued until William was left with no choice but to leave.

Attending one last board meeting, William told them, "I must stand up for the millions of common people, who like myself, have never had more than a basic education. How can we withhold from them the clear understanding of our Lord Jesus? How can we surrender the authority of God's Word to the will of this Society?"[194]

Once again William found himself having to leave one group to create another. He created the American Bible Union and got them working on a new translation to put the Bible in modern English. This time he tried to keep the other directors focused on what really mattered.

William believed, *"Producing a faithful revision of the English Bible for the common people has been for many years an object as dear to me as life. I have confidence that the Bible Union will do the work."*[195]

This translation was finished in 1864 and named the *"Common English Version."*[196]

William continued serving on the Board of the Bible Union for the rest of his life. He also served on the board of the Baptist Missionary Association, sending money to spread the Gospel around the world. And he would continue standing for truth even when it meant taking on the whole denomination by himself.

At one point, William was protesting the unnecessary cost of moving a seminary from one location to another. The opposing side felt that the seminary would gain more students and make more money if it relocated to a bigger city. William felt the resources were better preserved by remaining in its current location with buildings and classrooms already built.

When the seminary decided to follow William's advice in defiance of the denomination's leaders, William got in trouble.

When William was confronted over how he could defy the entire denomination on this issue, he boldly replied, *"The voice of the denomination will—in the end—answer to the voice of God."*[197]

He won that battle. The seminary stayed where it was and was able to continue attracting many students.

Along the way, William fell in love and married a nice lady named Mary Gilbert. Together they raised three sons—Robert, James and Samuel Colgate. William taught them the soap business, making them equal partners. Meanwhile, he continued innovating with various ideas for large scale factory production and creative advertising.

After a long life full of many accomplishments, in his later years he became very ill.

Finally at seventy-four years old with family gathered around him, in the last moments of his life, he looked up, saw something and exclaimed, *"My precious Jesus."*[198] With that he passed into eternity.

His children followed in his footsteps, running the family business and generously supporting many Christian ministries.

To them that was an important investment because as Samuel Colgate described, *"Without God's presence and the teachings of the Bible, we would be enshrouded in moral darkness and despair. May the Earth be full of the knowledge of the Lord, as waters cover the sea."*[199]

Samuel Colgate would also innovate the business with his own ideas. Figuring that the customers would need something more than soap, in 1873, he began selling toothpaste.

By 1876, he was rapidly prospering even in a difficult economy. Describing events in his journal, he wrote, *"Finished the yearly accounts of my business for 1876, while many firms have suffered, we have had made money. I feel thankful for the great prosperity I enjoy and trust I may share it by working for my Lord."*[200]

Samuel Colgate would also be involved in producing a biography of his father's life called *William Colgate the Christian Layman.*

The biography would be written by the young pastor W.W. Everts who had helped Colgate establish his free seat church.

The Colgate family allowed Everts to include some private papers of William Colgate in the biography so that people would know that the legacy of his life was his love for God.

As William had once written in his journal, his goal in life was *"To love Christ. To be pleased when He is pleased and grieved when He is grieved."*[201]

6

Entries and Exits

"The Lord brought us out from there
to bring us into the land He had promised."
Deuteronomy 6:23 (NLV)

God has something better for you than anything you've ever had before. He has planned out a great future that you can move into one step at a time. Yet sooner or later we will need to let go of something we have to get what God has waiting for us.

As hard as this can be, we can find comfort in the promise of Jesus: *"Everyone who has left their home, brothers, sisters, mother, father, children, or farm for me and for the Good News about me will get a hundred times more than they left."*

"Here in this world they will get more homes, brothers, sisters, mothers, children, and farms. And with these things they will have persecutions. But in the world that is coming they will also get the reward of eternal life."[202]

Going through changes means different things for different people. It could be graduating school, leaving home, buying a house, starting a job or ending a bad relationship.

While these major life decisions can be scary, God has promised, *"Good will come to you when you come in, and when you go out."*[203]

Before you make any major decision, take the time to seek God. Even Moses who had talked with God face to face—still didn't feel he knew enough to lead the Israelites through the wilderness. So he prayed to God, *"If You don't go with us, then don't make us leave this place."*[204]

God responded, *"I myself will go with you. I will lead you."*[205] Stay close with the Lord and you'll stay on the right track.

Think About:

God promises, *"Remember, I will be with you and protect you wherever you go, and I will bring you back to this land. I will not leave you until I have done all that I have promised you."*
Genesis 28:15 (GNT)

"Overcome the habit of grabbing at the nearest dollar as though it were the only dollar in the world."[206]
-Henry Ford

"The road to success isn't easy, but it's much happier than the road of leisure, ease and comfort."[207]
-Harvey Firestone

7

Henry Crowell

"There's an opportune time to do things,
a right time for everything on the earth."
Ecclesiastes 3:1 (MSG)

Henry Crowell
1855-1944
From Ohio

At close to ninety years old, Henry Crowell still showed up for work every day. Even after creating Quaker Oats had made him a lot of money, Crowell had no desire to retire. He loved running his company. And it felt great to prove that the doctors were wrong when they said he would die before his twenty-first birthday.

Crowell had been only nine years old, when his father died of tuberculosis at the young age of forty-three. Crowell had two younger brothers—Edward and Charles. While his mother had been left alone to raise three children under age ten, she was also left with the resources to do it.

Their father had started a shoe company, which had been so successful that he was able to leave them a well supplied trust fund. At nine years old Henry Crowell inherited $27,000 dollars.

His brothers had also inherited money but they wouldn't live long enough to enjoy it. Tragedy returned to that family. Both Edward and Charles became very ill with the same lung disease. Edward died at age twenty-eight. Charles fought for his life, until passing away at age thirty-nine.

Henry Crowell was also suffering from the same illness. By age seventeen he had to drop out of high school. The doctor told his family, *"He has lung trouble just like his father. Crowell will have to stop school or die."*[208]

That was hard. As Crowell later described, *"I was athletically inclined. Thoroughly enjoyed the gym, good at baseball, a leader in athletics, and pretty well developed. I was never sick at the beginning. But gradually my health failed. I was taken out when I was seventeen."*[209]

By age nineteen, he was bedridden. As he lay helpless, wondering what would happen, he read the Bible and prayed for answers. One morning, as he opened the Bible, a verse jumped off the page.

In Job 5:19, he read that God, *"Shall deliver you in six troubles: yes, in seven there shall no evil touch you."*[210]

He heard the Holy Spirit telling him to slow down and rest for seven years.

In his own words, Crowell described, *"I had been reading the Bible enough to realize the emphasis God put on the number seven. Seven years! Perhaps I might get well in seven years!"*[211]

Crowell also remembered something that he had learned in high school. The principal at his private high school had been a strong Christian who prayed and sought God's will. Principal Benjamin Mills cared deeply for his students. He always took time to sit and listen to them whenever they wanted to talk.

When they asked for his advice, the one thing that he always taught them was *"Take your time. Be sure to find the will of God."*[212]

That became the motto of Crowell's life. Even as he lay helpless on his bed, he kept thinking about how to do that. Just then the doctors came in and told him that spending more time outdoors would help his health.

The doctors actually recommended seven years of as much outdoor activity as possible. Then he might recover.

Seven years. That's what the Holy Spirit had just told him. Crowell described, *"I felt assurance in my heart that I would get well."*[213]

For the next several years, he focused on as much time outdoors as possible. The more time he spent outdoors, the better he felt. Slowly his strength began to return. When he felt up to traveling, he took a long cross country trip to find warmer weather in California. Taking his time, when he got to California, he rode horseback on a tour across the state, admiring the scenery. After that trip, he was feeling so much better that he decided to find something more challenging to keep busy.

Maybe he could buy a farm. Then he could work outdoors, plowing fields and planting crops. Crowell heard from a friend about a place called Fargo, North Dakota. The friend raved about how the farmland there was wonderful and the conditions perfect.

Crowell traveled there and spent several weeks fishing and relaxing outdoors. The scenery was beautiful and the town peaceful. Things looked right to settle down. He bought a farm, plowed the fields and planted a wheat crop.

Then came a tornado.

Crowell had gone to town for supplies when he saw the dark cloud headed straight for his property. Since the town was twelve miles from his property, Crowell could only wait in town and watch helplessly as the storm destroyed everything in its path.

The next morning after the storm had passed, Crowell drove back to his farm, wondering if anything would be left. He was in for a big surprise. His farm hadn't even been touched. The storm had traveled a straight path for several miles until it reached his property. Then it had made a sharp left turn.

Crowell couldn't believe his eyes. Every building on his farm was intact while other buildings for miles around were completely destroyed. Crowell was amazed as he realized his prayers had been answered.

"God must have changed the direction of the tornado."[214]

The next day, Crowell was approached by someone wanting to buy his farm. He thought: *"The Lord preserved the buildings and the property. Now He sends a man to buy, and pay cash. It seems like the Lord doesn't want me on this farm."*[215]

Crowell sold the farm and moved to South Dakota. Once again he bought a farm and planted wheat. Just as the crop was growing well, another storm came. This time a very heavy hot wind blew across the prairie, shriveling up the plants. What was supposed to be a bumper crop became a complete disappointment.

Crowell could only watch in frustration. Maybe farming wasn't his calling after all. *"I was turning against farming. I felt I would rather get into a business where if I made a mistake I could correct it."*[216]

Not knowing where life would take him next, *"I was confident of one thing—God was guiding me. I felt that I was now in good health again, but I would just wait awhile and see what God would do next. I knew He would soon show me what He wanted."*[217]

At eighteen years old, Crowell had made a covenant with God after attending a revival service preached by Evangelist Dwight L. Moody.

Moody had thundered from the pulpit, *"Think of big ways you can be used for God. The world has yet to see what God can do with and for and through and in a man who is fully devoted to Him."*[218]

Hearing those words, Crowell quietly slipped out of the service to have a private conversation with God.

There was a lake nearby. Crowell walked over and for a long time paced around the lake as he prayed about his future.

Did he even have a future? At the time he was still devastated over how his education had been interrupted by his illness, but maybe things had happened for a reason. Crowell would later describe how that night he realized God had a plan.

"Moody's words were the words of the Lord to me. I saw now that the wrecking of my school plans didn't really matter. God didn't need his men educated, or brilliant, or anything else! All God needed was just a man. Well, I decided to be that man."[219]

Crowell wanted to do big things for God, but how could a seriously ill young man ever make a difference in the world? The more Crowell thought about it, the more he realized something.

"To be sure, I would never preach like Moody. But I could make money and help support the labors of men like Moody. Then I resolved, 'God, if You will allow me to make money to be used in Your service, I will keep my name out of it so You will have all the glory.'"[220]

The rest of his life would be devoted to keeping that promise. In everything he did, he looked for ways to honor God.

After selling the farm, he began looking for other ways to make money. Then he heard from his uncle that an oatmeal processing mill was for sale back in his hometown. *"When I heard about this, I immediately thought—This is probably what God has planned for me. I had been seven years in search of health, and health was found. No longer was I obliged to live outdoors."*

Crowell knew, *"As I grew better and became well, God evidently did not want me to be a farmer. He took me out of one farm by a tornado and out of the second by a hot wind. And now that the seven years were finished, He was opening the way for me to secure the Quaker Mill. I felt compelled to go to my room and for a long time, I thanked God for all His blessings."*[221]

Crowell also learned something else from reading the Bible, *"I saw too, that my gratitude to God must be expressed in tithing."*[222]

During the seven years that Crowell had been trying to get well, technology had advanced. Someone had invented a new machine for processing oats.

In 1875, William Heston had patented this new invention and then launched the Quaker Mill Company. Things hadn't worked out. Too much competition from oat processing companies had destroyed his business. Running out of resources, in 1881, Heston sold his company to Warren Corning, who tried to make it work. After two years of struggling, Corning sold the Quaker Mill to Crowell for $25,000.

Twenty-six year old Henry Crowell knew nothing about the oatmeal business other than that the market for selling oats was very limited.

At that time, oatmeal was primarily used for feeding horses and other farm animals. It was never considered proper food for humans.

Typical American breakfasts in the 1800's were described by the renowned British Astronomer Francis Baily during his travels in America. While visiting Virginia he noticed that breakfast was something like *"Coffee, buckwheat cakes, and some fried venison or broiled chicken, meat being inseparable from an American breakfast."*[223]

Not everyone could afford that nice of a breakfast. Crowell thought about many families on the western frontier, struggling to make a living. They needed healthy, affordable food that could stand the harsh conditions of frontier life. But how could he convince people to eat something that they thought was only good enough for the animals? And what was it about oatmeal that disgusted people?

Crowell hired a team and sent them around America to find out. After visiting stores around the country, they reported back to Crowell what the problem was. Oatmeal was typically sold by stores in bulk containers: often barrels that sat open and unprotected. All kinds of things were frequently falling into the open barrels and contaminating the oatmeal but no one cared because only the animals would eat it. The team had seen cats napping on top of the oatmeal, leaving countless hairs behind. Rats scampered in and out. Sometimes the barrels accidentally tipped over, spilling oatmeal all over the dirty ground. Then the grocers would simply sweep it up, putting it right back into the barrel.

The team told Crowell: *"These goods were all clean when they left the factory. So are the bulk pickles, fish, crackers, etc. Most factories are sanitary nowadays. But even the careful grocer, no matter how hard he tries, cannot protect bulk goods from contamination—vile and dangerous to health."*[224]

The answer was simple. Packaging fresh oatmeal into smaller family sized portions that would sit on the shelf, safe from germs was Crowell's idea. First he had to convince people to eat it by launching an advertising campaign, emphasizing that his brand could be trusted for quality and purity.

Advertising was expensive. It was also considered unnecessary by the other oatmeal millers. So when Crowell approached the other oatmeal millers, inviting them to create an association to pool their resources, they stonewalled him.

Why did they need to spend money on advertising when they had gotten along just fine for years without it? Besides, what could this young Crowell know about oatmeal that they didn't?

The largest miller in the area, Ferdinand Schumacher blasted Crowell's ideas by saying, *"Advertising is silly business! We'll save our money—let our competitors advertise."*[225]

Even with resistance, Crowell still managed to bring several millers together to form the Consolidated Oatmeal Company in 1887. The board of directors included various different oatmeal millers. Crowell was elected President of the Board. Schumacher served as treasurer.

Yet the association collapsed because the millers insisted on doing things the way they had always been done.

Crowell tried again, forming The American Cereal Company. Once again, no one listened to his ideas. Everything Crowell tried to do was opposed. Slowly Schumacher took control until eventually Crowell was kicked out of his own organization.

"It was a shaky setup," Crowell recalled later, *"I knew Mr. Schumacher's policies would not work, but I just kept still."*[226]

Years passed.

The other millers began to realize the problems Schumacher was causing. Finally they reached their limit.

Raising enough money to buy out Schumacher, they went to Crowell and begged him to return. He did. This time they followed his advice and created the Quaker Oats Company in 1901.

Twenty years had passed before the millers had listened to him. Crowell didn't hold that against them.

He quickly got to work, pouring money into advertising. His marketing strategies paid off. Little by little, families across America began eating oatmeal for breakfast.

Crowell saved the oatmeal industry from extinction just in time for the industrial revolution when the automobile came and rapidly decreased the demand for horses and animal feed.

Oatmeal would help many families survive the food shortages that came during World War I. When the economic markets collapsed into the Great Depression, oatmeal again helped many families survive.

Even during rapid economic decline, Crowell reported to his company, *"The demand for our products has been so consistent, both in the United States and Europe, that the mills have been driven under high pressure."*[227]

Quaker Oats became such a massive success that Crowell soon had another problem. When the federal government began going after corporate monopolies in an effort to level the playing field, Crowell found himself locked into a massive court battle. Was Quaker Oats a monopoly? Crowell was accused of controlling ninety percent of the oatmeal industry.

In the long court battle that ensued, Crowell was able to prove that his business only had fifty percent of the market. By taking his time, even while under intense scrutiny on the witness stand, Crowell showed how he had saved the entire industry from becoming obsolete and was making money for many other smaller companies. Crowell won the case by proving that he was keeping the rest of the industry afloat.

Crowell also succeeded in a completely different industry through his wife's advice. Through mutual friends, Crowell had met the beautiful Susan Coleman. They married in 1888 and raised a family.

At the time, most families across America still cooked their meals over an open fire. Then the industrial revolution moved many families from rural areas to the cities to live in apartment buildings where open fires were a huge safety hazard. Stoves and ovens were desperately needed.

A local man had invented a new compact, oil-fueled cooking stove. It was just what people needed as they moved from farms to cities, looking for work. The inventor approached the local general store and convinced them to sell his stoves. One of the store clerks, Francis Drury, realized the potential for these modern stoves and suggested to his boss that they buy the rights to this invention.

The boss wasn't interested. The clerk didn't have enough money to buy it himself so he approached his friend Susan Crowell, who convinced her husband to launch the Perfection Stove Company.

It succeeded from the start. Within a few years they were selling so many stoves that they caught the attention of John D. Rockefeller.

At that time Rockefeller's company, Standard Oil, had more oil than they could sell. Cars and airplanes hadn't been invented yet so the oil was getting pumped out of the ground faster than it was needed.

When Rockefeller heard about this stove, he realized that this was a whole new market for oil.

So he approached Crowell with an offer. Could Standard Oil send their three thousand salesmen out to sell Crowell's stoves? They did. Those salesmen sold millions of stoves across America giving Rockefeller new customers for his oil and making Crowell a fortune.

Yet even with more money than he had ever dreamed, Crowell remained faithful to God. As their wealth opened doors into high class society, he and his wife brought Jesus everywhere they went.

Friends noticed they had a heart for sharing Christ with everyone they met. One friend described how impressed they were that *"This millionaire couple kept it up, talking with anyone and everyone about the Lord."*[228]

Susan started a ladies Bible study which quickly drew many ladies from the highest levels of wealth and power. Many lives were touched by their testimony. One corporate executive admitted, *"I'm not much of a churchman, but I can go for Mr. Crowell's type of Christianity."*[229]

When the Crowells moved to Chicago, they continued reaching many people for Christ. William Robinson was one of Chicago's leading businessmen who was deeply touched by his friendship with Crowell. He described how during his business lunches with Crowell, *"All my doubts, my skepticism of the Scriptures, one by one my objections fell away. Then and there I decided—just as I would decide a business question—to come to God."*[230]

Meanwhile, Crowell also worked to improve the city of Chicago. He poured money into helping the poor, paying for doctors and nurses to provide life changing medical operations to those who couldn't afford it. He was also involved with organizations that passed legislation to shut down human trafficking and protect women. In every way he could, Crowell worked tirelessly to keep the promise he had made to God.

Crowell always kept his name so far out of it that very few people knew where the money was coming from. He supported many missionaries around the world, paying for supplies and Bibles.

One local organization he supported heavily was founded by Dwight Moody. After Moody himself passed away in 1899, his Moody Bible Institute struggled. Just when it was running out of resources and about to close its doors, Crowell came into his business success and was able to help.

For the next several years, Crowell's donations enabled them to train many evangelists and ministers who took the Gospel around the world. The Moody directors responded to his generosity by offering to place Crowell's name on their building.

When they told Crowell about their plans, he responded, *"No! Years ago I told the Lord that if He would allow me to make money for His service, I would keep my name out of it so He could have all the glory."*[231]

That devotion to God also caused him to make a very tough choice. While Crowell had been heavily involved for many years in a local church that he loved, something happened in that church that disturbed him.

The church leadership began to openly reject the authority of the Bible. New doctrine infiltrated the church, turning the hearts of young people away from the simplicity of Christ. Disturbed by the growing trend, Crowell confronted the leadership. He pleaded with them to return to Scriptural guidelines. They wouldn't listen.

That made Crowell leave. Publishing an open letter to his denomination, he warned others about what was happening. Crowell made his: *"Forceful protest against changing standards and the weakening of the church's loyalty and devotion to Jesus Christ. I can serve the Lord elsewhere with a clear conscience."*[232]

When church leaders realized they had lost Crowell's money, they panicked. How could they get him to return?

When they begged him to reconsider he refused because
"If I ever found the will of God, it was in this matter."[233]

Then Crowell took steps to protect his money. Taking a lot of time to work with attorneys, he developed an ironclad trust.

Strong rules were written and five trustees were appointed to make sure that the money in the trust would always serve the Lord, even after Crowell himself passed.

At age sixty-two, Susan passed in 1922 before the trust was finished. In a time when this was considered unheard of—Crowell insisted on putting her name on the trust as he felt the money had belonged to both of them. It had been something that *"She and I dreamed together."*[234]

When the trust was finally completed, Crowell was happy to know that *"Our money will go to the work of the Lord Jesus—but be protected from the tricks of evil people who want the loaves and fishes, but not the Gospel."*[235]

Today that trust is still fully funded, donating about $5,000,000 each year to Christian organizations who meet the strict requirements.[236] The main goals of the trust include taking the Gospel to the furtherest corners of the globe, helping the oppressed and empowering women.[237]

The trust's founder, Crowell lived to be eighty-nine years old. Even in the last years of his life, good health followed him. He stayed in shape by taking walks down the busy streets of Chicago. Every day he walked to and from the train station to get to work.

On October 23, 1944, he walked briskly to the train station and boarded a train headed downtown. After sitting down, he opened his Bible to read, then closed his eyes and died peacefully.

Upon hearing the news of his passing, Moody Bible Institute honored his legacy by engraving Crowell's name on its headquarters in Chicago.

They had also engraved on their wall something that Crowell had once scribbled on a paper in his desk. *"If my life can always be lived so as to please God in every way, I'll be supremely happy."*[238]

7

Take Your Time

"Being excited about something is not enough.
You must also know what you are doing.
Don't rush into something,
or you might do it wrong."
Proverbs 19:2 (ERV)

When Crowell began the journey of seeking health, he couldn't see that one day he would launch the Quaker Oat Company. He just kept moving ahead in life, one step at a time.

You have a destiny too. That destiny is revealed one piece at a time as you move through the various seasons of life.

While we would love to know our future right now, God reveals each piece of the puzzle through a process so we have the time to develop the skills we need for the next level.

Things don't happen overnight because we aren't ready yet. Time is needed to develop the skills required for your future.

When things take a long time, God has not forgotten us. He is preparing us. *"He controls the times and the seasons."*[239]

God has a perfect timing for the various seasons of our lives. When He created the Earth, He gave us different seasons of nature.

"As long as the earth continues, there will always be a time for planting and a time for harvest. There will always be cold and hot, summer and winter, day and night on earth."[240]

Farmers know the right time to plant and harvest crops. While nature has seasons for planting and harvesting, our lives also have various seasons of time for different phases. Times to study. To develop a career. To start a family. Life becomes easier when we focus on making the most of whatever season we are in.

Still life moves really fast. People move faster, trying to keep up. And that's how we can get into trouble. If we move too fast, we could get ahead of God's timing.

In the Old Testament when God's people were moving into their new land they were told not to move too fast, but to stay behind the priests as they crossed the Jordan River. *"When you see the Levite priests carrying the Box of the Agreement of the Lord your God, follow them. But do not follow too closely. Stay about one thousand yards behind them. You have not been here before, but if you follow them, you will know where to go."*[241]

Why did God say that? Today we are led by the Holy Spirit, but the principle is the same. Stay behind the Lord so you can see where to go. Getting ahead of God could cause you to not see the right direction and possibly miss the provision which is attached to His timing.

"Learn well how to wait so you will be strong and complete and in need of nothing."[242] Haste can make mistakes because once something is done you can't take it back.

If you want to save time, slow down. When you take the time to do it right, you don't have to lose time doing it over.

There's a balance we can find. Psalm 32:8-9 describes how to find this balance by not being too fast like the horse or too slow like the mule but listening to God as He guides us.

"Learn to be patient, so that you will please God and be given what He has promised."[243] Slow down. Take more time to focus on doing fewer things and let your stress levels disappear.

"For even young people tire and drop out, young folk in their prime, stumble and fall. But those who wait upon God get fresh strength. They spread their wings and soar like eagles, they run and don't get tired, they walk and don't lag behind."[244]

Think About:

"You must be willing to wait without giving up. After you have done what God wants you to do, God will give you what He promised you."
Hebrews 10:36 (NLV)

"Move slowly. Guard against debt. Get it done right. Some people might get impatient at delay, but God takes time for a great work."[245]
-William Colgate

"It took God a long time to get me ready for the job He had for me. All my years of experience, trial and error, hard work, and disappointment were necessary before I could be guided to form this company."[246]
-Mary Kay

8

Merrell Vories

"Since Jesus went through everything you're going through and more, learn to think like Him. Think of your sufferings as a weaning from that old sinful habit of always expecting to get your own way.
Then you'll be able to live out your days free to pursue what God wants instead of being tyrannized by what you want."
1 Peter 4:1-2 (MSG)

Merrell Vories
1880-1964
From Arizona

At age twelve Merrell Vories felt God drawing him towards being a missionary. So he ran from it.

Merrell's early childhood in Kansas was complicated by a mysterious illness, which kept him too sick to attend school. The doctors couldn't figure it out. They suggested his family move to a warmer climate. So his family moved to Flagstaff, Arizona.

There Merrell recovered enough to begin attending school. He learned how to play the piano, composed poetry, and fell in love with architecture.

When he got to high school and felt the Holy Spirit nudging him to be a missionary, he resisted. He wanted to pursue a career in architecture to earn enough to send other people to the missions field.

In botany class, one of his high school assignments was attempting to grow peas without soil. The botany teacher hoped it would help students understand that it was impossible to grow plants without dirt. Yet Merrell figured out how to make peas sprout on a piece of cotton with the roots dangling in water. This little success taught him a much bigger lesson. *"It taught me not to give up any idea or undertaking just because someone who ought to know, declared it impossible."*[247]

After graduating high school, Merrell enrolled in Colorado College to study architecture. He paid his own way through school by selling office products part time.

After finishing his degree, he found a job at the YMCA. There he was able to bring in more donations anyone else had done at that office before. The YMCA rewarded him by paying his way to a Christian conference.

Five thousand college students attended the *Student Volunteer Convention* in Toronto. One was changed forever. Little did Merrell know that he was going to have a powerful encounter with God at this conference.

It happened while he was sitting in the front row, listening to a lady missionary describing her work. She had just returned to the United States after working in Asia for several years. As Merrell listened to her describing the challenges she had faced, suddenly he could no longer hear her words. It felt like everything around him disappeared. He experienced a supernatural vision.

Merrell later described the vision as one moment he was looking at her face, then she completely disappeared and he saw the face of Christ inside of her. Merrell looked at Jesus and wondered what to say.

In the vision, Jesus looked right at him and asked if Merrell was going to do anything about the call of God on his life. Then the vision ended and Merrell was back in his seat, listening to the service.

Merrell went home and couldn't sleep. For the next several days, every time he closed his eyes, all he could see was Jesus looking at him and asking him to make a choice.

Finally, he surrendered. Writing to a Christian organization, he asked for an opportunity to go to some desolate, remote part of the world. Some far away place where no other missionary would want to go.

Several months later he received a reply. Would he like to teach English in a remote region of Japan? There was a paid teaching position available at a public Japanese high school in the Omi province.

Merrell looked up information on Japan and found only about one percent was Christian. Many missionary organizations warned against going to the Omi province because of the remote location, lack of resources and vast difficulties.

When Merrell asked the missionary group, offering him the position for advice, they told him, *"You will have three quarters of a million people all to yourself. You will find nothing prepared for you—but everything against you. Do not be discouraged if after two years, you can see no results."*[248]

They were right. Merrell had no idea how difficult it would be until he arrived on February 2, 1905. The first thing he noticed was that he was the only westerner in the whole area. Only a few locals could understand and speak English with him.

Merrell didn't speak a word of Japanese. Feeling loneliness descend on him, Merrell's first impulse was to turn around and go home.

That was not an option. Having spent the last dollar he had on the travel to get there, he didn't have any money to leave.

Merrell arrived at the home he had rented only to realize that this house was three hundred years old. Nothing in that house had ever been renovated. The roof was leaking. The walls had no insulation to protect from the bitter cold outside. There was no heating. Merrell shivered himself to sleep, thinking it couldn't get any worse.

Things got worse. Late at night, a sudden earthquake rocked the house, jolting him wide awake. What had he gotten himself into?

Unable to go back to sleep, Merrell pulled out his journal and scribbled, *"Homesick, cold, headache, lonely. But here!"*[249]

The next day he showed up for work at the high school to find out that God was already turning all things for good.

Merrell had prayed for someone that could be a good friend and ministry partner with him. God had already answered that prayer.

One of the other teachers at the school, Miyamoto, introduced himself to Merrell in perfect English, saying he was assigned to be the English translator. Miyamoto thanked Merrell for coming to Omi because Merrell was an answer to _his_ prayer.

Several years before, Miyamoto had given his heart to God through the influence of another Christian teacher at that school. When that Christian teacher had been transferred to another district, Miyamoto had prayed God would send someone else to that school to strengthen his faith.

Miyamoto also told Merrell there were a few Christians in the town who met together each week. They had been praying God would send someone to their town to teach them the Bible. Would Merrell like to join them? By the end of his first day at work, Merrell had several new friends. The loneliness was beginning to fade.

Merrell quickly settled into his new life. By day teaching English. At night, holding Bible studies in his home.

To his surprise forty-five of his own students from the high school began attending his home Bible studies. They asked lots of questions. Miyamoto translated. It wasn't long before one student approached Merrell to ask *"Please, teach me how to pray."*[250]

Pretty soon, Merrell had a thriving church meeting in his home with a congregation of new believers excited about walking with God.

That bothered some of the village leaders. Fearing loss of influence over the locals, they stirred up the local young men to violence.

Bullies at the high school began attacking the students who were converting to Christ. Several students were brutally beaten, suffering brain concussions. One almost drowned after being thrown from a bridge into a lake and not allowed to get out of the water.

As the violence escalated, Merrell was at a loss for how to respond. The police turned a blind eye. But when he asked his students what they wanted, they prayed for courage to endure. Persecution only made them stronger.

As Merrell's influence grew, one student took matters into his own hands. He decided to put an end to everything by killing Merrell. Hiding a gun under his clothing, he went to Merrell's house late at night and asked to talk with him.

They talked for a long time. The more they talked, the more the Holy Spirit melted the anger in that student's heart. By the end of the night, he had become a Christian. That student would later become a full time pastor who brought many others to the Lord.

In the months that followed, the Holy Spirit moved through that village, touching hearts. Even the worst bullies began to change. Merrell was shocked when the ringleader of the bullies came to him with tears in his eyes asking, *"Can God forgive me after what I've done?"*[251]

By the end of his first year in Japan, Merrell had baptized several of the former *"tormentors."*

Merrell's success only further aggravated the local village leaders. They pressured local government officials, who pressured the high school principal to fire Merrell.

After two years of teaching in Japan, Merrell was called to the principal's office for an ultimatum. If he wanted to keep his job, he was going to have to cease all Bible studies at his home because as the principal described, *"They all expected you to teach the Bible, but they did not expect anyone to believe."*[252]

Merrell insisted that he had only taught Jesus on his own time and in his own house. How could that possibly interfere with his teaching job at the school? Yet he was still fired.

Merrell wondered how he was going to stay in Japan. His only income was the teaching salary. The missionary organization that had sent him there would not give him any money.

"It was a panicky, nightmare feeling of defeat," Merrell later recalled, *"What could I do? I had not yet learned the true question—What was God going to do for Omi?"*[253]

The answer came when the students raised enough money to cover Merrell's expenses. They couldn't stand the thought of losing him. For the next several weeks, Merrell was able to minister to them full time.

Then one day Merrell received a letter with twenty-five dollars in it. As he described, *"An American businessman traveling in Japan heard about the situation and even though he never visited us, he arranged to send us twenty-five dollars a month through a friend, without his name being mentioned. The money came just when we had to have it and I learned a lesson about looking towards the right source for a way out."*[254][255]

Three years later, Merrell's home Bible study had grown into a full size church, being pastored by one of Merrell's former students. The church offerings were more than enough to cover the cost of the pastor's salary and purchase a building for them to meet in.

Yet they still had to meet in homes because no one in the town would sell them property. That town and much of Japan were still under the control of some very powerful people who crushed anyone who tried to interfere.

Merrell found out how powerful they were as every attempt he made to buy a building was blocked. Door after door slammed shut in his face. Still he continued knocking on doors, looking for a building and hoping things would change.

Then one day everything changed. Someone knocked at Merrell's door. Opening the door, Merrell saw a very wealthy Japanese man.

This man had just bought the best property in town and wanted to give it to him. As Merrell's mouth dropped open in shock, the gentleman explained that he had been born and raised in that town.

After leaving the town he had launched a very successful dairy business in Kyoto. He had also become a Christian. The Holy Spirit had told him to return to his hometown and help Merrell buy a building for the church to meet.

As the miracle unfolded Merrell marveled, *"How we had worried, and fretted, and despaired over our inability to buy some little back street lot! And for fifteen years our God had been preparing for us the best spot in the town!"*[256]

The church moved into their new building and continued to grow. Meanwhile, Merrell felt the Lord guiding him in a different direction to use his education in architecture to open a business to fund the ministry.

Merrell described, *"While traveling around Japan, I had noticed that a good deal of uneconomical building had been done and cost too much where the builders were at the mercy of local contractors. The thought came to me that I could help other projects while earning support for our own."*[257]

To his surprise, as soon as his office opened, work poured in. There was tremendous demand for skilled architects. Merrell had to hire several other architects just to keep up with the flood of projects. Then he expanded the business by hiring construction crews to build the projects.

In the years that followed, they completed sixteen hundred buildings across Japan, including both industrial and residential.

Money from those projects expanded Merrell's ministry even further. He was able to support many full-time pastors who ministered in towns all across Japan. Demand for Merrell's business continued to grow so he opened new branches in Tokyo and Osaka. Little did he know that his business would transform business in Japan forever.

Japan was still deeply rooted in a type of caste system. Workers were treated like property. Everyone toiled twelve hours a day, seven days a week except Merrell's employees. They went home after eight hours and got the weekend off.

People noticed how even with their shorter hours, Merrell's employees completed building projects faster than anyone else. This inspired other Japanese companies to experiment with giving their employees one day off per week. As production improved, companies also started following Merrell's example in offering extra benefits for workers.

As Merrell continued building projects, he noticed that the parts and supplies seemed really expensive. Investigating the situation revealed that suppliers were deliberately driving up supply costs by overcharging.

Merrell put an end to that by importing his own construction supplies and equipment, saving his customers lots of money. The more money he saved his customers, the more new customers they referred to him. Soon Merrell's business had expanded way beyond anything he had ever expected and his work continued to change lives.

One of his customers was a highly educated, physics professor who came from a wealthy family. Suzuki-San could easily afford to pay Merrell fifty thousand dollars to build him a dream home. While they worked on the plans, San asked Merrell about God. San didn't believe in God because he knew that science could solve every problem.

Yet he believed in Merrell because *"You are a notorious American Christian and I am an atheist Japanese, but I like your ideas and I trust you."*[258]

Merrell chose his words carefully, focusing on doing his best on the project. The home was finished on time and under budget.

Months passed. One day San came to see Merrell. His heart was broken. The woman San had planned to marry, had fallen ill and died. Nothing had been able to heal the pain in his heart from losing her, but he wanted to hear more about God.

San gave his life to God and studied the Bible every day. He was so fascinated by the Bible that he studied it in several different languages. Then he quit his teaching job to begin preparing for the ministry.

After three years of preparation, San became a missionary. Drawing from his personal wealth, he moved to a remote village where no missionary had been before. There he bought land, built schools and used his education to install electricity for the town. He made a powerful difference in a place which had previously had little contact with the outside world.

Meanwhile, Merrell built the first hospital in Japan, fully equipped to treat the epidemic of tuberculosis. The best equipment money could buy was installed and immediately put to work saving lives. That hospital quickly overflowed with patients receiving the care that they could not afford.

Yet no matter how much Merrell accomplished, deep inside he was still very lonely. He wanted to meet someone special but wondered if any woman would ever want to share his crazy life. Who would want to move to the remote Omi Province? Little did he know he was about to meet that woman.

Born into the top of the caste system, Maki Hirooka had everything that money could buy. And she knew what she wanted.

Growing up she had seen her mother suffer under the culture. So Maki decided never to get married. Maybe that way she could free to make her own choices in life.

Maki's family was not happy with how she kept declining all the men who wanted to marry her. Still Maki insisted on completing her education. Could she attend college in America?

Her family granted her request. For the next several years she studied in America.

When she completed her education and came home, the family held a special dinner for her. Several family friends were invited to the dinner. Maki's brother invited his friend Merrell Vories.

Sitting at dinner, Merrell couldn't take his eyes off Maki. It was love at first sight for both of them. After the dinner ended, Merrell went home and wrote a long letter to Maki.

When the letter arrived in her mailbox, Maki realized Merrell wanted to marry her. She accepted. Her family was shocked. Never in two thousand years of Japanese history, had a member of the royalty married a commoner. Much less a *foreigner!*

On June 3, 1919, they married in a church, which had been built by Merrell. The nation noticed. People were deeply moved by how Maki had defied the social structure by marrying for love. They admired this beautiful bride in a gown accented by a stunning jade and gold necklace from her father.

Moving into Merrell's home was a major change for her. It was the first time she had been without maids and personal servants. Yet she was happy to do the housework herself. This was the first time that she had the freedom to make her own decisions and a husband who valued her ideas and suggestions. She also had a lot of curious neighbors who wondered why a royal would want to move to their humble village.

They stared at her, everywhere she went. The town had never been visited by royalty before. Yet day after day they could see Maki going out of her way to treat them as equals. She even visited the *"untouchable"* group of local residents who were forbidden to interact with the locals.

What was even more shocking was when Maki invited the *"untouchables"* to come to her home for dinner.

She personally prepared and served a meal to them, breaking down generations of tradition in a way that touched many lives.

Then she decided to open a school where all children in the town were invited to enroll.

Her school was soon filled with pupils, growing into a full kindergarten and elementary school. Everything was going great until things suddenly changed.

Death came to Japan on September 1, 1923.

The violent 7.9 earthquake destroyed many buildings. Lots of aftershocks followed. Half of Tokyo went up in flames. A tsunami swept over the coast. One hundred thousand people died. Many of the buildings, Merrell had built, withstood the shaking only to be consumed in the fire.

Panic ruled the country. Martial law was imposed as rumors spread. Immersed in relief efforts, Merrell noticed treacherous men seizing power by force. Desperation opened the door to a violent new ruling class. Japan headed in a dangerous direction as the balance of power shifted.

The new authorities tried to shift anger towards the foreigners in the country. People fled the country as violence towards foreigners was encouraged. The writing on the wall was obvious. As World War II came and Japan prepared to bomb Pearl Harbor, Merrell was forced to make the most painful decision of his life. Should he return to the comfort of America or stay and suffer with the people he loved?

Merrell decided to stay in Japan. There was no other way. That decision required him to surrender one of the most precious things to him—American citizenship. The only way to stay in Japan was to complete a lengthy process to become a naturalized Japanese citizen.

Many American missionaries criticized Merrell for it. Merrell replied that he was ready to die in the will of God. He wrote, *"If I fail, at least they cannot say I died shot in the back while retreating! If I succeed, Omi shall know the Gospel of love."*[259]

Merrell's decision to remain in Japan was greeted with suspicion by his neighbors. Was he an American spy? The neighbors shunned him.

Local police raided his house, ripping out wiring and an antenna. Surely Merrell must be secretly transmitting messages to America. Why else would he stay in Japan?

The government stepped in and shut down all churches in Japan linked to Merrell. The tuberculosis hospital, which had been his labor of love, was seized for military use. Maki was kicked out of her own schools, as government officials began controlling all education.

Persecution came to Christians. While many believers suffered, Merrell and Maki were protected by her friendship with the Emperor and Merrell's decision to become naturalized.

He wrote, *"Being granted Japanese citizenship made me escape from either being deported or put in a concentration camp. Not only was I undisturbed in our own work, but I was even invited to teach English at the Imperial University."[260]*

While Merrell continued teaching, the war took its toll on the nation. As most of Japan's resources went to fight the war, consumer goods became scare. Food shortages filled Japan. People went hungry. Maki tried to supplement their meager rations by growing vegetables in a little garden. But anything that grew in their garden was stolen by hungry neighbors. Living on the edge of starvation, they scoured the woods for any edible looking plant. What they found brought illness. No matter what they did, things looked worse and worse.

Merrell felt like a failure so he gave his private journal the title *The Anatomy of a Failure*. As he watched Japan turn in a dangerous direction, he wondered if things would ever change.

When the war ended and peace returned to Japan, Merrell hoped to return to his ministry. Little did he know how his ministry was about to change.

As things progressed, American forces under the command of General Douglas MacArthur arrived in Japan to help the nation rebuild after World War II.

The Prime Minister of Japan asked Merrell to visit General MacArthur on his behalf with a private message.

Merrell went to the General's office and found someone he known long before the war.

Sam Bartlett, aide to the General, had grown up in Japan as the child of missionaries. He had known Merrell long before the war. While they had once been friends, their lives had gone in separate directions. They hadn't seen each other in years. When Merrell came to visit the General, Bartlett didn't recognize him.

Starvation had eaten away at Merrell's body until he was skin and bones. Worried for his health, Bartlett stopped everything to feed Merrell. Then he took him to see the General.

Merrell delivered the message that the Prime Minister of Japan wanted to work with the General but was being threatened by powerful leaders of Japan who didn't want him working with the General. General Macarthur offered to arrange a meeting, along with a strong military escort for protection.

Then they discussed the future of Japan. Merrell asked for Maki's lifelong dream. That dream came true. In 1946, General Douglas MacArthur made sure that women voted for the first time in Japanese history.

Next came the question of how the Japanese people, who had long suffered under the tyranny of dictatorship, could transition to democracy. MacArthur wanted Merrell's advice to better understand Japanese culture.

Merrell explained how the people wanted the stability of seeing their own Emperor retained in leadership. And the Emperor was ready to make a historic announcement.

For years, some people in Japan's leadership had demanded the people worship the Emperor as God to keep them under control. That belief had resulted in the deaths of many Japanese forces as kamikaze pilots. Dark forces had caused the Japanese people to suffer by forcing Japan into war in an attempt to seize world power.

When the Emperor tried to stand up to them by deciding to end the war by surrendering, they tried to stop him with an assassination attempt. These dark forces at the top of society were not about to allow any changes to Japan.

To counteract their power, the Emperor volunteered to make a major announcement.

On January 14, 1946, Emperor Hirohito went on national radio to declare that he was not God. This controversial speech opened the door for establishing the civil rights of Japanese citizens.

In the days that followed, General Macarthur asked both Merrell and Maki to become advisors in the reconstruction of Japan. Maki was placed in charge of rewriting all the public school curriculum.

Merrell's ministry exploded with massive growth. Everywhere he went, people wanted to know about Jesus. Even the high school, which had once fired him, begged him to return to their faculty and teach on anything he wanted. Watching his success, the Omi Province was very proud of their hometown hero. Their local newspaper printed that Merrell's ministry was the town's *"chief asset."*[261]

Food was still scarce. General MacArthur sent twenty American troops with supplies to take care of Merrell and Maki. They brought something that Merrell and Maki had not seen in years—butter!

After the war, many of Merrell's friends visited them. One day, Merrell was surprised to look up and see Suzuki-San. Merrell hardly recognized him. San's once strong body had become only skin and bones.

During the war, his fervent preaching for Christ had gotten him locked up in prison. That hadn't stopped San's ministry. He had preached to everyone in the prison, resulting in several dramatic conversions.

As he told this to Merrell, San's face radiated happiness. He explained, *"In no other way than being a prisoner could I have brought the gospel to the military personnel, who otherwise wouldn't have listened to me two minutes."*

Yet that ministry had come at a great cost. San had been treated very harshly in the prison, enduring frequent beatings and interrogations.

He endured the suffering with such peace, even his jailers wondered why. He described, *"When my inquisitors asked me how I could bear punishment without even being nervous, I explained, 'They beat my master, Christ, also.'"*[262]

After the war, San returned to full time ministry, reaching even more people for Christ.

Meanwhile, in the later years of his life, Merrell developed cataracts on his eyes and had to travel to America for medical treatment. After a successful surgery, he returned to Japan, where he lived the rest of his life.

General MacArthur was still working in Japan. Many times the General sent for Merrell and Maki to listen to their advice. When Merrell thanked the General for doing everything he could to help the Japanese people, Macarthur responded, *"I am just trying to follow the Sermon on the Mount."*[263]

Merrell also followed that Sermon on the Mount until he passed away on May 7, 1964 from the lingering effects of a stroke.

Japan greatly mourned his loss.

The Emperor honored him with the prestigious Blue Ribbon Medal, *"For social and spiritual services to Japan."*[264]

Maki was also honored with the prestigious *Third Order of the Sacred Treasure.* The tuberculosis hospital they had built was renamed *Merrell Vories Memorial* to honor their legacy.

To tell their story to the world and inspire a new generation of missionaries, Maki published Merrell's private journal.

Merrell's writings revealed what he had learned walking with God. *"My spirit is unbroken,"* he had once written, *"I have learned to believe that all things work together for good to those that love God (Romans 8:28)."*[265]

8

Proving Your Love

"You should keep a clear mind in every situation. Don't be afraid of suffering for the Lord."
2 Timothy 4:5 (NLT)

God tests our hearts. Sooner or later, every Christian gets the chance to prove their love when we face the trial of our faith.

"Consider it a sheer gift, friends, when tests and challenges come at you from all sides. You know that under pressure, your faith-life is forced into the open and shows its true colors."[266]

Yet what God asks of us is much easier than what people do to themselves. There are two types of suffering: God's plan and our mistakes. Our choices make our own lives harder or easier.

"You don't gain anything by being punished for some wrong you have done. But God will bless you, if you have to suffer for doing something good."[267]

The Bible warns us not to add extra suffering to ourselves.

"If you suffer, it must not be because you are a murderer or a thief or a criminal or a meddler in other people's affairs."

"However, if you suffer because you are a Christian, don't be ashamed of it, but thank God that you bear Christ's name."[268]

As we walk with God, *"We go through exactly what Christ goes through. If we go through the hard times with him, then we're certainly going to go through the good times with him!"*[269]

Every one of us will encounter four tests:

1) Obedience

When Jesus walked the Earth, *"Though he was God's Son, he learned trusting-obedience by what he suffered, just as we do."*[270] Will you obey God when you don't feel like it? What would have happened if Merrell Vories had never gone to Japan? Or if he had given up after getting fired?

At some point, we all must choose between getting our own way or choosing God's. Even Jesus Himself wrestled with this decision to the point of sweating blood over it.

He prayed, *"My Father, if it is possible, take this cup of suffering from Me! Yet not what I want, but what You want."*[271]

As we follow in Jesus' footsteps He has promised, *"Those who really love me are the ones who not only know My commands but also obey them. My Father will love such people, and I will love them. I will make Myself known to them."*[272]

2) The *"why"* question

Something will happen to us that we don't understand. We will wonder why it happened. We will be shaken to our core. Then we will end up trying to figure it out.

When something really bad happens, do you look up at God and ask, *"Why?"*

Jesus did. Hanging on the cross, He cried out, *"My God, my God, why did you abandon Me?"*[273]

Even Jesus wondered why certain things happened. The hardest test for most of us is the why question. Can you trust God when you don't understand why something happened?

Life is not fair. After tragedy, people either shake their fist in the air, or continue trusting God to turn things for good.

Will you remain loyal to God, when nothing makes sense?

"God will bless you for this, if you endure the pain of undeserved suffering because you are conscious of His will."[274]

3) Keeping a thankful heart

Can you find something to be thankful for even when other things are really hard? God asks us to, *"Be thankful in all circumstances. This is what God wants from you in your life in union with Christ Jesus."*[275] This is not easy. That's why it's called the sacrifice of praise. *"Let us give thanks all the time to God through Jesus Christ. Our gift to Him is to give thanks."*[276]

4) Persecution

"Everyone who wants to live a godly life in union with Christ Jesus will be persecuted."[277] People will not understand why you're living for God. Your faith will be scorned. Are you strong enough to withstand pressure?

Jesus did. *"He did not retaliate when He was insulted, nor threaten revenge when He suffered. He left his case in the hands of God, who always judges fairly."*[278]

The Apostle Paul wrote, *"We do not try to please people, but to please God, who tests our motives."*[279]

So what happens after you pass these tests?

God promises, *"If we suffer and stay true to Him, then we will be a leader with Him."*[280]

Parents often keep a scrapbook to record family memories. In Heaven, God also keeps a book of all the things you do for Him.

Every sacrifice you make. Every little thing you do simply motivated by love is recorded in that book.

Malachi 3:16 describes how God keeps a book of remembrance on you. He will reward you for your faithfulness to Him.

Think About:

"With this hope you can be happy even if you need to have sorrow and all kinds of tests for awhile.
These tests have come to prove your faith and to show that it is good. Gold, which can be destroyed, is tested by fire.
Your faith is worth much more than gold and it must be tested also. Then your faith will bring thanks and shining-greatness and honor to Jesus Christ when He comes again."
1 Peter 1:6-7 (NLV)

"He is no fool who gives what he cannot keep to gain what he cannot lose."[281282]
-Jim Elliot

"Looking back to my earliest business experiences, now I realize that what I had once thought was hardship and sacrifice, turned out to be open doors to future endeavors. Thank God for it. We were being guided by Him."[283]
-J.C. Penney

9

Albert A. Hyde

"God takes care of us richly. He gives us everything to enjoy."
1 Timothy 6:17b (ERV)

Albert A. Hyde
1848-1935
From Kansas

Imagine starting a business in a risky field known mostly for fraud. Risking everything, while fighting to keep your own home out of foreclosure and having to dig out from under the crushing failure of your last venture. That's where Albert Hyde started but not where he finished.

Hyde was born into a strong Christian family. His grandfather was a pastor. His father was a groundbreaking teacher who had pioneered a new school to improve the local educational opportunities.

Hyde grew up finding his own way in life. At age seventeen he left home and moved to Kansas. There he went to work as a bookkeeper for a local bank. He did so well that he was promoted into managing his own branch at twenty-four.

Now making enough to provide for a family, he fell in love with a beautiful girl named Ida Elizabeth Todd. They married and raised nine children together.

With their family growing, Hyde began to think of other ways to support those nine children. In 1887, he launched a dry goods store specializing in books, toys and games for children. As the town boomed, his store became very successful. Hyde took the profits he made at the store and began investing in real estate. Everything was going great until a drought came.

As crops failed, incomes in the town evaporated. Tough economic conditions made families leave town, lowering the value of the properties around the town. Eventually the local real estate market totally collapsed.

Hyde was left holding mortgages on investment land that he couldn't pay. As he described, *"With everybody poverty stricken and a great many becoming bankrupt, it was apparently impossible to make this business pay."*[284]

Finding himself one hundred thousand dollars in debt, Hyde closed his store and filed for bankruptcy.

Then unable to pay the mortgage on his own home, Hyde turned it over to the bank. The bank didn't want it. They couldn't sell it. Too many homes were being foreclosed and sitting vacant in the city. So they offered to let him keep his home if he would pay rent of ten dollars a month. Hyde agreed, grateful to keep a roof over his family.

Now how was he going to afford that ten dollars a month? There were no jobs in the town. Just as everything looked hopeless, Hyde's brother-in-law approached him with an idea for a new soap business. With no other options, Hyde decided to take it. Needing another person to help with the work, Hyde invited a third partner to join them. Hyde launched this business with the few dollars he had because *"I had to finance them both, as they were without funds."*[285]

The business quickly failed. While Hyde aggressively tried selling the soap door to door, the local people just didn't have any money.

The brother-in-law and their friend quit, leaving Hyde to hold the business together. However, the brother-in-law had also left Hyde with something of value—his formula for a new cough medicine.

Hyde decided to develop the product, never realizing that his little company would pioneer the entire cough medicine industry. Hyde just knew that his pastor at church always seemed to have a sore throat. Maybe this could help him.

Hyde gave the pastor some of the cough medicine. It helped him preach better without having to clear his throat as much. The pastor, Charles Bradt, told other ministers about this new cough medicine. Soon Hyde had plenty of customers buying his product.

Realizing that he had something with a lot of potential, Hyde began to experiment with the cough medicine. Seeking out advice from doctors and pharmacists about the main ingredient, menthol, he discovered that for thousands of years the Japanese had used menthol to relieve aches and pains. Yet surprisingly menthol was still hard to find. Hyde had to buy his menthol supplies from people who imported it from the Japanese Island of Hokkaido. Yet even with the extra cost of importation, the more Hyde tested out his product, the more it helped people.

Back then, access to doctors was limited and very expensive. So many people relied on over the counter remedies to treat ailments like the common cold. However, there were no laws regulating the formulas of these remedies.

Before the Pure Food and Drugs Act of 1906, manufacturers could put anything in their formula. They could write anything on their product label, resulting in many products on store shelves that promised miracle cures but only disappointed consumers.

The market was flooded with all kinds of fake medicines. Thus, most consumers were skeptical about buying cold medicines. For Hyde's product to be successful, he had to overcome strong consumer skepticism.

Hyde started by developing a simple, effective label. Then he approached local drug stores, asking them to leave jars of his products on their counters. When it sold, the stores received bonuses.

Hyde avoided the typical advertising of the time because people were very skeptical of it.

Instead he focused on paying commissions to salesmen and drug stores that sold his product because he preferred to *"Pay men instead of billboards."*[286]

He paid women too. Long before America accepted women in the workplace, Hyde opened doors for them. He wrote essays like *Women and Law*, saying, *"Woman's power in the world is a willingness to sacrifice for her ideals far beyond man's endurance."*[287]

Women were always welcome to work at his company. His first traveling salesman was a woman named Ella Veazie. In 1896, she went from town to town, opening new doors and adding new clients. She made enough money to put herself through medical school, yet she continued working the job she loved at Hyde's company for forty years.

Employees at Hyde's company appreciated the generous employee benefits he provided, which were way ahead of the time. Hyde actually pioneered the idea of a paid vacation. Not only did employees get paid time off, they could travel at company expense to vacation spots.

Benefits like disability pay were once radical, new ideas of Hyde. He welcomed anyone who was a hard worker, even blind people, who often turned out to be more productive than the rest of his workforce.

That workforce was needed as sales continued to grow. Mentholatum quickly expanded across America. Soon it was being exported to over one hundred countries.

Yet all the money never changed Hyde's heart for God. He believed: *"Right relationship to God and service to men as taught by Christ, is the best thing into which we can put our lives and our money."*[288]

Knowing that God had called him to fund missionaries around the world, he helped as many as he could. The one he helped the most was Merrell Vories.

Five years after Merrell had moved to Japan, he returned to America to attend the Men's National Missionary Conference in Chicago. Hyde was the keynote speaker of that conference. They met on May 6, 1910.

During his session, Hyde shared his heart with the audience with story after story of how rewarding it was to make money serve Christ.

"We all say that we believe the teachings of Jesus Christ. And yet a man does not believe a thing unless he acts on his belief."

"In other words, 'By their fruits you shall know them.' And then our Savior said, 'It is more blessed to give than it is to receive.' The pleasure of giving money is fulfilling the Lord's command and helping, if he cannot go personally, to preach the gospel to all the earth."[289]

That speech deeply touched the audience. Afterward, there were many people lining up to talk with Hyde. Merrell Vories had been sitting in the audience listening to the speech. He also wanted to shake hands with Hyde, but stood back waiting his turn.

What happened next was later described by Merrell. *"In Hyde's speech, he described helping Phil Gillett's ministry complete a building project in Korea. Gillett and I were both alumni of Colorado College, and I had recently visited him in Korea."*

"After Hyde's speech, I went up to the stage and introduced myself, telling him what I had seen of Gillett's work which he had helped. This immediately interested Hyde, who was very friendly and asked me something about my work in Japan."

"Another man tried to pull Hyde away at this point, but he insisted upon hearing more about me while we stood there on the stage for an hour."

"Two things began at that first meeting—Hyde invited me to visit him in Kansas on my way west, to report on the progress of my own fundraising in America. And he gave me a sample jar of Mentholatum."

"Several months later, I stopped in Kansas and had a second interview with Hyde at his office. He was interested in my (fundraising) efforts in America and asked me to write him a final report before I sailed for Japan. We talked a little about the possibility of our architectural office introducing Mentholatum into Japan."

"After I boarded the ship to return to Japan, I wrote to Hyde that I had managed to raise $640 in cash and pledges. As soon as a reply letter could be delivered from America to Japan, he wrote back with a check for $700. And he asked me to notify him of any more financial shortage in our ministry projects."

"We began sending Hyde regular hand written reports of our activities. He wrote back that he enjoyed our letters so much that he was sending a typewriter. And he included another large check."[290]

Hyde became the largest supporter of Merrell's ministry in Japan, building the school for Merrell's wife Maki and helping with other projects.

Merrell had been trying to send out ministry teams to remote areas of Japan where transportation was very limited. Since Merrell was working in a territory of sixteen hundred square miles without roads that could be traveled by car, Hyde bought them a houseboat capable of housing and transporting ministry teams to remote villages.

Hyde did a lot more. Wanting to give Merrell a steady income stream instead of occasional donations, he gave Merrell the franchise rights to sell Mentholatum in Japan. This was one of the first American products to succeed in Japan. Merrell built a factory in Japan, hired local workers and reinvested all of the profits into local ministry projects.

Merrell also made a big statement by paying good wages and benefits to his workers. At the time, regular wages in Japan were so low that the only way most families could survive was by having every family member work full time. For years, many teenage girls in Japan had missed out on a high school education, because they had to support their families by working long hours.

Merrell gave them a better opportunity. He opened a special high school where teen girls could receive half a day of classroom instruction, then get paid to work the other half of the day in the factory. Thus they could earn the money they desperately needed while still being able to graduate with the diploma and job skills to escape the cycle of poverty. This made a huge difference for many families. It also became some of the best product advertising.

Mentholatum became one of the best selling products in Japan. Even when World War II came, closing down most factories in Japan, Merrell's factory stayed open. Throughout the war, the Japanese government continued buying Mentholatum for the military.

Merrell described, *"Only the Army and Navy's need for Mentholatum finally saved that factory from confiscation. It became the sole source of livelihood for our entire staff of more than three hundred workers, with their families totaling more than twelve hundred people."*[291]

Meanwhile, back in the United States, Hyde devoted the rest of his life to giving. In his own words he described, *"This is a happy feeling that money, satan's greatest tool, is being used to overthrow his reign and help establish the Kingdom of God on the earth."*[292]

One of the leading evangelists of the time, Reverend John Mott, described how Hyde's impact was felt around the world. Mott wrote, *"I could not name one of the fifty-eight nations of the world which I traveled over in the past twenty years where I have not seen the great influences which have come forth from the life of Albert Hyde. It is inspiring to think that a man can sit in a Kansas office and cause streams of service to flow forth to every continent on earth."*[293]

But Hyde was still very cautious with giving the money. He avoided emotional giving, never allowing people to manipulate or control him. While he was deluged with requests for donations, he was careful to decline the projects that he didn't feel right about.

One time a friend asked for money, emphasizing that a crisis was happening and *"The cause of Presbyterianism would suffer!"*

Hyde replied, *"That doesn't matter—it is the cause of Christ that should enlist our support."*[294]

His secretary, Ethel Willard, noticed that Hyde *"Spent a lot of time learning about the group or individual he sent money or help to. He'd get all the details down before he gave them a nickel."*[295]

When selecting projects, Hyde focused on following the guidance of the Holy Spirit. He described, *"I have a habit of praying for anyone who comes into my mind when I wake in the night. Sometimes it is a sense that some friend needs help and I ought to pray for him or her. Then I write a letter if I feel moved to do so, and wonderful things happen."*[296]

Following his heart, Hyde often included large checks in letters to missionary friends. One friend was Sherwood Eddy who had devoted his life to taking the gospel into remote areas of the world.

Hyde was an answer to his prayer, helping them cover a massive budget shortfall. Eddy wrote: *"At Christmas time things looked very dark. It seemed we could not possibly close our books without God's supernatural intervention in touching the hearts of people to give. We needed nearly $140,000. Some men had donated $5,000 each. Then came Hyde's telegram. We were in tears finding out that Hyde trusted us."*[297]

Throughout his life, Hyde stayed focused on the simplicity of walking with God. He wrote, *"We've made the religious life too complex. Over exalting intellectualism and our own philosophy gets us nowhere. I long for the childlike faith which Christ taught. I believe thoroughly in the Holy Spirit and His work in my heart."*[298]

Hyde's personal motto was: *"I got all my money from the Lord and it all goes back to Him."*[299]

Hyde believed, *"The danger is that getting money develops egotism and selfishness. Accumulated wealth whets selfish appetite, hardens character, shortens life, and has been the downfall of individuals and of nations since history began. It is the means that satan uses many times in the final effort which draws us away from God."*[300]

Many people admired his generosity. Even the local newspaper editor wrote: *"If he did, he erred in the right direction."*[301]

Hyde's son Charles wrote about him, *"He'd be getting along all right, if he could just get the Lord paid off. That's all that's worrying him."*[302]

Hyde made the mistake of ignoring his son's advice when he suggested purchasing their main business competitor—Vick's. Hyde felt that was unnecessary because *"Nothing's going to happen with it—it's not worth the money."*[303]

Time would prove that failure to purchase Vicks would be Hyde's biggest missed opportunity. However, Hyde still made a lot of money and continued giving generously as the years passed by quickly.

In the later years of his life, Hyde suffered from cancer. After enduring a painful surgery, he had to wear a colostomy pouch. It irritated him so much that he invented a much better one. That invention turned into a whole new income stream.

After a lifetime of success, by the time he reached eighty-seven years old, Hyde was finally ready to retire. He thanked all of his staff for their help as he reminisced over their shared history, saying, *"Looking back over the years of the Mentholatum Company and the Hyde family, I can't help but feel that the Lord has guided us in many ways."*

"I think you all know that we started without a cent; I was bankrupt. But somehow, we have gone ahead. We used our brains, our muscles, and all the help we could get, to put Mentholatum over, which now supports a good many families."

"Here I am on the verge of the grave looking back and finding a great joy in having helped in the service of teaching the gospel of Jesus Christ here, at home, and abroad. That is a real satisfaction to me."[304]

Knowing his life was drawing to a close, Hyde notified all the ministries—that he had supported—how his contributions would cease when he passed away.

That sudden announcement caused wide spread panic. The ministries that had relied on him for years, worried. How could they fund church budgets without him? Couldn't Hyde just invest his resources into a trust and continue donating from beyond the grave?

When they asked Hyde to reconsider, he responded, *"My place must be taken by others."*[305]

When Hyde died in 1935, his dream was accomplished. Everything he owned was sold and the money given to various Christian projects. Nothing was left to his own children because Hyde feared money could only *"handicap or curse."*[306]

However Hyde's children pooled the finances they had earned by working for his company and bought back ownership of the company. For the next hundred years, the Hyde family passed ownership of the company down through four generations. Then the company was sold to Japanese investors in 1988.

Meanwhile, Merrell Vories turned what Hyde had given him into a long-term income stream. Merrell formally incorporated his franchise and kept the money supporting the ministry for many years after Hyde had passed.

9

Drinking From the Faucet

"The best thing we can do is eat and drink and enjoy what we have earned. And yet I realized that even this comes from God. How else could you have anything to eat or enjoy yourself at all?"
Ecclesiastes 2:24-25 (GNT)

God knows that you need stuff. Jesus recognized that in Matthew 6:32. So God sends us a stream of blessing flowing into our lives like the water flows from the faucet in our kitchen. Drinking from the faucet means using that financial provision to meet your own material needs, before you try to help others.

What God gives you is for you. Not just everyone else. Yes, helping people is important but only in balance with helping yourself.

No matter how much you give away, *"There will always be poor people in the land."*[307] Thus, Jesus taught us to *"Love your neighbor the same as you love yourself."*[308]

Taking care of yourself is not selfish. It's the only way you'll be able to fulfill God's plans for you. By spending money on yourself, you actually will be able to do more for others.

Think about it. Eating food gives you energy during the day. Putting gas in your car enables you to go places. If you stop doing either one, you won't get very far. Plus, having fun is also part of God's plan for your life.

God wants you to enjoy what you've earned. His dream is that *"People will build houses and get to live in them—they will not be used by someone else...They will fully enjoy the things that they have worked for."*[309]

So why do we feel guilty for enjoying the good things in life? Even Jesus was criticized for it. One day a woman wanted to honor Jesus with her best. Taking an expensive bottle of perfume, she went to where Jesus was having dinner. *"She poured the perfume on Jesus' feet. Then she wiped his feet with her hair. And the sweet smell from the perfume filled the whole house. Judas Iscariot, one of Jesus' followers, was there—the one who would later hand Jesus over to his enemies."*

"Judas said, 'That perfume was worth a full year's pay. It should have been sold, and the money should have been given to the poor people.' But Judas did not really care about the poor. He said this because he was a thief. He was the one who kept the moneybag for the group of followers. And he often stole money from the bag. Jesus said, 'Let her alone. She's anticipating and honoring the day of my burial. You always have the poor with you. You don't always have me."[310]

Like many Christians, Judas criticized extravagance and *Jesus rebuked him for it!* While Jesus had given money to the poor many other times, He did not allow Judas to give that particular money away. He enjoyed something that cost an entire year's pay. So why do we feel guilty about taking care of ourselves?

Albert Hyde felt guilty about enjoying the money he had earned. He only felt spiritual when sacrificing. Let's take a closer look at his opinion and compare it with the Bible.

Hyde: *"Without study and attention, it is impossible to wisely give away millions of dollars. With the constant care for accumulated wealth we cannot find time to properly study and help Kingdom causes."*[311]

Having money enables you to hire a staff to help—we will study the Bible verses on this subject in the chapter about Mary Kay.

Hyde: *"If men would stop spending on themselves and family and give to the Kingdom of God, a new meaning would come into life."*[312]

You can do both—help others and help your own family. In the New Testament the Apostle Paul wrote, *"Parents should save to give to their children."*[313] And, *"They should take care of their own family."*[314]

Hyde: *"Leave no estate over which heirs can quarrel. Luxury is a degrading influence. An inheritance can only handicap or curse."*[315]

The Bible says:
"A good man leaves what he owns for his children's children."[316]
"House and riches are handed down from fathers."[317]

While we admire Hyde's heart for God and remarkable lifetime achievements, we believe that his mistake was dying penniless instead of controlling his own money from beyond the grave. He could have left his fortune in a living trust to serve Christ forever. LeTourneau and Crowell did. They proved you can balance between supporting God's work and providing for your family.

Plus, one of the organizations that Hyde supported was the YMCA, which has since drifted from its Christian roots. Hyde might have felt differently if he had known what would happen to them.

God wants you to enjoy what you have.

"All of us should eat and drink and enjoy what we have worked for. It is God's gift."[318]

Think About:

"Take care of yourself, have a good time, and make the most of whatever job you have for as long as God gives you life."
Ecclesiastes 5:18b (MSG)

"Wherever you are, be all there. Live to the hilt every situation you believe to be the will of God."[319]
-Jim Elliott

"The giving of money demands just as careful study and as painstaking attention as the making of money."[320]
-John D. Rockefeller Sr.

10

Henry Heinz

"If you humble yourself, you will be honored."
Luke 18:14b (CEV)

Henry Heinz
1844-1919
From Pennsylvania

Bankruptcy is not where you expect to find successful people. Yet Henry Heinz was digging himself out of it, when he got the business idea that worked.

Heinz started his first successful business when he was only eight years old. As a young child, he helped his mother work in her garden to raise food for their family. The garden produced more food than they could eat. That gave Heinz the idea to try selling the extra produce door to door.

Heinz started with one basket of produce that he carried door to door until it was all sold. Then he invested the money into a wheelbarrow that could transport more produce to his customers.

Little by little, for the next several years, his business continued to grow. By the time he had turned sixteen, he had hired three workers and bought a horse and wagon.

To protect his supply, he had also built a greenhouse to continue growing produce year round. By this time the local grocery stores had become dependent on his deliveries. Heinz catered to their needs, offering deliveries at 8PM the night before they were needed. That way grocers no longer had to wake up at 4AM, which had been the industry standard for receiving deliveries.

One grocer remarked, *"I like to buy from Heinz. I always pay a little more than I pay anyone else, but I never lose money on anything he sells me."*[321]

While things were going good, Heinz expanded his business by adding additional products. During the winter months, he drove a horse drawn wagon eighty miles to the lake, picked up blocks of ice and sold them to the locals. It was a great idea, but it didn't work. Too many other people had the same idea. Heinz was stuck with a load of ice that he couldn't sell. The answer was simple. He gave it away, then had to drive his empty horse drawn wagon all the way home.

That gave him a lot of time to think. How could he turn a mistake into a profit? Instead of driving straight back, he pulled off the road and began to visit local merchants. Asking them if they needed anything to be hauled somewhere, he found someone who had extra milk, eggs, and butter. Heinz bought the load, hauled it home and sold it, turning his mistake into a twenty-five dollar profit.

Later, when using his own experience to advise others, he would teach them, *"The trouble with most men is that they are looking all around for nickels that are scattered about them, when just ahead of them is a twenty dollar gold piece."*[322]

As Heinz continued to excel in business, he found ways to help his family. Heinz had always been close with his parents. He described, *"I had an honest father and a mother with a Christlike spirit."*[323]

When his parents took a long vacation to Europe in 1868, they asked Heinz to look after their brick-laying business while they were gone. Weeks later, they returned to a big surprise. Heinz had built them a beautiful new home which cost them nothing. By collecting the overdue and previously uncollectible customer accounts of their brick-laying business, Heinz had financed construction on the dream home they had always wanted.

Meanwhile, Heinz was building his own home. He fell in love with a beautiful girl named Sarah Young. They married and raised four boys and a girl. Heinz cared deeply for his wife, paying attention to little things like how much effort she put into preparing meals. When she used horseradish in a recipe, it took a lot of time to prepare the raw horseradish roots. That gave Heinz a new idea. Maybe if he prepared jars of horseradish, ladies would appreciate not having to do the work of preparing it themselves.

So Heinz launched a new food processing company. He bottled vegetables to be sold on store shelves, making preparing dinner faster and easier. To distinguish the purity and quality of his product, Heinz utilized clear jars that showed attractive ingredients. They sold. Heinz was quickly overwhelmed with demand, forcing him to rapidly expand. He began buying more and more produce to make as much as possible.

But there was one thing he didn't prepare for. Overbuying. With no way to accurately predict consumer demand, Heinz made the mistake of buying too many supplies. There was not enough demand for his canned goods. His business collapsed and he went bankrupt in 1875.

Creditors began harassing him. Determined to publicly humiliate him, one creditor went out of his way to smear the Heinz reputation in his hometown.

Yet Heinz still forgave him. Years later, when news spread that particular man had lost everything financially and his own property was about to be sold at auction, Heinz intervened.

He paid whatever it took to enable the man to keep his home and household possessions. Everyone was shocked that Heinz would do that for someone who had hurt him deeply.

The man came to thank Heinz because the one person, *"Whom I treated as an enemy has proved to be my friend and saved me in my trouble."*[324]

But before Heinz was able to help others, first he had to dig himself out of bankruptcy.

At thirty-two years old, when he went broke, he felt like a failure for being unable to support his family. Even worse, he had lost the money invested by family and friends.

Resolved to pay them back, he started a new company and gave them stock in what would become known as H. J. Heinz, Inc.

This time horseradish was not the main product. Heinz had a better idea for something called ketchup. While various versions of it had been around since the 1600's, they had never been very popular. So Heinz began working on a formula to please the taste buds. Once again, he insisted on clear bottles to catch customer's attention. He patented his bottle design in 1882.

By 1900, Heinz was America's largest pickle, ketchup, and mustard manufacturer.[325] His creative advertisements had captured consumer attention. He introduced the first ever electric sign in New York. He also built an entire pier for Atlantic City. The rest of his ads ran regularly, but never on Sundays. And the most successful idea he had was for adding *"57 Varieties"* to the label.

That idea came to Heinz while he was riding a train. Seeing a sign about *"21 styles"*, he started counting how many products he had.

"I counted well beyond 57, but 57 kept coming back into my mind."

He remembered. *"I got off the train immediately, went down to the lithographer's, where I designed a street car card and had it distributed throughout the U.S.. I myself did not realize how highly successful a slogan it was going to be."*[326]

As his company grew, the profits were poured back into generous employee wages and benefits. Yet what workers remembered most was his kindness and respect.

People noticed how Heinz *"Studied men more than books, for men were the tools with which he had to work."*[327]

Loyal to his own workers, he always promoted from within. *"He never hired stars,"* one employee recalled.[328]

Unlike many bosses of that time, Heinz always chose his words carefully. Inscribed on his own office wall was the motto: *"Not so much what you say, but how, when and where."*[329]

Even his own Pastor described how *"No one who worked with him could feel 'under' him."*[330]

Protecting the feelings and dignity of workers was always a priority. His gentle methods motivated them. Heinz didn't want to have any of the harshness which was typical of the work environments of that time. He sought to guide, not threaten people. While company rules were enforced, he didn't break people with them. He sought to help workers understand the why, instead of just forcing them to follow meaningless policies.

Heinz was often heard quoting from the Bible: *"The written law brings death, but the Sprit gives life."*[331]

Teaching his workers the Golden Rule he insisted on *"Placing yourself in another's shoes, and never expecting from anyone that which you would not care to do."*[332]

One day Heinz noticed that one of his workers was improperly weighing some apples that the company was purchasing. By just slightly tilting the scales, the employee was getting a few extra pounds without paying the supplier for it.

Heinz asked the employee to come to his office. Then he asked what was happening. The employee explained he was trying to save the Heinz Company a few bucks on the cost of apples because *"You know, a quick eye, a quick hand and you can always slip over a few pounds extra."*

Heinz replied, *"You were robbing a man who was selling to me and you were robbing me of something more precious. There is only one way to weigh or do anything else—be as square to the other fellow as to yourself."*[333]

That employee was fired. All others were warned to deal honestly with their suppliers.

Heinz also felt a strong responsibility to the consumer. Paying attention to even the smallest details of production, he sought to maintain high standards in the food processing industry, even when he had to fight his own industry to do it. While other manufacturers fought the pressure to improve processing methods, Heinz lobbied for it. His efforts convinced Congress to pass the 1906 Pure Food and Drug Act.

That was important to him because he believed *"Quality is to a product what character is to a man."*[334]

Meanwhile, Heinz was always a strong force in the church.

For twenty-five years, he volunteered as the local Sunday School Superintendent because *"It has paid me the largest dividends of any invest-ment I ever made."*[335] He specialized in working together with Christians across denominational lines. And he insisted on proper money man-agement in church groups.

While attending a national Sunday School convention in 1895, he was disturbed to hear desperate pleas for donations.

Heinz hated the idea of pressuring people to give. So he stood up and publicly confronted the leadership. Suggesting that if they would stay out of debt, *"Pay as you go, and not use the time of your conventions in raising funds,"* then he would provide a generous donation.[336]

The audience responded with applause. The organization itself was so impressed by Heinz that they nominated him to be their new president.

For over ten years, Heinz ran the Sunday School organization, stay-ing on track and under budget. His strategy in both philanthropy and business was simple. *"The worst mistake you can make is to let immediate convenience dictate a makeshift solution for any troublesome problem."*

"Get at the fundamental principle involved, and settle your problem on that basis, and no other. The problem itself is nothing to worry about, no matter how big. In fact, the bigger the problem, the easier it is to see the principle on which it ought to be settled."[337]

Working with the Sunday school organization gave Heinz the opportunity to pursue what was on his heart. Spreading the gospel around the world was the command of Jesus and Heinz wanted to be part of the process. Yet he didn't just want to send money to mission-aries. A closer look was needed at how ministry funds were spent.

So in 1913, Heinz led a group of twenty-nine Christian business leaders on a five month world tour. Their purpose was to bridge the gap between cultures, open new doors for ministry, understand the deepest spiritual needs, and find the most effective ministry solutions.

For the next five months they traveled to Hawaii, Japan, China, Korea, Philippines, Russia and even Siberia.

The trip was a cross cultural success. Everywhere they went, they were warmly welcomed by local business and government officials.

Heinz and his team listened to the concerns and learned everything they could about the other cultures.

When they went to China, Heinz marveled at how Chinese civilization had existed long before Moses saw the burning bush. Meeting with government leaders they found, *"In the Chinese House and Senate, which was visited by our party through special permission, many of the leaders are Christians. Before the republic it was not possible for a Christian to get elected to office."*[338]

The Chinese honored his visit by proclaiming April 27, 1913 as a national day of prayer.

Heinz and his team continued on, visiting Christian hospitals, organizations, and churches, and encouraging the people wherever they went.

In Korea, Heinz was impressed by how aggressive the Korean Christians were in sharing their faith. He heard the story of how a missionary traveling in Korea had once gotten lost and ended up way off course at a remote village. There he shared the gospel, left Bibles and moved on. One year later, he returned to the village to find a thriving church with over one hundred faithful members. Hearing this story and getting to meet the people, Heinz was happy to see the harvest coming from the seeds of the Gospel.

When Heinz reached Japan, the Japanese were fascinated by the idea of Christian business people. They enjoyed talking about both God and business. New friends were made. New Sunday Schools were opened in Japan.

After five months and thousands of miles traveled, the trip ended as they visited an international Christian convention in Switzerland. Heinz would be asked to share about what they had seen.

After discussing what they had learned from listening to people around the world, he closed with a prayer that the seeds they had planted would be used by God. *"We now lay down our work at the feet of our Lord. It was ours to sow the seed. Our Father will prepare the harvest. It has been a labor of love."*[339]

Once Heinz returned home, he was overwhelmed with requests for involvement in other Christian organizations. He helped as much as he could.

The years passed by quickly. Heinz physically pushed himself to keep up with all the requests he received. One morning, he woke up with a cold. The doctor told him to rest. He refused, having to leave for another church meeting. The cold Heinz caught became pneumonia. He passed away in 1919 at seventy-five years old.

The world grieved. Heinz had touched so many lives that condolences poured in from every direction.

John Wanamaker, famous for inventing the modern department store, said, *"He was always an inspiration to me."*[340]

Christians in Tokyo held a special memorial service to honor his legacy. Sunday School students in Japan even sent someone nine thousand miles to Pittsburgh to lay a special wreath on his grave.[341]

Employees of the Heinz Company issued a public statement grieving the President they had loved.

"He was sympathetic, considerate, kind, helpful. Though a strong personality and a dominant force, he was always receptive to suggestions and always desired to develop the judgment of the younger men about him."[342]

Heinz left a fortune to fund charitable organizations. He also left strong instructions and trustees appointed to watch over each dollar to make sure it was spent well.

Taking care of his own family, he left an inheritance to his children because he believed, *"The means to provide education and other opportunities should be a great advantage to a boy, not a handicap. It is the father's duty to see to it."*[343]

Then for everyone else, he had left a note in his will. How did Heinz himself want to be remembered?

The very first thing written in his will was:

"The most important item in it—a confession of my faith in Jesus Christ as my Savior. I also desire to bear witness to the fact that throughout my life—in which there were the usual joys and sorrows—I have been wonderfully sustained by my faith in God through Jesus Christ."

Heinz concluded, *"To it I attribute any success I may have attained during my life."*[344]

10

The Power of Humility

"The reward for humility and fearing the Lord is riches
and honor and life."
Proverbs 22:4 (NET)

You're smart. You're really good at something and it's hard to stay humble about it. But humility is worth it. If you want to keep moving up the ladder of success *"Humble yourselves before the Lord, and he will lift you up."*[345]

How did Jesus demonstrate humility? By seeking and fulfilling God's plan for His life. Jesus *"Humbled himself by being fully obedient to God."*[346]

When Jesus walked the Earth, He set the example of being humble and teachable. Before picking His disciples, Jesus spent all night praying over the decision because *"I cannot do anything on my own. The Father sent Me, and He is the one who told me how to judge. I judge with fairness, because I obey Him, and I don't just try to please Myself."*[347]

Jesus taught us that humility is the easier way in life. *"Come to me all of you who are tired from the heavy burden you have been forced to carry. I will give you rest. Accept my teaching. Learn from me."*

"I am gentle and humble in spirit. And you will be able to get some rest. Yes, the teaching that I ask you to accept is easy. The load I give you to carry is light."[348]

Humility is trusting God instead of worrying. *"And God will exalt you in due time, if you humble yourselves under his mighty hand by casting all your cares on him because he cares for you."*[349]

Humility is worshiping and focusing on God. *"The Lord says: 'Don't brag about your wisdom or strength or wealth. If you feel you must brag, then have enough sense to brag about worshiping Me, the Lord.'"*[350]

Humility is being honest and open to correction. We cannot afford to allow pride in our lives. *"Pride is the first step toward destruction. Proud thoughts will lead you to defeat."*[351]

Think About:

"Clothe yourselves with humility toward one another, because God opposes the proud but gives grace to the humble."
1 Peter 5:5 (NET)

"Carelessness and overconfidence are usually more dangerous than deliberately accepted risks."[352]
-Wilbur Wright

"Great mistakes have been made in exalting a man-made organization or church rather than the Kingdom of God on Earth such as Christ continuously taught, promoted, and illustrated by His own life. Meditation on His Word will make us grow in humility and optimism."[353]
-A. A. Hyde

11

Harriet Tubman

God says, "I will teach you and guide you in the way you should live.
I will watch over you and be your guide."
Psalm 32:8 (ERV)

Harriet Tubman
1822-1913
From Maryland

What Harriet Tubman accomplished is astounding. Before the Civil War, she personally guided hundreds of slaves to freedom in the North. During the Civil War, she led special forces troops on covert operations for the Union Army. After the war, her home became a place to care for those in need.

How could one woman accomplish so much in the face of such tremendous opposition? According to her, *"Wasn't me, was the Lord! I always told Him, 'I trust You. I don't know where to go or what to do, but I expect you to lead me and He always did."*[854]

In her own words Harriet described her childhood. *"I grew up like a neglected weed, ignorant of liberty, having had no experience with it."*[355]

Born into slavery on a plantation in Maryland, she suffered horrible abuse throughout her childhood. She was beaten, sleep deprived and forced to work long hours. She suffered permanent damage when she was hit in the head with a lead weight thrown by the overseer.

That injury caused her to experience headaches, dizziness, sudden sleepiness and memory loss for the rest of her life.

The abuse continued when she grew up and married.

Her husband told her that she was worthless, she would never amount to anything, and if she ever tried to escape from the plantation he would violently interfere.

Yet through all the pain she could hear another voice. Late at night, when she fell asleep, God would speak to her through dreams. In her dreams God showed her if she stepped out in faith and ran from the plantation, she would find complete strangers who would help her escape.

Harriet didn't know anything about the outside world. Having been denied any chance at an education, she couldn't read. She had no map showing where to go and no money to get there. Yet night after night in her dreams, she saw that something was waiting for her in the outside world.

One day she heard through the grapevine that the master's family was planning to sell her to a plantation farther south.

Time was running out for her to escape to the north. Late that night, she told her brothers that she was going to leave. She did not tell her husband or her parents but she asked her brothers to come along. Her brothers volunteered to guide her out to the main road. They went with her for a short way, hugged her goodbye and then turned back to the plantation for fear of being caught.

Everyone knew that all the main roads were patrolled by law enforcement looking for fugitives. Anyone caught without a written pass would be brutally punished but that was a risk Harriet was willing to take.

As she would later describe, *"I had made up my mind that I had a right to either have liberty or death. If I could not have one, then I would have the other; for no man was going to take me alive; I was going fight as long as my strength lasted."*[356]

For days she traveled at night and hid during the day. Very carefully, she followed the North Star, trying to stay on back roads as much as possible. Sometimes she tried to eat what she found in the woods.

Other times she knocked on people's doors and asked for food.

Asking for help was very risky. There were many people who would gladly turn her in for the reward.

Still somehow she managed to find the right people to ask for help. The Holy Spirit helped her discern whom to approach and whom to avoid.

After many days on the road, she finally reached the free state of Pennsylvania. As she crossed the line into freedom, *"I looked at my hands to see if I was the same person now that I was free. There was such a glory over everything. The sun shone through the trees and I felt like I was in Heaven."*[357]

She began a new life. She found work, earned a paycheck and rented a place to live. However she had trouble enjoying it knowing her family and friends still suffered. As soon as she had saved some money, she went back to the South and rescued a few family members and friends. Then she returned again and helped more escape. And returned again. And again. Each time people found freedom. As groups of slaves began mysteriously disappearing from the plantations, people noticed.

Robert Smedley, who was operating the Underground Railroad in Pennsylvania at that time, would later describe how Harriet worked behind the scenes.

"She was active in helping hundreds to escape. She would go fearlessly into the slave states, talk with the slaves, tell them how to escape, direct them on the road, and thus during one visit among them, would start numbers on their way northward to freedom."

"Large sums of money were offered for her capture, but all in vain. She could elude patrols and pursuers with much ease and unconcern. She had faith in God and would consult with God just as one would consult a friend upon matters of business. She said, 'God never deceived me.'"[358]

Harriet Tubman became one of the most successful conductors on the Underground Railroad. She outsmarted some of the most educated minds in the nation as her strategies always stayed one step ahead of law enforcement.

Those who knew her recalled, *"She always came in the winter when the nights were long and dark, and people who have homes stay in them."*[359]

She planned escapes for the weekend, giving them a head start before they could be reported missing on Monday.

She even recruited a team of people to follow the slave catchers and tear down wanted posters, shortly after any were posted on the roads.

One day she was riding a train in the South, when she overheard two other passengers reading her wanted poster which mentioned that she was illiterate.

Hearing that, Harriet calmly pulled out a book and pretended to read it. The other passengers looked right past her, never seeing what was right in front of them.

Another time she was walking through the market in her old neighborhood, when she recognized her former master walking right towards her. Harriet was wearing a sunbonnet that covered most of her face but there was a real possibility she would be recognized.

Fortunately, she was prepared for this exact scenario. Harriet had just purchased some chickens at the market and had them attached to a leash.

She tugged hard on the leash, causing the chickens to squawk and flutter and make so much noise that everyone got distracted. She made a big show of trying to calm down the chickens as her old master walked right by her. He never even noticed.

Then there were other times when her plans failed. If something went wrong on the trip and it looked like they were about to be caught, she would put the people on a train heading south, knowing that only trains headed north were searched. Then they would rendezvous at a different location to continue north again.

No matter what happened she always had a different strategy for each trip, as some of her friends would later describe, *"They hid in potato holes by day, while their pursuers passed within a few feet of them."*

"They were passed along by friends in various disguises; they scattered and separated; some traveling by boat, some by wagons, some by railroad cars, others on foot, to meet at some specified station of the Underground Railroad."[360]

They also had a well planned network of safe houses. One was run by William Still who kept some of the most detailed records of the Underground Railroad while working for the Pennsylvania Anti-slavery Society.

After helping Harriet's group several times on their way to freedom, he wrote, *"Her success was wonderful. While others greatly worried for her safety, she herself completely lacked any fear."*[361]

The more successful she became, the more of a target she became. Slaveholders began to catch on to what she was doing. They met together to plan how to stop her. Law enforcement was warned to watch all the roads for her. The State of Maryland offered a massive reward of twelve thousand dollars for her capture, making her the most wanted outlaw fugitive in America!

The best bounty hunters tried to hunt her down. They never found her. She outsmarted some of the most brilliant minds in the nation simply by listening to the Lord.

She only went where the Lord led her to go. He never failed her, not even when she rode trains displaying her wanted poster, or when fellow passengers shoved her aside to examine the rewards posted on the train for her capture. She was as fearless in her old southern neighborhood as she was in the safety of the North.

Many people admired her courage including John Brown who called her, *"The best and bravest."*[362]

Many people helped her on these secret travels. One of the most helpful was Thomas Garrett, a devout Quaker businessman, who paid a heavy price for helping hundreds of slaves escape. When he was caught, law enforcement seized and sold all his property.

In his trial the judge told him, *"Let this be a lesson to you."*

Garrett replied to the court, *"Judge, you haven't left me a dollar, but if anyone knows of a fugitive who wants shelter and a friend send him to Thomas Garrett!"*[363]

Even though Garrett had to start again from scratch, in the years that followed God prospered Garrett's business until his resources were restored. Then he continued helping Harriet.

Garrett's kindness would be repaid. During the Civil War, when violence filled the country and civilian homes were being looted and burned, the African American community protected Garrett's home.

Just before the Civil War came, Garrett wrote, *"The roads have become much more dangerous, as they are being constantly watched."*

"Yet we have hope, seeing Harriet seems to have had a special angel to guard her on her journey of mercy. I have never met anyone else who had more confidence in the voice of God, as spoken direct to her soul. She has frequently told me that she talked with God and He talked with her every single day."[364]

Garrett also knew about many narrow escapes Harriet had. Once she had been traveling a regular route at night with a group of fugitives when God told her to stop. She did. Then she asked God what to do. "He told her to leave the road and turn to the left. She obeyed and soon came to a small stream of water. There was no boat, no bridge; she again inquired of her Guide what she was to do. She was told to go through."

"It was cold in the month of March, but having confidence in her Guide, she went in. The water came up to her shoulders. The men refused to follow till they saw her safe on the opposite shore. They then followed. She soon had to wade a second stream; soon after which she came to a cabin of colored people, who took them all in, put them to bed, and dried their clothes, ready to proceed the next night on their journey."[365]

Later it was discovered that law enforcement had been lying in wait on the road up ahead. The law enforcement would never know how Harriet had completely escaped the hidden ambush, when this was the road she often traveled.

However, running the Underground Railroad required significant money. Harriet received much of the finances needed from a strong network of abolitionist groups who believed in her work.

Oliver Johnson got to know her well as he worked at the American Antislavery Society office in New York, where she regularly came for supplies. He would later describe, "Her skill in avoiding arrest and her courage to face hardship and danger was phenomenal."

What impressed Johnson the most was Harriet's strong humility. When she was asked to describe her adventures, she never bragged about what she had done or even acted "like it was remarkable at all."

Johnson continued, "I remember one day when she came into the office, there was a Boston lady there who was working for the antislavery cause."

"Harriet was telling, in her simple way, the story of her last journey. A group of fugitives were to meet her in the woods, that she might conduct them north. For some unexplained reason they did not come."

"Night came on and with it a blinding snow storm. She protected herself behind a tree as well as she could, and remained all night alone and exposed to the fury of the storm."

"'Why Harriet,' said the Boston lady, 'Didn't you almost feel when you were laying there alone, as if there was no God?'"

"Harriet replied, 'Oh no. I just asked Jesus to take care of me and He never let me get frost bitten one bit.'"[366]

By 1857, she had a feeling that it was time to rescue her parents. While they were still on the plantation, their cabin was a vital gateway to the Underground Railroad. Harriet had a bad feeling that her parents were about to get caught. Knowing her father was in poor health and unable to walk very far, she knew she would have to find a horse and wagon to transport them. How would she pay for that?

Praying for guidance, the Lord told her to talk to a particular friend. That friend had just received donations for her from antislavery groups, who had heard about her and wanted to help. When she visited this friend he handed her sixty dollars—more than enough to pick up the horse and wagon for the trip. She would successfully rescue her parents just in time to prevent the betrayal that had been planned for them.

Harriett later described how she had rescued them from prosecution for helping slaves escape. *"I saved them the expense of the trial by removing it to a higher court."*[367]

When the Civil War came, the Union Army asked for her help. No one knew how to move through the backwoods of the South like she did. She became a spy for the Union Army, silently moving behind Confederate lines to gather intel from the slaves on the plantations.

Many of these slaves would tell her military secrets they would not tell anyone else. The info that she received would later be described in U.S. Government reports as: *"This source of information represented the single most prolific and productive category of intelligence obtained and acted on by Union Forces throughout the Civil War."*[368]

According to Brigadier General Rufus Saxton, *"She was very valuable to us in both South Carolina and Florida. She worked as a spy, often going behind enemy lines with remarkable courage, zeal, and reliability."*[369]

Another U.S. Army report documented: *"Her spying and scouting evolved into a kind of special forces operation under Colonel James Montgomery."*[370]

Once Harriet led a unit of three hundred Union soldiers on a covert operation behind enemy lines. The team, *"Slipped up the river, eluding torpedoes that they had spotted. Undetected, the raiders swarmed ashore, destroyed a Confederate supply depot, torched warehouses, and liberated more than seven hundred fifty rice plantation slaves."*[371]

Many of those slaves would volunteer to serve in the army. General Saxton wrote, *"This is the only military command in American history wherein a woman, black or white, led the raid, and under whose inspiration it was originated and conducted."*[372]

After the war, Secretary of State William Seward petitioned Congress to grant Harriet a pension for her military service. He explained, *"The cause of freedom owes her much; the country owes her much."*[373]

Congress refused. That bothered Seward, so he figured out a way to get Harriet a home. When Seward offered to help Harriet purchase a home, Harriet insisted on paying for it herself. A deal was worked out where Harriet wrote a memoir of her life. The book royalties of twelve hundred dollars paid for her new property.

Harriet would later donate some of her land to the local church so that another home could be built to care for the elderly.

Harriet also turned her own home into a place to care for others. She took in many people who were struggling and needed a fresh start. Living in that home was where love would find her.

One day, a handsome young soldier knocked at her door.

Nelson Davis had fallen in love with her while they both served in the military during the war. When his military service ended, he hunted her down. It didn't matter that he was twenty-one years younger, she was the woman of his dreams.

They married in 1869 and enjoyed twenty years together. After he passed away from tuberculosis, she received a pension as the widow of a veteran. Years later, in 1899, President McKinley signed a bill to honor her military service by raising her government widow's pension to $20/year.

In the last years of her life, she fought a new battle. This time it was for women to have the right to vote. Harriet became a strong leader in the suffrage movement, working alongside people like Elizabeth Cady Stanton and Susan B. Anthony. Harriet was often invited to speak at women's suffrage conferences and she would also be the keynote speaker at the inaugural meeting of the National Federation of Afro-American Women in 1896.

She lived into her nineties, finally passing away from pneumonia in 1913 and she was laid to rest with full military honors in the Fort Hill Cemetery.

Booker T. Washington was invited to speak at the dedication of a special memorial made to honor her in the city of Auburn, New York, where she had settled after the war.

He summed it up best. *"Success is not to be measured so much by the position that one has reached in life as by the obstacles which he has overcome while trying to succeed."*[874]

The memory of her remarkable life would be honored in many ways. The *SS Harriet Tubman* was built and served in World War II. The state of Maryland would develop a national park to honor her achievements.

In 2002, Congress finally paid her estate her own long overdue military pension she had earned while serving her country.

11

Learn the Leading

"The true children of God are those who let God's Spirit lead them."
Romans 8:14 (ERV)

How did Jesus make decisions? He followed the Holy Spirit. Before starting His ministry, *"The Holy Spirit led Jesus into the desert."*[375]

There he spent forty days alone with God and defeated the devil's temptations. Then Jesus began ministering to the people but still found time to seek God's plan. Before choosing the twelve disciples, *"Jesus went up a hill to pray and spent the whole night there praying to God."*[376]

When Jesus left the Earth, He promised, *"I will ask the Father, and He will give you another Helper, who will stay with you forever. He is the Spirit, who reveals the truth about God. The world cannot receive Him, because it cannot see Him or know Him. But you know Him because He remains with you and is in you."*[377]

How does the Holy Spirit help us? *"The Spirit shows what is true and will come and guide you into the full truth."*[378]

The world is full of deception but we can escape that as the Holy Spirit helps us discern truth from error.

God doesn't want us to learn the hard way. He is always there with us, trying to show us which direction to take.

What happens if we're too busy to listen to him?

"Our leaders are stupid; they do not ask the Lord for guidance. This is why they have failed, and our people have been scattered."[379]

So how do you recognize the Holy Spirit's voice? The story of Elijah in 1Kings 19:11-13 describes how God speaks through a still small voice in our hearts. Very rarely does God speak audibly. He doesn't write messages in the sky.

He speaks to us through the Bible and by an inner knowing. That gentle nudge, directing towards certain things and away from others is the Holy Spirit communicating with your spirit.

The stories in this book describe people hearing God's voice, but only Harriet Tubman and Merrell Vories actually heard the audible voice of God in a vision. Everyone else was being guided through that deep inner knowing.

Because Harriet Tubman never had a chance to learn to read and couldn't read the Bible for herself, God directed her through dreams and visions as she needed them. Yet she still mostly relied on the deep inner knowing from the Holy Spirit to guide her.

We also need to focus on that still small voice of God that we hear in our hearts, instead of trying to seek dramatic visions or angelic encounters. When we need to know our future the Holy Spirit, *"Will let you know what is going to happen."*[380]

Reading the Bible helps you learn to hear God's voice, because the Holy Spirit will open your eyes to understand it. *"His Spirit teaches you about everything."*[381]

Sometimes it will feel like certain verses jump off the page at you, as He brings to your attention the answers you need.

Guidance is also felt through the peace of God. *"The peace that Christ gives is to guide you in the decisions you make."*[382]

"The Spirit doesn't speak on His own. He will tell you only what He has heard from me."[383]

Jesus explained how to discern the Holy Spirit. That everything He does will honor God and remain true to the Bible.

"The Spirit will bring glory to me by taking my message and telling it to you. Everything that the Father has is mine. That is why I have said that the Spirit takes my message and tells it to you."[384]

Think About:

"I am the Lord your God, who teaches you to profit,
Who leads you in the way you should go."
Isaiah 48:17 (NASB)

"If you are sensitive enough to listen,
the Creator will speak to you."[385]
-Dr. George Washington Carver

"Daily reading of the Bible prepares the mind and the heart for hearing the will of God."[386]
-James Kraft

12

Booker T.
Washington

"The things that are impossible with people are possible with God."
Luke 18:27 (NASB)

Booker T. Washington
1856-1915
From Virginia

Booker T. Washington was born under the cruel system of slavery, just before the Civil War. As he grew up, he would walk past the schoolhouse, wishing that he could attend school and learn to read.

He never dreamed that one day he would hold a degree from Harvard. That he would open the door for many others to receive a college education as well.

When he watched the plantation owner's family having tea and eating little cakes, he wished for the chance to try one of the delicious looking pastries.

He never thought that one day he would be invited to enjoy tea and pastries with Queen Victoria.

Or that he would become a close friend and advisor to several U.S. Presidents including William McKinley and Theodore Roosevelt. That a ship would be built to honor his memory. God had big plans for him, way beyond anything he had ever thought possible.

Washington never knew who his biological father was. In his memoir he described, *"I have heard that he was a white man who lived on one of the nearby plantations. Whoever he was, he never took the least interest in me."*[387]

Yet even though he was raised under *"The most miserable, desolate and discouraging surroundings,"*[388] he chose to forgive.

"I will allow no man to drag me down so low as to make me hate him."[389]

One of Washington's most vivid childhood memories, *"Was early one morning before day, when I was awakened by my mother kneeling over her children and fervently praying that Lincoln and his armies might be successful, and that one day she and her children might be free."*

"Though I was a child during the Civil War, I recall the many late at night whispered discussions that I heard my mother and the other slaves on the plantation indulge in."

"From the Bible, they had learned the story of the children of Israel and always believed that some day they would be free. From the time that Garrison, Lovejoy and others began to agitate for freedom, the slaves throughout the South kept in close touch with the progress of the movement. Freedom was in the air. We had been expecting it."[390]

The day that changed his life was when the war ended and a government official visited the plantation to read the Emancipation Proclamation.

Washington described, *"The most distinct thing I recall was that some strange man, a U.S. Officer, made a little speech and then read a rather long paper."*

"We were told that we were all free and could go when and where we pleased. My mother, who was standing by my side, leaned over and kissed her children, while tears of joy ran down her cheeks. She explained to us what it all meant, that this was the day for which she had been so long praying, but fearing that she would never live to see."[391]

During the war, Washington's step father had escaped and headed north to West Virginia. There he worked and saved up as much money as he could. When the war ended, he sent word to Washington's mother to come.

Washington, his mother and two siblings, left everything they had ever known and traveled to West Virginia. There Washington got a job working in the coal mines, trying to help his family even though he was about ten years old. It was miserable work in harsh conditions but what could he do?

The answer came one day when he overheard people talking about a boarding school in Virginia. The Hampton Institute welcomed students who couldn't afford tuition, allowing them to earn their room and board by working for the school. Maybe they would accept him. But the school was five hundred miles away. How could he get the money to travel there?

Working in the coal mine, Washington also heard about something else. There was a job opening, working in the home of the coal mine owner. That job would pay more than he was making.

Dreaming of earning enough money to attend school, Washington applied and was hired. For the next two years, he saved every penny that he could. At night he studied whatever books he could find, teaching himself to read. As he became a teenager, he finally felt ready to pursue his dream of an education. Taking a leap of faith, he quit his job and left town to apply at the school.

The trip to the Hampton Institute was five hundred miles. He traveled by stagecoach, since none of the railroads went directly there. When the stagecoach stopped for the night and all of the passengers went to the hotel, Washington quickly found out that he could not book a room at the hotel because of his skin color.

That left him with nowhere to sleep for the night. His only option was to curl up underneath the town's sidewalk, trying to stay warm in the cold.

The next morning, dirty and disheveled, he decided to look for work in the town because he needed money to continue the journey. Looking around, he found a man working on a ship who looked like he could use some help.

Washington asked for work and the man hired him. For several days, he worked for the man. Each night, he slept under the sidewalk.

When he had finally earned enough money to finish his trip, he got on the next stagecoach and continued on his journey.

When he finally reached the Hampton Institute, everything he saw at the school was totally different than his normal life. His new surroundings felt like pure luxury.

According to him, *"Life at Hampton took me into a new world. Having meals at regular hours, eating on a tablecloth, using a napkin, the bathtub, toothbrush, even sheets on the bed were all new to me."*[392]

More importantly, for the first time he knew, *"What it means to be a man instead of a piece of property."*[393]

Plus, his new school gave him something else he had never had. *"One of the most valuable lessons I ever learned at Hampton Institute was the value of the Bible. For the first time in my life, I had my own copy. And ever since, no matter how busy I may be, I never let a day pass without reading at least a few verses."*[394]

Washington continued his studies, while working as a janitor at the school, until graduating with honors in 1875. With his new degree he went home only to find his old town had changed.

Factories had shut down—his old job was long gone. His friends were struggling under the crushing weight of poverty. Their despair broke his heart. Knowing that education could open new doors for people, Washington started a night school, so that people in the town, who worked full time, could still receive the education that they had always wanted.

His school was an overnight success. Many of his students were able to utilize their education to find better jobs.

News of Washington's success reached his former principal at the Hampton Institute, retired General Samuel Armstrong.

When Alabama state officials approached Armstrong asking him to nominate someone to run a new school, he immediately thought of Washington as *"The best man we ever had here."*[395]

Washington was invited to become dean of the new Tuskegee Institute in Alabama.

In 1881, Washington arrived at Tuskegee to find nothing. No buildings, no classrooms, no furniture, no books and no supplies. Only a bunch of students eager to learn.

The government funding of two thousand dollars a year, wasn't anywhere near enough to cover the expenses. Washington wondered how he could possibly raise enough funds to get the school running.

He wrote, *"During the first years at Tuskegee, night after night I would roll and toss on my bed, without sleep, because of the anxiety and uncertainty in trying to construct buildings and provide equipment for a school when no one knew where the money was to come from."*[396]

The easiest answer was to simply charge tuition to cover expenses. But Washington didn't want to do that because he wanted to give other students the chance that had once been given him.

He did. To allow students to earn their tuition by working for the school, he invited them to help him build Tuskegee from the ground up.

That's exactly what they did. The first students rolled up their sleeves, poured their own concrete foundations, made their own bricks and built their own buildings to make Tuskegee Institute. They even made the furniture, desks, and chairs.

The hardest part of the process was brick making. As motivated as they were, none of them actually knew how to make bricks. They kept trying and failing which further depleted what little resources they had for construction.

When the money ran out, Washington sold his watch to buy the supplies to try again. This time it worked. And it gave them a new source of income. Once they figured out how to make bricks, they found out that the local community also needed bricks to build buildings.

This turned into a brick making factory which funded the school by selling over one million bricks a year. And it caught the attention of the steel billionaire Andrew Carnegie.

Carnegie was so impressed by their hard work and determination that he volunteered to donate whatever it would cost to build a nice library at the school. Washington thanked him for the generous offer, saying that if he could donate the money for supplies they could save on the construction cost by having the students build it themselves.

That impressed Carnegie even more. He became one of the largest financial supporters of Tuskegee, also making sure to provide for Washington's family.

By this time, Washington had fallen in love and married Franny, a fellow graduate of the Hampton Institute. She gave birth to their daughter Portia, then pass away at an early age.

Washington fell in love again, marrying a beautiful lady named Olivia. She helped him in his work at Tuskegee, but the heavy stress wore her down until she collapsed. She died in 1889, leaving Washington as a single father to three young children. Once again Washington had to grieve a deep personal loss.

Then he fell in love again and married a lady named Margaret who worked at Tuskegee.

Meanwhile, Washington focused on doing everything he could for the students at Tuskegee. He knew that having an education could make a huge difference in lifting people out of poverty.

So he focused the curriculum at Tuskegee on practical job skills so that students would be able to find the best paying jobs upon graduation. And he taught life skills, like the importance of property ownership, which enabled many graduates to overcome the cycle of poverty.

The new Tuskegee graduates quickly gained a reputation as being some of the best employees a company could find. This led to many companies offering higher salaries to recruit Tuskegee graduates.

Tuskegee graduates also became known for scientific breakthroughs that benefited their communities. As they studied better ways of farming, new ideas were discovered.

According to Washington, *"One of our graduates had produced two hundred and sixty-six bushels of sweet potatoes from an acre of ground, in a community where the average production had been only forty-nine bushels to the acre. He had been able to do this by reason of his knowledge of the soil chemistry. The white farmers in the neighborhood respected him, and came to him for ideas regarding the raising of sweet potatoes."*[397]

That student had learned a few things from the most well known teacher at Tuskegee—Dr. George Washington Carver.

Washington had recruited Carver, knowing that if the school could grow its own crops, they could save money on cafeteria costs. They did.

In just the year 1905 alone, the Agriculture department produced, *"Two hundred thousand pounds of meat, and eight thousand bushels of sweet potatoes."*[398]

Yet Washington and Dr. Carver didn't get along. Trying to stretch every penny, Washington micro managed the entire school. He pushed Dr. Carver to do things his way, while not recognizing that Dr. Carver had his own ideas. Washington tried to save money by not giving him the laboratory and equipment that he requested. Why should one professor get extra funding?

Washington missed the fact that Dr. Carver could produce much more with better equipment.

Dr. Carver was frustrated when he had no other option than making his own equipment from what he found in the trash. He complained but no one was listening.

Washington continued with his unreasonable demands, pushing Dr. Carver to focus more time on running the campus dairy and less time in the laboratory. Dr. Carver explained how the dairy was already producing hundreds of dollars a year in cafeteria necessities.

Washington replied that milk, butter, and cream weren't enough. They should start making cheese.

Dr. Carver responded, *"Fresh milk was worth five times the value of the cheese they could produce from it."*[399]

Washington retaliated by demoting Dr. Carver, putting another man in charge of the department.

Dr. Carver resigned. Why put up with this nonsense when Thomas Edison and Henry Ford were begging him to come and work for them?

Just as Dr. Carver was about to walk out the door, things changed. Washington apologized. The laboratory funding Carver needed was approved. Washington showed more respect for Dr. Carver, acknowledging that he was *"One of the most gifted men."*[400]

Despite all the challenges, Carver spent the rest of his career at Tuskegee because he felt that God had called him there.

Through that laboratory, Dr. Carver made Tuskegee famous. He published several bulletins with answers to the everyday problems faced by farmers. For example, he suggested they could cut costs on feeding farm animals by collecting acorns and mixing them with corn. That was less expensive than buying feed and also enhanced egg and milk production by improving nutrition.

Dr. Carver's ideas worked so well that soon farmers weren't the only ones seeking his advice. Government officials from the U.S. Agricultural department sought Dr. Carver for help in solving all sorts of farming problems. Dr. Carver amazed them by finding practical answers to what had been considered impossible situations.

Tuskegee's success made Booker T. Washington a celebrity. He was invited to speak all over the nation, including: Harvard, Yale, Williams, Amherst, University of Pennsylvania, and University of Michigan. Harvard gave him an honorary degree.

In 1898, President William McKinley personally visited Tuskegee to congratulate him on the success and to tell the students: *"What you do will affect not only those who come after you here, but many men and women whom you may never meet. The results of your training and work here will eventually be felt, in nearly every part of the country."*[401]

When Theodore Roosevelt became President, he often consulted Washington for advice on selecting the right candidates for top government positions. Washington was also sought out for advice by Rockefeller on how to disperse money in philanthropy to achieve the most good for the most people. Rockefeller would also become a large donor to Tuskegee.

While Washington would achieve greater success than he had ever dreamed, he would always feel like his greatest accomplishment was in how his students achieved the financial independence that had once seemed so impossible.

Tuskegee had such a powerful impact on the community that according to Washington's own great grandchildren, *"By 1910 roughly two and a half million black Americans were living in homes that they owned, that black farmers owned and operated more than a billion dollars worth of cultivated farms, and that black businesses were thriving throughout the country."* They also documented that by 1905, remarkable numbers of Tuskegee graduates had become highly successful entrepreneurs.[402]

Washington himself was proud that: *"While we stress the industrial side of the work at Tuskegee, we do not neglect the spiritual training. The school is strictly undenominational, but it is thoroughly Christian. Our preaching service, prayer-meetings, Sunday-school, Christian Endeavour Society, Young Men's Christian Association, and various missionary organizations, testify to this."*[403]

Washington's health suffered from the constant stress of managing the school. Pouring everything he had into this dream, broke his health. He never took a day off. When his friends demanded that he take a vacation, they had to raise all the money themselves. Not just to pay his way to Europe, but to finance the school's budget while he was gone. He was amazed when they accomplished it.

For the first time in his life, he experienced a vacation.

In 1899, when he and his wife Margaret boarded the ship to travel to Europe, they were shocked to discover their friends had even paid for him to travel first class.

"The whole thing seemed more like a dream than like reality, and for a long time it was difficult for me to make myself believe that I was actually going to Europe," He wrote. *"As soon as the last goodbyes were said, and the steamer had cut loose from the wharf, the load of anxiety, and responsibility, which I had carried for eighteen years, began to lift itself from my shoulders. It was the first time in all those years that I had felt free from worry."*[404]

Together with Margaret, he toured England and Europe for four months. To his surprise, people everywhere had heard of his work. And they wanted to support it.

When the British welcomed him, he was invited to the palace to sit down for tea at Windsor Castle with Queen Victoria. He described, *"In our party was Susan B. Anthony and I was deeply impressed with the fact that one did not often get an opportunity to see, during the same hour, two women so remarkable in different ways as Susan B. Anthony and Queen Victoria."*[405]

When the trip finally ended, he went home and continued pouring every ounce of energy into the school. His body wore out from the stress. Soon kidney stones were hurting him. By 1915, his health had rapidly declined. He would die at the young age of fifty-nine, getting buried where his heart was at Tuskegee.

The nation mourned. Condolences poured in from around the world. President Taft remembered, *"I knew Booker T. Washington well and valued him highly as a friend."*[406]

Rockefeller said, *"He will be greatly missed and his memory will be cherished with grateful affection for generations to come."*[407]

Former President Theodore Roosevelt believed, *"Booker T. Washington lived up to Micah 6:8, 'What more does the Lord require of you than to do justice and love mercy and walk humbly with your God.' I benefited very much by my association with him and valued greatly his friendship and respect."*[408]

After Washington's death, the work at Tuskegee continued. Following World War I, as wounded veterans returned home from the war, the federal government chose Tuskegee as the location for building a veteran's hospital. This facility would also house the new medical department of Tuskegee, training the next generation of doctors, nurses and medical professionals.

That infuriated the Ku Klux Klan. Once the veteran's hospital was built, the KKK planned a late night attack to burn it down. When the night came, they gathered a convoy of cars and drove down to Tuskegee. They had no idea that Tuskegee was waiting for them.

Two hundred military veterans had come to the hospital at Tuskegee for treatment of injuries they had sustained while serving their country.

These vets were not about to let the hospital be destroyed. When the alarm sounded through the campus that the KKK convoy was on its way, the veterans walked outside and formed an armed perimeter around the hospital.

Campus security had also been tipped off about the planned attack. Firefighting equipment was prepped and ready. As they set up defenses around the hospital, everyone moved into position.

When the KKK drove up to the hospital, they were shocked to see they couldn't even get close to the hospital. The entire perimeter was covered with veterans standing their ground with guns drawn and pointed right at the convoy.

Not a single shot would be fired. The older veterans kept a sharp eye on the younger vets to make sure that no one pulled the trigger until absolutely necessary. Their plan worked. The KKK drove away and never returned. That hospital would never be attacked again.

When World War II arrived, Tuskegee trained the first African American fighter pilots. The movie, *Red Tails,* documents the courage of these brave men. After the war, several of these pilots would become leaders in the Civil Rights Movement.[409] And also during the war, on September 29, 1942, the SS *Booker T. Washington* was launched. Washington's daughter Portia dedicated it.

Tuskegee still stands today. Washington's legacy lives on in the countless graduates and their immeasurable contributions to business, science, education, military, and government.

His life would inspire many others including the Rev. Martin Luther King who said it best. *"From an old clay cabin in Virginia's hills, Booker T. Washington rose up to be one of the nation's great leaders. He lit a torch in Alabama, then darkness fled."*[410]

Booker T. Washington
Photos

Tuskegee class on history

Tuskegee graduate building the ship

Launch of the SS. Booker T. Washington

Booker's daughter Portia at the ship launch

12

Shatter the Limits

"Behold, I am the Lord, the God of all flesh:
is there any thing too hard for Me?"
Jeremiah 32:27 (KJV)

God's dream for you is better than you could imagine. It goes way beyond what you think you could have.

"No eye has ever seen or no ear has ever heard or no mind has ever thought of the wonderful things God has made ready for those who love Him."[411]

How do we get those things?

"God has shown these things to us through His Holy Spirit. It is the Holy Spirit Who looks into all things, even the secrets of God, and shows them to us."[412]

God is not limited by your past, your education, resources, or any other circumstance. Everything that seems to be holding you back is easy for God to solve.

The Bible tells about someone named Jonathan who put his faith in God instead of his circumstances. Israel had been attacked by the Philistines and things looked pretty bad.

"When the Israelites saw that they were way outnumbered and in deep trouble, they ran for cover, hiding in caves and pits, ravines and brambles and cisterns—wherever."[413]

While Jonathan's father, King Saul, just sat and did nothing, Jonathan believed that God was not limited by the overwhelming odds against them. He decided to do something about the situation.

"Jonathan and the soldier who carried his weapons talked as they went toward the Philistine camp. 'It's just the two of us against all those godless men,' Jonathan said. 'But the Lord can help a few soldiers win a battle just as easily as he can help a whole army. Maybe the Lord will help us win this battle.'"[414]

The armor bearer agreed with him. *"Whatever you want to do, I'm with you."*[415]

Together they faced their problem head on by attacking the entire Philistine army by themselves. And God fought for them.

"Jonathan crawled up the hillside with the soldier right behind him. When they got to the top, Jonathan killed the Philistines who attacked from the front, and the soldier killed those who attacked from behind."

"Before they had gone a hundred feet, they had killed about twenty Philistines. The whole Philistine army panicked—those in camp, those on guard duty, those in the fields, and those on raiding patrols. All of them were afraid and confused. Then God sent an earthquake, and the ground began to tremble."[416]

The rest of Israel's army saw the tide of the battle turning and came to help. By the time it was all over, they had won a major victory. God delivered the entire nation because of the faith of two people.

Yet God can only do big things for you when you believe His promises written in the Scriptures.

The Bible also tells a story of what happens when people refuse to believe God.

One time the Israelites were suffering a severe food shortage. People were starving.

God sent the prophet Elisha to comfort everyone with the promise that things were about to change. He prophesied that by the very next day they would have more food than they could handle.

Most people believed. One person doubted.

"Then the officer who was close to the king answered the man of God. The officer said, 'Even if the Lord made windows in heaven, this could not happen.' Elisha said, 'You will see it with your own eyes, but you will not eat any of that food.'"[417]

God kept His promise. *"Food prices dropped overnight."*[418]

Yet that officer never got to enjoy any of it.

"It so happened that the king of Israel had put the city gate under the command of the officer who was his personal attendant. The officer was trampled to death there by the people and died, as Elisha had predicted when the king went to see him."[419]

God wants to do mighty things for you too. When He reveals that awesome future to you, can you believe it?

"Today when you hear his voice, don't harden your hearts as Israel did when they rebelled."[420]

Even though God had prepared a good future for them, *"They were not allowed to enter and have God's rest, because they did not believe."*[421]

Several different times, *"They complained about Him and said, 'Can God give us food in the desert?'"*[422]

How did that make God feel? *"When God heard that, he was furious."*[423]

Those words *"Brought pain to the Holy God."*[424] And it cost them the Promised Land.

Every one of them died in the wilderness, never getting the better things in life. So the Bible warns us, *"Don't let evil thoughts or doubts make any of you turn from the living God."*[425]

Even Jesus was limited by people. Visiting one particular town, *"Jesus did not do many miracles there, because the people did not believe in Him."*[426]

As the cost of living rises and incomes fall, don't trust in the world's ability to ruin your life.

Look to God who can do *"Far more than you could ever imagine or guess or request in your wildest dreams! He does it not by pushing us around but by working within us, his Spirit deeply and gently within us."*[427]

Think About:

"For the eyes of the Lord run to and fro throughout the whole earth, to show Himself strong on behalf of those whose heart is loyal to Him."
2 Chronicles 16:9 (NKJV)

"No airplane will ever fly from New York to Paris. That's impossible. What limits the flight is the motor. No known motor can run at the requisite speed for four days without stopping, and you can't be sure of finding the proper winds for soaring."[428]
-Wilbur Wright
March 25, 1909

"Refuse to recognize that there are impossibilities. No one knows enough to be sure what really is and isn't possible. Everything is possible. Faith is the substance of things hoped for, the evidence of things not seen. (Hebrews 11:1)"[429]
-Henry Ford

13

Madam CJ Walker

"She works late into the night
to make sure her business earns a profit."
Proverbs 31:18 (ERV)

Madam CJ Walker
Birth name: Sarah Breedlove
1867-1919
From Louisiana

At twenty years old, Sarah Breedlove was left to raise her daughter alone after her husband passed away. All she wanted was a better life for her daughter. Little did she know that she would make history by pioneering the cosmetics industry, creating thousands of jobs and inspiring a new generation of entrepreneurs.

Sarah was raised by her sister after being orphaned at a young age. At fourteen, she moved out to marry her first love. Three years later, they had a beautiful baby daughter.

Then her happiness was shattered. *"I was left a widow at the age of twenty, with a little girl to raise."* [430] (The exact details of how her parents and her husband passed are unknown).

Sarah moved to St. Louis, fell in love again and married a man named John Davis. Soon she realized this was a mistake. First her husband refused to work. Sarah had to struggle to make enough money to pay the bills while he kept making excuses for not working. Then he betrayed her by having an affair. Sarah found out and confronted him over it. He responded by beating her. She left. Once again, she felt alone as she struggled to make it on her own.

This was a time in American history when very few jobs were available to women. One of those few paying jobs was doing laundry. In the days before the invention of the washing machine, doing laundry was so physically difficult that most homemakers used what little money they had to pay someone else to do their laundry.

Laundry methods had not changed much since the Middle Ages. Clothes were boiled over an open fire. Dirt was removed by hand scrubbing. Drying was done on an outdoor clothesline. The book *Miss Leslie's Lady's Manual* explained how to do laundry in 1850:

- *"In America most families have their washing done once a week. This is much better than the European custom of monthly or quarterly washes."*
- *"For a laundry, a large fireplace is better than a stove, as the latter will make the room intolerably hot in the summer."*
- *"A large brass or copper kettle is an indispensable tool for laundry; as an iron pot will stain the clothes."*
- *"After soaking clothes overnight, begin early in the morning so clothes will dry by evening."*
- *"Mix two quarts of lye in the water of a large tub. You should have a long round hickory stick, somewhat flattened at one end, to stir the clothes while boiling—and a long stout hickory fork, with which to lift them out of the hot water without scalding your hands."*
- *"When the washing is over for the day, the tubs, buckets, etc., should be make clean and turned up to dry; all the articles used should be put away in their proper places, and the floor wiped up with a mop or cloth."*[431]

That's the heavy labor Sarah was doing every day, all day long. While this enabled her to make a steady income while staying at home with her daughter, month after month of working with harsh chemicals began to affect her health.

Over a period of time, the endless hours of heavy physical labor also took a heavy toll on her.

According to Sarah, *"I was at my tubs one morning with a heavy wash before me. As I bent over the washboard, and looked at my arms buried in soapsuds, I said to myself, 'What are you going to do when you grow old and your back gets stiff? Who is going to take care of your little girl?'"*

"This set me to thinking, but with all my thinking I couldn't see how I, a poor washerwoman, was going to better my condition."[432]

Things went from bad to worse. The heavy chemicals for cleaning laundry began causing her hair to fall out. She covered her head with a scarf and tried every scalp remedy available. Nothing worked. Then she cried out to God for help.

As she later described, what happened next was a miracle. *"He answered my prayer. For one night I had a dream, and in that dream a big black man appeared to me and told me what to mix for my hair."*

"Some of the remedy was from Africa, but I sent for it, mixed it, put it on my scalp and in a few weeks my hair was coming in faster than it had ever fallen out. I tried it on my friends. It helped them."[433]

She continued, *"Something told me to start in the business in which I am now engaged. This I did. I went to Denver Colorado, and began my business career on a capital of $1.25."*[434]

When Sarah moved to Denver she rented a room and found a job as a chef. That way she had the money to pay bills so she could continue experimenting with her formula in her free time at home.

When she had finally figured it out, she put it in a jar and began selling it door to door. Ladies invited her into their home where she did their hair and told them about her product. Many of these ladies became long term customers.

Madam CJ Walker Driving an Automobile photo is from the
Indiana Historical Society Madam CJ Walker Collection.
Photo is used with permission. The front passenger is her
daughter. In the backseat is Lucy Flint and Alice Kelly who
both work for her. Lucy is the bookkeeper and Alice is the
factory forelady. The brick building behind them is owned by
Madam Walker as her place of business.

In that time most homes lacked the convenience of running water.

Without access to running water, most women could not wash
their hair very often, sometimes only once a month, resulting in many
women experiencing scalp and hair problems.

When Sarah knocked on their door, she brought the solution to
their problem. Soon Sarah had more customers than she could manage
on her own. Turning to her church for help, Sarah invited her friends
to help her in the business.

Sarah had always been involved in the local church, where she had
long been a driving force behind many community outreaches. Now
that she needed help with her business, other church members with
business experience helped her organize her company, advising her on
production, distribution, and marketing.

While all this was going on she had fallen in love with a journalist named Charles J. Walker.

Marrying him changed her name to Madam CJ Walker. So she named her new company—Madam CJ Walker Manufacturing. She worked on advertising her brand name as much as she could.

One reporter described, *"She always had a respect for printer's ink, for as fast as she earned a little money she spent it in advertising."*[435]

Her advertising was very successful. Sales rose. Money poured in. Eventually she reached a point where even by working night and day she still couldn't keep up with the orders. It was time to open a factory and hire employees.

Then she opened a beauty school, to train students in cosmetology.

Graduates of her school went out and sold her products as independent sales reps, making more money from commissions than the typical salaries available to women at that time.

Watching their success made Sarah very happy. She insisted, *"The girls and women of our race must not be afraid to take hold of business endeavors."*[436]

Yet while her business was doing well, her husband was becoming jealous of her. The more she succeeded, the more he tried to sabotage her. Instead of respecting her success, he began stealing from her.

One of her friends warned her that her husband was *"Meeting the postman, getting the mail, not filling orders."*[437]

It was worse than that. He was also having an affair with one of her closest friends. Sarah came home from a hard day's work to find her husband in bed with another woman.

That deeply hurt her but she chose to forgive and move on. She filed for divorce, turning the matter over to her attorney and ceasing all direct communication with her now ex-husband.

Her husband soon regretted his mistake. He married his mistress only to find out she had never wanted him.

The mistress had only been trying to get the formula for the products. Once she had it, she launched her own cosmetics business but failed miserably. Eventually Sarah's ex-husband begged her to take him back, but she saw right through his lies and did not allow him in her life. Instead, she moved on to bigger and better things.

In 1912, she was invited to attend the National Negro Business League Convention where she shared her remarkable story. *"I am a woman that came from the cotton fields of the South. From there I was promoted to the wash-tub."*

"Then I was promoted to the cook kitchen, and from there I promoted myself into the business of manufacturing hair goods and preparations. I have built my own factory on my own ground. I am not ashamed of my past."[438]

After her speech, Booker T. Washington passed a resolution recognizing Walker as the *"Foremost business woman."*[439]

Five years later, she was making enough money to buy a mansion in Rockefeller's neighborhood. This purchase of a $250,000 home put her on the front page of the newspaper. People were stunned to see that a woman could make that much money.

The reporter covering the story wrote, *"Twelve years ago she was a washerwoman, glad of a chance to do anyone's family wash for $1.50 a day."*[440]

Now the reporter was in awe to see no expense had been spared in furnishing her residence. Four cars, including a Model T, sat in the garage. There was a full household staff employed to wait on her, including a driver and a private tutor.

In the interview with the reporter Madam Walker said, *"If I have accomplished anything in life, it is because I have been willing to work hard. Perseverance is my motto."*

"I got my start, by giving myself a start. It is often the best way."[441]

The reporter also noted in the article was that she had recently been invited to the White House to meet with President Woodrow Wilson.

With more money than she had ever hoped, Madam Walker was able to enjoy everything she had ever wanted. Lavish possessions, rare art, elaborate musical instruments, expensive vehicles, expensive travel, and the best of everything filled her life.

Still she emptied her bank account to help others. Visitors noticed her kindness and generosity to the servants. She also gave scholarships to many students at Tuskegee Institute. She loaned money to other ladies trying to start businesses and never hesitated to help anyone she could.

Yet no matter how much money she had, she never forgot to honor God. One guest who stayed with her at Christmas noticed how she insisted on everyone kneeling down to give thanks to God. *"The theme of her prayer was humility and awe in the presence of God."* [442]

As the years passed by, her health took a turn for the worse.

She sought the best medical treatment money could buy, but they were unable to treat her high blood pressure and hypertension.

At age fifty-one she passed away, still holding firmly to her lifelong trust in God. She reminded all those around her, *"It was through His Divine providence that I am what I am, for all good, perfect gifts come from above."* [443]

By then her company had grown to making annual revenues of what would be millions of dollars in today's money.

Her personal fortune is estimated to have been about twenty million dollars in today's currency, making her one of the wealthiest people in America at the time. [444]

She left a will directing that part of her fortune would go to her daughter. Part went to help charitable organizations and part was left to maintain her home and grounds that people would be reminded of what one woman can accomplish with a dream.

Since then her memory has lived on to inspire many other people. New York City named a street after her.

In 2010, Congress issued a proclamation honoring her achievements in pioneering the cosmetics industry by *"Establishing a groundbreaking national and international business empire, first selling products door-to-door, then developing a marketing strategy, which included selling products through the mail."*

"Madam CJ Walker is one of history's greatest businesspersons, and a role model for women, African-Americans, small business, entrepreneurs, and the nation's young people." [445]

And in the Guinness Book of World Records, Madam Walker lives on as the first American woman to become a multi-millionaire. [446]

13

Developing Your Ideas

"Diligence brings wealth."
Proverbs 10:4b (MSG)

Madam Walker's secret to success was developing ideas and products people needed and getting paid every time they sold. Instead of working a regular job and getting paid one time for the work, she figured out how to work once and keep getting paid for it by inventing products and developing relationships with customers who would buy her products on a regular basis.

"Whoever gathers little by little has plenty."[447]

Madam Walker is a powerful example of the Biblical woman, described in Proverbs 31, who develops products, turns a profit, then builds on the future by reinvesting her earnings into further endeavors.

Proverbs 31: *"She makes clothes and belts and sells them to the merchants. She looks at land and buys it. She uses the money she has earned and plants a vineyard."*[448]

While Madam Walker pioneered multi-level marketing and found remarkable success, multi-level marketing is not for everyone.

Trying to sell someone else's products can be very frustrating. You don't have to market other people's ideas when God has brand new, creative ideas He can give you, if you will seek Him.

Starting a business is also not for everyone, but there are many other ways to do things. Ask God to reveal to you the right pathway for your own ideas. Then go search out how best to develop your ideas.

Remember the heart of God even back in the Old Testament was wanting to help people reach the point that *"You will lend to many nations, but you will not have to borrow from any."*[449]

Think About:

"Blessed is she that believed for there shall be a performance of those things which were told her from the Lord."
Luke 1:45 (KJV)

"Man's impossibilities are God's opportunities."[450]
-James Kraft

"The secret of staying afloat, is to create something that people will pay for. I didn't work at inventions, unless I saw a market demand for them."[451]
-Thomas Edison

14

President William McKinley

"People who listen when they are corrected will live,
but those who will not admit that they are wrong are in danger."
Proverbs 10:17 (GNT)

President William McKinley
1843-1901
From Ohio
Entered office as the 25th President of the United States
on March 4, 1897

President William McKinley never hid his love for God. After taking the oath of office at his inauguration, he leaned down to kiss the Bible. He was never ashamed to kneel in the Oval Office, seeking God's guidance.

Night after night, he walked the floors of the White House, quietly praying for the country. Yet like all other Presidents he made mistakes. His biggest one was ignoring the warning from the Secret Service.

Long before reaching the White House, McKinley had proven his courage under intense Civil War combat.

In 1861, he quit a comfortable post office job to volunteer for the military. During the most intense battles of the Civil War, he never flinched. Not even when a sniper shot his horse right out from under him. That courage was soon recognized.

By 1865, President Lincoln had promoted McKinley to the rank of Army Major. After the Civil War, McKinley passed the bar exam in 1867, becoming the local district attorney.

Then he was elected to serve in Congress. After serving several terms in Congress, in 1891, he ran for Governor of Ohio. On the campaign trail, he traveled to Dayton and gave a campaign speech at the local county fair. The Wright Brothers attended the fair, listened to McKinley's speech and were impressed.

Orville Wright described in a letter to his father, *"We had a great time here yesterday. McKinley made an afternoon speech, which was a success. He looks like an honest man."*[452]

McKinley won his election and served as Ohio's thirty-ninth Governor.

In 1896, McKinley ran for President and won by a landslide. He was hugely popular, easily winning re-election in 1900. Every where he made a public appearance, massive crowds came to see him. People patiently waited for hours to shake his hand, knowing that he loved connecting with people. He would stop everywhere he went to greet people, even when the Secret Service warned him about the danger.

The Secret Service was concerned about the rise of violent anarchist groups, who were brutally attacking heads of state around the world. Trying to overthrow several different governments, they carried out attacks against leaders in France, Austria, Italy, and Spain. As news spread across the Atlantic of attack after attack, the people around McKinley worried about him, sensing that danger was drawing near.

After receiving death threats, the Secret Service cancelled the public reception the President was scheduled to host in Buffalo, New York.

McKinley had it rescheduled.

The Secret Service cancelled it again.

McKinley refused to listen to them. *"I have no enemies. Why should I fear? No one would wish to hurt me."*[453]

Frustrated at McKinley's determination to put himself in harm's way, the Secret Service increased the number of men guarding the President. Yet three Secret Service agents, four soldiers and four police officers wouldn't be able to save the President from his own bad decision.

On September 6, 1901, President McKinley showed up at the scheduled public reception and mingled with the people. Dozens of people came to shake his hand.

Leon Czolgosz came to kill him.

At twenty-eight years old, Leon wanted the total elimination of all government. Knowing he could get close to McKinley, he showed up at the reception, getting into the receiving line with a weapon hidden in his pocket.

When his turn came to meet the President and McKinley extended his hand in greeting, Leon pulled out his gun. He fired pointblank.

Two shots hit McKinley. One only grazed him. The other sank directly into his stomach. Feeling the pain, McKinley didn't cringe or cry out. Silently he sat down in a chair, then told everyone that he was fine.

The first person to tackle Leon was not the Secret Service. McKinley had not allowed them to stand next to him. The people standing next to McKinley were politicians who weren't about to take the bullet for him. Fortunately, there was still the crowd of regular people swarming the President.

James Parker was six feet six inches of pure steel. He was down on his luck, having just lost his job in the food service industry. He had come to hear his President.

When the shots were fired, Parker grabbed Leon by the throat knocking his arm away. They wrestled for the gun. Leon was strong. Parker was stronger and ripped the gun right out of his hands.

That's why only two shots were fired. Leon had more ammo and could have hurt more people, if Parker had not fought back.

The crowd couldn't believe what had just happened. Shocked and enraged, the crowd began beating Leon. Still bleeding from his wounds, McKinley forgave the shooter, telling the crowd to stop hurting him.

Law enforcement was humiliated they had not protected McKinley. They did not want to admit James Parker (a black man) had heroically tried to give his life to save the President. Parker was not invited to testify at Leon's trial.

However, several newspapers interviewed Parker who said, *"I'm glad I was able to be of service to the country."*

To make sure the truth was not forgotten, on September 27, 1901, the black community held an event to celebrate Parker. They read a public statement honoring *"The heroic act of James Parker in having thwarted the purpose of Leon Czolgosz."*[454]

President McKinley was rushed into emergency surgery. As the nurses were prepping him, they could hear him quietly whispering the hymn *"Nearer My God to Thee."*

The surgery lasted several hours but the doctors were unable to find the bullet.

To help the doctors, Thomas Edison sent his latest invention—the x-ray machine. But this invention was in such an early stage that it still didn't work right. The doctors weren't able to locate or remove the bullet. Gangrene set into the wound.

After several days of fighting for his life, the end came.

Looking at his wife for the last time before walking through Heaven's door, McKinley's last words were *"It is God's way. His will, not ours, be done."*[455]

Leon was tried and convicted of murder. He received the death penalty but died unrepentant as the nation mourned the President they had cherished.

President McKinley
Photos

President McKinley with his wife

Security at McKinley's inauguration

McKinley visits Tuskegee and Booker T. Washington

President McKinley with his cabinet

Crowds gathering to meet McKinley before he was attacked

Parker trying to save the President

McKinley's funeral

14

Does God Control Our Decisions?

God says, *"How I wish My people would listen to Me; how I wish they would obey Me! I would quickly defeat their enemies and conquer all their foes."*
Psalm 8:13 (GNT)

Is everything that happens to us, somehow part of God's mysterious will? Or are our lives shaped by our own choices?

We've often heard the saying *"God is in control."* Control of what? Everything? Even our own choices in life? Or do we have the ability to choose contrary to God's will? Does God's will automatically happen, regardless of what we do?

God answered this question in the Bible by saying, *"Today I have given you the choice between life and death, between blessings and curses."*[456]

The sovereignty of God gave us the power of personal choice when *"He put us in charge of the earth."*[457]

All of God's promises depend on our decision to obey Him. That's why the Bible has many IF/THEN type statements.

"IF you diligently obey the Lord....all these blessings will come upon you."[458]

"IF My people....will humble themselves and pray....I will heal their land."[459]

"All these good things will come upon you—IF you will obey the Lord your God."[460]

IF could not exist in a world where everything that happened to us was somehow controlled by God. There would be NO IF statements in the Bible if God's will just automatically happened. Instead, God gave us the ability to choose between good or evil.

God won't make those choices for us. God won't interfere if we choose the wrong path. God is a loving father who suffers the pain of watching His children go astray.

When Jesus walked the Earth, it hurt Him to watch people suffer by making bad decisions. As much as He wanted to help them—He could not help unless they allowed Him.

At times Jesus had to watch helplessly grieving, *"How many times I wanted to help your people. I wanted to gather them together as a hen gathers her chicks under her wings. But you did not let me."*[461]

Think about those words of Christ. *"You did NOT let me."*

Jesus was actually limited by people's decisions. Don't let that happen to you. You have the power to choose what's good for your life.

You can choose to open the door to God's good things for you and close the door to the bad things that come your way.

Jesus taught us the Lord's Prayer which specifically asks for God's will to be done on Earth as it is in Heaven, showing us God's will doesn't automatically happen.

In our own lives, we choose to fulfill God's dreams for our lives or go another way. Otherwise, why would we need to pray for God's will to happen, if it were just predestined to happen anyway?

"God made people good, but they have found many ways to be bad."[462] While God is very patient in dealing with our hearts, eventually, if we refuse to yield to Him, He will allow us to go astray. *"My Spirit will not struggle with humans forever."*[463]

Some things have happened to you because other people chose to do evil. That's not your fault. That's not God's will. God never needs someone else to sin to teach you anything.

Next time you hear someone trying to blame God for their own choices, remember: *"Don't blame God when you are tempted! God cannot be tempted by evil, and he doesn't use evil to tempt others."*[464]

According to Romans 12:2, there are three levels of God's will: good, better, and perfect. That gives you the choice of which level you want to have. The best part of having a free will is that if you don't like where you are, you can change it.

Remember the story of Jabez in the Bible? *"His mother had given him the name Jabez, because his birth had been very painful. But Jabez prayed to the God of Israel, 'Bless me, God, and give me much land. Be with me and keep me from anything evil that might cause me pain.' And God gave him what he prayed for."*[465]

Jabez knew that evil causes pain yet things can be changed.

"For God did not give us a spirit of fear. He gave us a spirit of power and of love and of a good mind."[466]

The power God gave us is the ability to change our circumstances. Instead of being trapped by fear, we can change things. We can choose to forgive and fulfill God's dreams for our lives.

If you have the ability to change the situation for good—do it. If you've done everything you can, researched every possibility, forgiven people that hurt you and still can't change things, then trust the sovereignty of God to make *"All things work together for good."*[467]

Think About:

"If you wander from the right path, either to the right or to the left, you will hear a voice behind you saying, 'You should go this way. Here is the right way.'"
Isaiah 30:21 (ERV)

"The trouble with most of us is that we try to fit God into our plans rather than fit ourselves into His plan."[468]
-R. G. LeTourneau

"My concern is not whether God is on our side; my great concern is to be on God's side."[469]
-President Abraham Lincoln

1 5

Irene Spencer & Susan Schmidt

God warns, *"My people would not listen to Me. So I let them go their stubborn ways and do whatever they wanted."*
Psalm 81:11a-12 (GNT)

Irene Spencer
1937-2017
From Utah

Susan Schmidt
1953-
From Utah

Irene Spencer was dealt a very difficult hand in life. She was born into a Utah religious group that preached plural marriage. Getting to Heaven required sharing your husband with as many sister wives as he wanted to have. Children were seen as trophies for men, ensuring their eternal power. Misery and poverty were the norm. And everyone believed this was God's will.

God forbids polygamy. So does the Mormon Church, which out-lawed it over a century ago. In 1879, the U.S. Supreme Court declared it unconstitutional. Congress outlawed *"bigamous cohabitation"* in 1882. Utah had turned it into a felony by 1935.[470]

Yet some men refused to change. To continue their lifestyle, several polygamist groups left the Mormon Church and went their own way.

In 1924, Alma LeBaron was thrown out of the Mormon Church for being a polygamist. When federal marshals threatened to arrest him for violating the bigamy laws, he moved his wives to Chihuahua, Mexico. He had eight children including Joel, Ervil and Verlan LeBaron. When Alma died in 1951, he left control of the group to his son Joel Lebaron.

Joel LeBaron decided to move the group from Mexico back to Utah. There Joel formed his own church, claming that he was God's direct mouthpiece and anything he wanted to do was God's will.

The one person in that group that knew that Joel was wrong was his brother Ervil LeBaron. After all, Ervil knew for a fact that Ervil was God's true prophet! Ervil tried to convince the group to follow him. When no one would pay attention to Ervil, he left and formed his own group. Then he convinced that group to kill Joel. Making up his own rules as he went, Ervil married thirteen wives and had twenty-five children.

Joel's church wasn't interested in Ervil's leadership. They promoted his other brother, Verlan LeBaron to lead the church. Verlan was a much kindler, gentler leader. He didn't want to kill anyone, just sleep several different women. Soon he had his eye on a young lady named Irene Spencer.

Irene was born into another Utah polygamy group, which was involved with the LeBaron group. The leader of that group was Irene's uncle, Rulon Allred, who married sixteen wives.

Irene's mother was the sister of Rulon Allred. She had a mind of her own. Through the years she had started questioning their doctrine. Eventually Irene's mother recognized that something was wrong and left the group. That meant she also left what little provision she had.

Life in the outside world was very difficult. With minimal job skills she had no other choice but to try homesteading and farming the tough soil.

It was a hard life. When a good looking guy came her way, she fell in love. Little did she know that he was violent. For the next several years, Irene's mother suffered dearly.

Irene grew up watching her stepfather's rage leave her mother bruised and bleeding. Yet Irene believed it was God's will, because that's what she had learned in church. According to her, *"I lived in constant fear that my mother would go to hell because she gave up polygamy. So when she married in monogamy and I saw the abuse she endured, I felt it was God's punishment for her abandoning polygamy."*[471]

Because her mom had left the group, Irene had a chance at a normal life. She attended the local high school and soon found herself getting attention from the guys. Irene had a great personality that attracted young men. Her high school days even included a steady boyfriend named Glen who begged her to marry him. Yet there was something holding her back from happiness with Glen.

Irene had been told her whole life by the polygamous group that she would receive a personal revelation from God on who to marry.

Yet they brainwashed her to believe that this personal revelation would involve becoming a sister wife. So at sixteen years old, when Irene heard a voice telling her to marry her sister's husband, Verlan LeBaron, that sounded like divine guidance. She followed that voice, not realizing that this was forbidden by God in Leviticus 18:18.

It was a miserable marriage. Verlan moved her down to where their group had a community in Chihuahua, Mexico. There she lived in brutal poverty. Their income was what crops they could raise by hand with very little equipment to make the work easier. Irene had thirteen children with Verlan, only to raise all those children by herself, as Verlan was gone most of the time, chasing other women.

Irene lived a very lonely life, feeling like there was no way out.

She described, *"I did not want to be accountable for breaking the religious laws that my forefathers had painfully sacrificed to live. When polygamy is your only identity, you cling to it."*[472]

Meanwhile, her husband Verlan had fallen in love with fifteen year old Susan Schmidt of Utah.

Susan had also grown up in church being taught that God would send a man to her, that she would have to share. But when Ervil LeBaron began pursuing her, Susan was terrified. Knowing his violent reputation, Susan wanted nothing to do with Ervil. Instead, she had met a handsome young man, who visited her church regularly, named Verlan LeBaron.

Susan had also been taught that God would reveal her husband to her through a personal revelation.

One night she had a dream that Verlan rescued her from Ervil. Since Verlan had already begun chasing her, Susan believed that dream was a confirmation from God that she should marry Verlan. She did. Then Susan was moved down to Mexico where she also found out how miserable it was to live plural marriage.

Susan got to know Irene as they lived in the same community and had to do the same heavy physical labor.

"We lived in small adobe houses. Mostly without toilets, running water or electricity. Food, medical attention or anything that cost money was scarce," Susan said. *"What mostly trapped me was fear. The overwhelming fear that I couldn't possibly make it on my own with five young children out in the scary, evil world."*[73]

The world was getting even scarier. Ervil put a hit out on Verlan. Turning his polygamous group into a thriving criminal enterprise, Ervil taught his people to steal American cars and sell them in Mexico, as well as drug smuggling and bank robbery. Whatever made quick money. Following Ervil's orders, they killed more than thirty people.

One of the people they killed was a Vietnam Veteran named Dean West. Coming home from the Vietnam War, Dean didn't have a lot of veteran friendly places to go.

So when Ervil offered him a job teaching military style tactics to the group, Dean tried to be respectful of their lifestyle choices.

Dean had only one wife named Cheryl. He deeply loved her. When Cheryl began seeing red flags in the group and wanted to leave, Dean listened to her.

That infuriated Ervil who didn't want anyone to leave the group. He set a trap for Dean. Ervil's pregnant wife, Vonda, asked Dean to come over and fix her washer.

While Dean's back was turned, Vonda shot him point blank. For that she would be convicted of murder and sentenced to life in prison.

Meanwhile, Ervil stayed on the move, trying to stay one step ahead of the authorities hunting him. Ervil needed money so he harassed other polygamist groups, demanding that they pay him ten percent of their income. When they refused, he would return with violence. Ervil never hesitated to take out anyone who stood in his way, even women and children.

The various polygamous groups began fighting back by posting guards and preparing for violent confrontations.

One group in Utah got so tired of being harassed by Ervil, that when he demanded a meeting with them, they showed up fully armed and prepared with a body bag to take him out. But they would not get a chance to kill Ervil. He would be smart enough to disappear before the meeting.

Ervil ordered the death of Irene's uncle, Rulon Allred. Ervil sent one of his wives to pull the trigger. Allred was shot at his own medical office in front of terrified eyewitnesses. Meanwhile, Ervil left a trail of death and destruction, taking out anyone he felt was a threat.

As one of Ervil's main targets, Verlan had to run for his life. That left Susan upset at his constant absence.

Life in polygamy was lonely. Was it really worth it? Finally unable to take the misery anymore, Susan began to question everything she had been taught. Picking up the Bible, she looked for answers.

Opening her heart, she asked God, *"To show me that this whole concept was as wrong as my gut instincts told me it was."*[474]

As she poured over the Bible, verses leapt off the page at her. Seeing things she had never seen before, she realized that God actually hated polygamy. In fact just before Noah's flood came, *"God obviously was angry at these men's choice to take more than one wife."*

"The only righteous man was Noah, who had one wife. Even the animals that were taken into the ark were in pairs, one male and one female."[475]

Reading further through the Bible, the Holy Spirit continued revealing more verses to Susan. By the time she realized the truth, it had set her free.

When Susan showed those verses to Verlan, *"He assured me that I just needed to have faith, to not worry about a thing, and leave the heavy scripture studying to the priesthood men."*[476]

Now that her eyes were opened, Susan was done. To escape, she turned to family members who had left the group. At her request, they came to Mexico, picked up her and the kids, and drove them back to Utah. There she stayed with her brother, until she could figure out what to do.

Yet just as Susan took her life back, Verlan showed up at her brother's house, trying to keep her under his thumb. Verlan threatened to take the children if she didn't return.

Susan stood her ground, offering to report him to authorities for having committed a felony by transporting her across state lines when she was underage. That scared Verlan. He left her alone.

Susan found a job, working as a waitress by day, while attending night school to earn her high school diploma. After graduating from high school she enrolled in college.

Along the way she met the man of her dreams. He loved her and the five children. They married and lived happily for twenty-nine years, until he passed away.

Now Susan ministers to others, showing them how to break free of religious tradition. Today she advocates for other victims of polygamy to get the resources and human kindness they need.

Now back to Irene's story....

Still living in Mexico, Irene was reaching the end of her rope. The pain and desperation was pushing her to think of leaving. In her own words she described, *"One day I looked around and realized they could not threaten me any more with hell. I was already there. I wanted to commit suicide. Some of my nieces and nephews already had."*[477]

As Verlan continued chasing new ladies, Irene finally reached her limit and decided to leave.

The way out came from her children. By this time her children had grown up, moved away, gotten good jobs and were making steady income.

They gave her money to escape, one even buying her a car. Finally owning something that no one could take away from her, she drove off to America in that car. She never looked back.

Yet there was still one more thing she wanted. Even through years of pain and suffering, Irene still deeply loved God.

Letting go of everything she had ever known, *"I cried out, 'God, whoever you are, I want to know you.'"*[478]

Irene went to visit her son, who lived in Alaska. He invited her to attend his evangelical church. While sitting in the congregation during the service she heard God's voice for the first time.

"The Holy Spirit simply revealed to me God's unconditional, divine love, fully available right now through the sacrifice already paid by His Son," she described.

"After years of religious sacrifice and suffering, I finally understood that Christ really is sufficient. Never again would I have to jump through strange, agonizing hoops in order to cajole God into accepting me."[479]

Irene also found her true love. Hector Spencer had grown up in the same group but escaped and lived a normal life.

After Irene left the group and began contacting old friends, they reconnected and fell in love. They enjoyed twenty-five years of happiness together until Hector passed away in 2013. Meanwhile, God used Irene to minister to many hurting people.

After years of pursuit, the FBI finally found Ervil LeBaron. He was sentenced to life in prison for the murder of Irene's uncle, Rulon Allred. One year into his prison sentence, Ervil died of a heart attack in 1981. His brother, Verlan LeBaron, also died that same year in a car accident.

In the last years of her life, Irene traveled America, helping people understand they don't have to earn God's love. She was able to minister to many people before passing to Heaven on March 12, 2017.

15

The Danger of Sacrifice

"People ruin their lives by their own foolishness and
then are angry at the Lord."
Proverbs 19:3 (NLT)

When you love God, you want please Him. You want to sacrifice for Him. But no matter how much you sacrifice, you'll probably still feel like you haven't done enough because Christian theology often overemphasizes the importance of sacrifice.

Yet is sacrifice really the most important thing to God? Nope.

God's Word says, *"Obedience is better than sacrifice."*[480]

According to the Bible, God is pleased by faith and obedience to Him, not by sacrifices.

King David realized this in the Bible when he wrote in the Psalms, *"You don't really want sacrifices, or I would give them to you. The sacrifice that God wants is a humble spirit. God, you will not turn away someone who comes with a humble heart and is willing to obey You."*[481]

Even in the Old Testament, God warned His people to be very careful on where and how they sacrificed.

"Be sure you don't offer your burnt offerings in just any place you see. The Lord will choose his special place among your tribes. Offer your burnt offerings and do everything else I told you only in that place."[482]

While lots of things need to be done and many people will ask for your help, if you say yes to everyone, you will wear yourself out.

Then you won't be able to help anyone. Instead, try to limit the sacrifices you make according to your actual responsibilities and what you want to do. Not what you feel that you have to do.

Jesus explained how to do this when He said, *"No one takes my life away from me. I give my own life freely. I have the right to give my life, and I have the right to get it back again. This is what the Father told me."*[483]

Even when sacrificing, Jesus stayed in control by not allowing other people use Him. He decided where, when and how to lay down His life.

The Pharisees tried to kill Jesus several times before He went to the cross, but He escaped each time. He waited until it was part of God's plan for Him to sacrifice Himself.

The Bible teaches us to make our own choices as to how we help others, not allowing ourselves to be pushed into doing things out of guilt.

"Each man should give as he has decided in his heart. He should not give, wishing he could keep it. Or he should not give if he feels he has to give. God loves a man who gives because he wants to give."[484]

Follow the Holy Spirit. Not guilt. Not fear of disappointing people.

Take the time to seek God's will so you won't waste time in the wrong direction.

"Watch your step when you enter God's house. Enter to learn. That's far better than mindlessly offering a sacrifice, doing more harm than good."[485]

Think About:

God says to us, *"I want your loyalty, not your sacrifices.*
I want you to know me, not to give me burnt offerings."[486]
Hosea 6:6 (GW)

"If you trust in your own good works, you'll never rest.
You'll always feel like you haven't done enough.
Just do the best you can and put your trust in Christ,
Who is our peace."[487]
-William Tyndale

"Experience has taught me
that when I yielded to pressure, things went wrong.
But when I followed God's Word in the Bible,
things worked out in the end."[488]
-William Colgate

16

Milton Hershey

"Good people might fall again and again, but they always get up."
Proverbs 24:16a (ERV)

Milton Hershey
1857-1945
From Pennsylvania

Milton Hershey was a failure. Not once. Not twice. Three times his business collapsed. And each time he got back up, believing he was one day closer to his dream.

Hershey's grandfather was a farmer. Through years of hard work, he made enough money from farming to retire early with a nest egg of $100,000, giving him the freedom to answer the call of God to enter the ministry. He became a circuit riding pastor, traveling many miles to preach everywhere from Ohio to Canada.

Meanwhile, back home on the farm, his daughter Fanny was pursued by a handsome neighbor named Henry. He promised her everything she could imagine. They married in 1856 and had a little son named Milton Hershey. But Henry made bad choices that caused Fanny all kinds of problems.

According to Fanny, "*I was only twenty at the time, and his flattery and impressiveness soon won me over. I should have prayed to the Heavenly Father and asked for His guidance before I married him, but I was willful. I thought that I could change him for the better. But Henry and work didn't get along very well.*"[489]

Henry was always making excuses for avoiding his responsibilities, finding every possible way to avoid working. While he had inherited a house from his family and moved Fanny into that home, he soon lost it. Hearing that oil had been discovered nearby in western Pennsylvania, he packed up his family and rushed off to find his fortune. Their trip was financed by mortgaging the family home.

"*It seemed a fool hardy thing to do, and so it turned out, for we hadn't been in Oil City very long before Henry had frittered away all of our money. Those were heart-rending days and they left their mark on me that I was never able to blot out,*" Fanny described.

"*Henry had sold everything he could lay his hands on. I had to take in boarders and do people's laundry. And when things got so bad that I couldn't carry on any longer, I appealed to my brothers Abe and Ben to come and bring us back home.*"[490]

Fanny's brothers received her letter and came to help her. When they arrived, they were shocked at the terrible poverty that Fanny and little Milton Hershey were suffering under. The brothers moved her back home.

Along came her husband. Nothing changed. Henry tried farming. Once again his refusal to work hard, left them struggling to make a living.

Fanny tried to raise vegetables to sell on Saturday mornings at the local farmer's market. By then little Milton Hershey was old enough to toddle around. Sometimes while Fanny was helping a customer, he would wander off. If she couldn't find him, she knew to check the local candy shop. She could always find him there.

From an early age, Hershey was fascinated by candy. He loved visiting the local candy shop and asking questions.

As he grew up and began attending school he always had a pocket full of candy. That candy made him many friends at school but his father was convinced that there was no future in candy. Instead, Henry pushed Hershey to learn a real job skill.

When Hershey was fourteen, Henry apprenticed him to a local printer, figuring he could learn an easier trade than farming. Hershey was totally miserable in this apprenticeship. It was long hours of work with no pay, learning a skill he had no interest in.

Quitting was not an option. If he ran away, he would be forcibly returned to the apprenticeship, because of the legal contract his father had signed. Feeling trapped, Hershey tried to think of a way out.

One day he dropped his hat in the printing press. The printing press broke. Everything came to a dead standstill. The printer was furious. Hershey was kicked out and told never to return.

That gave Hershey the chance to make his own decisions. He found a job working for a candy maker.

His dad was not happy. Henry believed, *"Such stuff is woman's work. The boy will never get anywhere making candy."*[491]

Yet even when his own father didn't believe in him, the candy maker, Joseph Royer, did. He was impressed by Hershey's strong work ethic and willingness to learn. According to Royer, *"He's smart and always applies himself to his work. I could easily see that he was determined to learn all there was to know about the candy business as quickly as possible."*[492]

Four years later, Hershey was nineteen year old and ready for a change. He decided, *"If I can make money for my employer, why can't I do just as well for myself?"*[493]

Thinking of how he could start his own business, Hershey realized that the city of Philadelphia was about to celebrate the one hundred year anniversary of America's independence. Two hundred thousand people were planning to come to that celebration.

Maybe those crowds would like to buy some candy. Hershey decided to move there and open his first candy store.

Just before Hershey left his hometown, his mother took him aside and said, "*Now that you are going out into the world alone, the best advice that I can give you is to put your faith in your Heavenly Father. Never lose that faith, even though things may not go as well as you think they should. In time, everything will come out all right.*"

Hershey replied, "*Never fear, mother. My faith is strong.*"[494]

His first store was an overnight success. As crowds thronged the city of Philadelphia, people discovered the tasty caramel candy in his shop. Everything sold so fast that Hershey could barely keep up with the demand.

Then the festivities ended. People went home. As the crowds left the city, his sales dropped overnight. Hershey was left with too much supply and not enough demand. How could he sell the rest of the candy? Maybe the local dry goods stores would be interested.

Approaching several dry goods stores in the city, Hershey was able to find new customers for his products. Several stores accepted his candy, selling it on consignment. Soon he had several regular wholesale clients and enough business coming in that he needed a staff.

He wrote home, asking his mother and aunt to come and help with the business. They did. But even with the extra help, the demand for his candy increased until they were working night and day to keep up with the orders.

Just when everything was going great, his father showed up. Having heard that they were making money, Henry wanted some. He came to the shop and asked Hershey for a loan.

Hershey loved his father but knew his father was still wandering from place to place, always in need but never willing to work. What was he going to do? Feeling guilty, Hershey gave him three hundred dollars. Maybe then he could leave town and leave them alone.

That cost them dearly. Hershey had been doing so well that he wasn't prepared when some of his customers didn't pay on time. Hershey ran out of money and needed more supplies while he was still waiting to get paid for the candy sitting on consignment in the stores.

The only solution to ask his uncles for a loan. They graciously bailed him out.

Yet just when Hershey's sales began to pick up again, his dad came back and begged for more money. Hershey loaned him fifty dollars. Once again the money disappeared quickly.

The third time his dad came back and begged for money, all the frustration Hershey had been feeling exploded. This time he told his father, "*No more of my money will slip through your fingers. From now on you can look out for yourself.*"[495]

While Hershey was having this difficult conversation with his father, the shop door opened. In walked the agent from the sugar company.

This sugar company had been giving Hershey the supplies he needed on credit, but when the agent walked in and saw him exploding at his father, the agent decided, "*A son who treats his father as you have done is a poor risk. From now on you'll pay cash.*"[496]

That set Hershey back even farther. Meanwhile the stores continued to delay paying him. As Hershey was stretched way beyond his means, things got worse.

One of his employees had a major accident with a full load of product. He reported, "*As I was crossing Market Street the fifth wheel of my wagon got caught in the tracks and the darned thing upset! The horse ran away, and the candies were scattered all over the street.*"

"*After I got on my feet, I ran after the horse and I soon had him under control, but not until the damage had been done. People came running from everywhere and filled their pockets. The wagon was knocked to smithereens.*"[497]

Once again Hershey had to plead with his uncles for help. They sent it. Soon after, his Mom reported to the uncles: "*We keep busy, but things are not as good as we would like to see them. Money seems to disappear like magic with us. The four hundred dollars was used almost immediately to buy sugar.*"[498]

This time, the uncles told them to quit. Seven years of trying to make the business work was enough. They needed a fresh start.

When they refused to bail him out again, Hershey shut down the shop and sold everything.

Starting over from scratch, Hershey tried to find a regular job. This was during an economic downturn when jobs were hard to find.

Hershey traveled from town to town, looking for any job he could find.

At one point, he answered an employment ad that directed him to a suspicious looking building. Something didn't feel right. This didn't look like a regular business but he was too desperate to care.

When he knocked on the door, the man who opened it, refused to answer any questions. He told Hershey to come in, sit down with a group of young men and just wait. Hershey obeyed, even as his gut feeling told him something was wrong.

Rumor on the street was that young men were being kidnapped into forced labor on merchant ships.

Knowing he had to get out of there, Hershey carefully studied the room, looking for a way out. Standing to his feet, he boldly walked to the door and turned the knob. It was locked. He was trapped.

Fortunately he was prepared for this type of situation.

Knowing that forcible kidnapping was happening to young men looking for work, Hershey had brought a gun with him for protection. Drawing his weapon, he turned to the man in charge and demanded, *"Let me out the door."*[499]

The man didn't argue. He opened the door and Hershey escaped. He never did find out what they were doing or what happened to everyone else there.

Meanwhile, that type of kidnapping was legal in America until 1915 when laws were written to address it.

As Hershey continued looking for work but finding nothing, it was time for a change of scenery. Moving to Denver, Colorado to stay with his father, he was able to find a job working for a caramel maker.

This was how he got the idea that would transform the candy industry. Day after day of working with his hands for the candy maker, Hershey kept thinking about how to make the candy taste better.

At that time, caramel candy was typically made through a process that involved adding paraffin wax to caramel. Instead, Hershey started thinking about adding milk. Would milk make it taste better?

For weeks, Hershey worked on different formulas for making the candy until he had greatly improved the flavor. He even figured out how to keep it from sticking to teeth.

As soon as he had saved up some money, he moved to Chicago and opened another candy store. It failed. Hershey moved to New York and tried to open a store there. That didn't work either. Finally he packed up and moved to Pennsylvania. This time he asked his mother and aunt to come and help. They did.

To launch the new business, his aunt mortgaged her house. With both his mother and aunt helping, this time the store succeeded. Moving back to Pennsylvania had put them close enough to local farms to get the finest fresh milk. Mixed with Hershey's new formula, they finally had the candy that would bring people back for more.

Business exploded. Within a few years, they had sold over a million dollars of caramel candy. Hershey now had a full time staff of hundreds and a family that was thrilled at his success. He had even made enough money to buy back his family's farm that had once been lost to foreclosure.

While his dreams had come true, his mother and aunt encouraged him to continue thinking of new ideas because as his aunt insisted, *"There's greater success for you ahead."*[500]

Six years later, Hershey received a big offer. Would he like to sell his company?

The offer was a lot of money. While Hershey didn't want to retire, the more he thought about it, the more he realized that maybe the caramel candy business *"Has reached its peak."*[501]

Noticing that his customers seemed to prefer the chocolate covered caramels, maybe the future of the industry was in chocolate. Letting the caramel side of the business go would open the door for him to focus on how to make the best possible chocolates. With that in mind, he sold the caramel business for a lot of money.

There was a time in American history when most people didn't like chocolate. It was rare, expensive and very bitter to the taste. Hershey figured there must be a better way. Maybe he could add milk to enhance the flavor. Would almonds make it taste better?

Hershey kept experimenting until he found something that tasted really good. According to him, "*I started with the intention of making the best chocolate that money or skill could make.*"

"*Regardless of the manufacturing cost, I made it just as good as I knew how. I wasn't going into the chocolate business to add to my wealth. I had all the money I needed. What I wanted to do is to find a way to put my money to work so that it would benefit others.*"[502]

Dreaming big, Hershey started looking to buy industrial property where chocolate could be manufactured on a big scale. Still a farmer at heart, he went way out into the country.

There he found a place to build an entire town with a big factory to employ people and nice homes for them to enjoy. In a time when most American homes still lacked electricity and indoor plumbing, Hershey made sure that every home in his town had that, hoping to make it a really nice place to live.

That town would become known as Hershey, Pennsylvania. People thought he was crazy to build an enterprise in the middle of nowhere.

Yet Hershey saw the bigger picture, "*I never liked cities. Why a farmer should want to move to the city is more than I can understand, for a farmer has a higher standard of living than a man who lives in the city.*"

"*The farmer, for instance, can build a house for the price of two or three years rent in the city. To me, the whole prosperity of our country rests on the intelligent industry of the farmer.*"[503]

After growing up in a family struggling to survive, Hershey knew how important it was for families to get a chance in life. His dream was to give that chance to others. So when he built the town of Hershey, Pennsylvania, he made it easy for families to own their own homes.

Hershey paid them higher than average wages and bonuses that helped with down payments. To him, the reward was watching employees succeed.

He described, "*Many of those who started at the bottom of the ladder, doing menial tasks, took advantage of their opportunity and are now in charge of their respective departments.*"[504]

Sometimes Hershey himself contributed spiritually towards the entire town. The town had its own printing press, which published a free newspaper called the *Press.*

One day Hershey found a Christian pamphlet that he wanted to share with everyone. The pamphlet told the story of a businessman who had found success by applying Scripture to his work.

Walking into the print shop in his town, Hershey told the printer, *"Here's a booklet that I want you to print in the Press (town's newspaper). It tells about the greatest book that was ever written—the Bible."*[505]

When the printer opened the booklet, he realized that Hershey had personally underlined several Bible verses in the pamphlet including:

"Where there is no vision, the people perish." (Proverbs 29:18)

"Trust in the Lord and do good; so shall you dwell in the land and be fed." (Psalm 37:3)

"No good thing will He withhold from them that walk uprightly." (Psalm 84:11)

Then Hershey had also underlined these quotes in the pamphlet: *"Those verses are the two greatest promissory notes in the world, signed by Almighty God Himself."*

"To know that you are walking side by side with the greatest Power in the universe—the Power that cannot fail—gives life a purpose and a meaning."[506]

Hershey would also find the romantic love that he had always hoped for. One day in 1898, while he was approaching retail stores to sell his candy, Hershey met the love of his life. A beautiful store clerk caught his attention. Her cheerful spirit would brighten his life.

Yet their happiness would be short lived. Soon after they married, his wife Kitty got sick with a mysterious disease. In the years that followed, their love grew while her health slowly deteriorated.

Hershey found the best doctors that money could buy, yet none of them could find the answer. Hershey remained fully devoted to her, always looking for a way to help. Desperately seeking a cure, he took her to Europe for medical attention. Nothing helped. Eventually they gave up and returned home to America. They returned ahead of schedule, just in time to miss their reservation to sail home on the Titanic.

When Kitty died at age forty-one, Hershey grieved deeply. Then he made her dream come true. Together they had explored ideas of how to put their wealth to work helping needy children. While they would never have a child of their own, at least they could make a difference for others. He poured their resources into making a home for those that needed it most.

For years, Hershey had been thinking about the children who faced the harshness of the world after losing their parents. He had visited many orphanages only to be disappointed to see cold environments where their stomachs were fed but their hearts neglected.

Hershey would be deeply affected by that experience, later saying that, *"Before I founded my school, I visited a number of orphan institutions so that I might learn things first hand. What troubled me the most was the lack of home atmosphere. I believe it is a great mistake to put a uniform on a boy and make him feel like an outcast. The school won't be worth much unless love is thrown in."*[507]

To serve their needs, Hershey gave his wealth to provide a home to care for orphans. Carefully planning every detail, his dream was to create a place where at risk children could grow up in a loving home environment. Trying to find the best staff to run the home, Hershey insisted, *"We want men and women who love and understand children. And we must not neglect the moral and religious training of the boys, either."*[508]

Then he built an entire school to provide the best education and job skills, hoping to help them find the trade that they would enjoy. He said, *"Our boys are the future itself growing up before our very eyes. Who knows, someday one of them may be at the head of the chocolate business."*

"Our school provides them with a thorough education, with instruction in carpentry, blacksmithing, agriculture, dairying and other trades. They graduate when they are eighteen at which time we give each $100 to tide them over until they get a job. That's more than I had when I was that age."[509]

This home for orphans would open its doors and its heart to many children. One of them was seven year old Lou Bocian.

After losing his mother and being neglected by his biological father, Lou was begging on the streets when he was found and brought to the home.

Years later as a grown man, Lou would recall his experience of meeting Hershey as he arrived at the school. *"He was right there when I first arrived at the school and they were giving me my clothes. He put his arm around me and said, 'From now on, we'll take care of you. You're one of my boys.'"*

"He'd come about every two weeks and watch us play. He was, to us, a very kind man whom we considered to be our foster father."[510]

While helping these children filled an emptiness in his heart, Hershey still felt the deep pain of losing his wife. One Christmas while he stared at the gigantic Christmas tree he was heard saying to a close friend, *"They tell me that I am the richest man in town, and financially speaking I am. But on Christmas I know that I am the poorest. I am reminded all the more of my aloneness in this world, having neither a wife or children."*[511]

Through the years, Hershey continued generously supporting both the children and many other charities. At one point he gave each church in his town a check for twenty thousand dollars, hoping to pay off their mortgages.

Yet he still worried that they wouldn't understand how to properly manage their finances. *"It won't be long before all of them will be in debt again."*[512][513]

When the Great Depression came, Hershey found a way to keep the business running. None of his employees were laid off, even during the darkest parts of the Great Depression.

He reasoned, *"Things are bad, but there's always a way out. We'll have to work harder and pay stricter attention to business."*[514]

While sales had declined, so did the cost of sugar. Hershey kept making money and pouring it into helping others.

After a long life of helping everyone he could, at eighty-eight years old he passed away in 1945.

Since then his fortune has continued helping thousands of children.

Today the profits of the Hershey Company still support that home for children. The charitable foundation that he pioneered remains one of the largest in the world.

This is advice that Hershey wanted to pass down to future generations. *"Luck had nothing to do with my success. As I see it, my success is the result of not being satisfied with mediocrity, and making the most of my opportunities."*

"You can only make money by giving people what they want. When I started making chocolate I didn't follow the policies of those already in the business. Instead, I made a better nickel chocolate bar than any of my competitors."[515]

16

Rise Again

God says, *"I will pay you back
for those years of trouble."*
Joel 2:25b (ERV)

Everyone makes mistakes in life. Sometimes those mistakes cost us dearly. Yet no matter how much you have lost, God can restore more.

The Bible tells the story of King Amaziah who made some really big mistakes. When trouble came, instead of turning to God for help, he tried to solve the problems his own way.

At one point he spent a fortune on hiring an army for protection. Yet God sent a prophet to tell him that only the Lord could protect him in battle. That he needed to send the hired army home and instead face the impending trouble with the military force that he already had.

King Amaziah asked what about all the money he had lost by hiring these soldiers?

The prophet replied, *"The Lord can give you much more than that."*[516] The end of the story is that he didn't listen to God and everything went wrong.

The Bible tells another story about someone named Joseph. He went through years of ups and downs. Years of frustrations and unfulfilled dreams.

Yet in the end, God brought him through a healing process where he could honestly say, *"God has made me forget all my sufferings."*[517]

Then there's also the story of Job in the Bible. Even after losing everything, the end of the story was: *"The Lord made him prosperous again and gave him twice as much as he had had before. The Lord blessed the last part of Job's life even more than he had blessed the first."*[518]

No matter what you've been through, God has something much better for you. Let God show you how His plan can get you to where in the end, *"All the wealth you lost will be nothing compared with what God will give you then."*[519]

Think About:

"The Lord guides us in the way we should go and protects those who please him. If they fall, they will not stay down, because the Lord will help them up."
Psalm 37:23-24 (GNT)

"There really isn't such a thing as failure if you learn something from it."[520]
-R. G. LeTourneau

"Failure is only the opportunity to begin again more intelligently. There is no disgrace in honest failure—there is disgrace in fearing to fail."[521]
-Henry Ford

17

J. C. Penney

"A worker should be given his pay."
Luke 10:7b (ERV)

J. C. Penney
1875-1971
From Missouri

There's a lot of reasons that pastor's children rebel. For J.C. Penney, it was just one. Stinginess.

Penney was one of twelve children born to a pastor and his wife. *"My father was an old-school Baptist preacher who served his people without pay. His farm was his only income."*

Penney later recalled, *"He was a man of but one occupation, that of serving the Lord. Whether he preached on Sunday, plowed on Monday, sowed on Tuesday, or reaped on Wednesday, it was all to the glory of God."*[522]

His father was a log cabin preacher willing to work long hours to help others. He had built the log cabin church from scratch to help the local community. Year after year, he poured his time and energy into helping the townspeople. Rain or shine, he was there when they needed him.

Then one day, they decided that they didn't want him. It was the day he asked for a salary. The congregation refused. They got offended. Then they asked him to leave his own church.

J. C. Penney was fourteen years old when he watched his family get kicked out of their own church. That made him furious at God. How could this happen to his family? He vowed never again to darken the door of a church.

Meanwhile, he watched his father react differently. His father chose to forgive and forget. Penney later described, *"His refusal to become bitter and his willingness to bear the cross of misunderstanding saved me from becoming a cynic to Christianity."*[523]

His father went back to farming. Then God gave them what the church didn't. Their farm prospered, giving them steady income and paying off the mortgage.

Six years later, Penney faced a deeper pain. His father became ill and suddenly passed away. Grieving the loss of someone who meant everything to him, Penney found comfort in the encouraging words his father had uttered on his deathbed. *"Jim's going to make it. I like the way he started out."*[524] Knowing that his father believed in him inspired Penney to never give up.

Penney had started out making money at a young age by working all sorts of odd jobs around town. *"I collected horseshoe nails from the blacksmith's floor, ran errands, cut grass, drove cows to pasture, delivered packages, fetched and carried for the ladies when there was a church supper or rummage sale."*[525]

One time Penney cut the grass for a lady who promised to pay him fifteen cents. When the work was finished, *"She tried to pay me off in cookies instead of the agreed fifteen cents."*

He refused. There were enough cookies at home; he wanted his wages. *"Blushing, she paid me the agreed fifteen cents but with a sniff, as though letting me know that it might be just as well if I looked elsewhere for grass to cut."*[526]

The first full time job he worked was as a store clerk. There he learned how to sell, by paying attention to the needs of customers.

Paying attention to details is also how he discovered that his boss was cheating the customers.

The store sold two brands of coffee. The good coffee was forty cents a pound. The cheap coffee was fifteen cents. However, Penney noticed that his boss would refill both containers with the cheap coffee. Then make the clerks pressure customers into buying only the more expensive coffee. Penney couldn't do it. He asked for his last paycheck and left.

Penney had saved up enough money that he was able to open his own business. His first venture was a butcher's shop.

It failed miserably. Embarrassed and out of money, he had to go back to working for someone else.

Yet he still believed in his dream. *"When I was a young man, it was generally accepted as a fact that a man could not create a fortune and remain a Christian. I wanted very much to do both."*[527]

Once again Penney worked as a store clerk, but this time his bosses noticed how good Penney was at selling. They offered to help him open his own store. Could he afford to invest his own money into purchasing the franchise?

That was the opportunity he had been hoping for. Taking a leap of faith, Penney looked around at various places to open the store and selected a location his bosses couldn't understand. Kemmerer, Wyoming? That was a small mining town in the middle of nowhere. How would his store survive? His bosses had already tried and failed at having a store there.

Penney saw something that no one else did. Listening to customers had taught him that people want good service, quality products, and lower prices.

Kemmerer was a great location because the only competition was one other store with high prices and bad service.

That store was run by the mining company, which took its customers for granted, feeling like they were doing the miners a favor to sell dry goods. Penney talked to the miners, asking what they wanted. The more he talked to customers the more he felt prepared to meet their needs.

Penney opened his first store in 1902. The Golden Rule was more than just the name of the store. Penney practiced it with enthusiasm, personally testing out all new merchandise, demanding to know its quality and limitations before the customers did.

In a time when nothing bought at a store could be trusted for quality, Penney insisted on having the best products at the lowest prices. He also kept the store open longer in the evening to give the locals enough time to shop when it was convenient for them.

He described, *"At the end of the first year alone we had done about $29,000 worth of business, at an overhead which was almost laughably low. I attributed our progress considerably to our understanding of people who worked with their hands: farmers, laborers, and their families. They were the kind of people who grasped what we were doing and because we dealt squarely with them, gave us their trade."*[528]

As his first store began to succeed, Penney dreamed, *"Someday I'm going to have a chain of dry goods stores that will cover these mountain states!"*[529]

The way to make his dream come true was through partnering with some of his best employees. Watching his employees carefully, Penney approached the hardest workers, offering them a chance to own their own franchise. Many of them took the deal. Within nine years, Penney had twenty-two stores because he had given others the same chance that was given him.

He believed, *"Men work best when they work for themselves."*[530]

His best business partner was his wife. Penney had fallen in love with a local girl named Berta. They married and raised two sons. She helped him open his first store, working just as many long hours as he did.

In their early years, as they struggled to get by, she saved every dollar possible. As they began to prosper, she still continued to save everything, trying to help her husband.

Her life was suddenly cut short. She became very ill in a time when medicine was not very advanced and doctors routinely made mistakes. In her case, the doctors decided the best treatment was to remove her tonsils.

The surgery was scheduled at a time when Penney was out of town on business. After the surgery was completed and she was released from the hospital, she decided to walk home to save paying money for a taxi.

She walked all the way home in bad weather on a cold day. The cold she caught became pneumonia. She died in 1910, leaving Penney to raise their two boys alone.

Losing the love of his life was a devastating blow. For months, Penney would struggle to concentrate on business when all he wanted to do was think about her.

To honor her memory, he fulfilled one of her lifelong dreams. Since she was the one who had brought him back to church, he gave the church they attended enough money to pay off the mortgage.

Still that couldn't heal the pain in his heart. In his own words Penney would later describe how *"the shock"* of losing her had been, *"So sudden and so severe that it came near to overwhelming me. It was the most difficult time of my life."*

"Many a night, I walked the streets battling with temptation and the darkness that had settled upon me. If it had not been for the memory of my father's faith in me, I might have faltered and fallen by the wayside."[531]

Trying to recover, Penney decided to take a vacation. Maybe getting away from everything would help him process this pain. Together with friends, he took a long overseas vacation.

They went to the Holy Land and walked where Jesus had walked. Then they took their time traveling across Europe, absorbing the history and culture.

Finally able to relax, Penney didn't think about how their travel plans included a return trip home on the Titanic. They just took their time enjoying the vacation. They took so much time that they missed the first trip of the Titanic.

One day Penney would open the newspaper and be shocked to find out how blessed he was to have scheduled his voyage home for the second Titanic voyage, not the first!

Months later, when Penney finally returned home, it was time for big changes.

Business competitors had been copying the his store's name without following the principle. So he figured out how to distinguish his brand by changing the name to J. C. Penney's. He continued expanding his stores by giving employees a chance to own their own business.

Penney's dream came true. He built one of most highly successful chains of dry goods stores across the country. Not even the Great Depression stopped his expansion. For forty years straight, Penney averaged opening one new location every ten days.[532] And he become much more than a millionaire.

He built a fortune of forty million dollars. That money would be used to help many others. While Penney was generous to many charitable causes, he always tried to help those who needed it the most. And he tried to honor those who had meant so much to him.

To honor the memory of his parents, he built a retirement community for pastors in Florida. This way they could be taken care of, after all the years they had taken care of others.

Meanwhile, he found happiness again. He fell in love again and remarried. As the years passed by, his wealth continued to grow. Life was great. Then suddenly it came crumbling down all around him.

Much of Penney's wealth was his stock ownership in his company. Trying to help others, he had borrowed too much money to finance many charitable causes. This money was borrowed by leveraging against the value of his stock holdings.

When the stock market suddenly crashed and the Great Depression began, Penney's wealth was wiped out.

The value of his stock disappeared. The banks came after him to pay the loans. Lawsuits swirled. What money he did have, disappeared into lawyer's fees, court costs, and creditor's demands. Eventually most of his assets had to be sold off to satisfy debt collectors, while he tried to figure out what to do.

By then his health had broken. As his body failed him, he became so ill that he had to check himself into the hospital. As the days passed and his condition continued to deteriorate, Penney wondered if he would make it. Knowing he didn't have much time left, he started writing goodbye letters to his family.

Time passed slowly. Hour after hour, unable to sleep, Penney lay in a hospital bed feeling at his weakest. One night, as he waited to die, he heard music. Wondering where the music was coming from, he went for a walk and found a church service.

This was a simple gathering of hospital workers in the hospital chapel. They were singing the hymn, *"God will take care of you."*

Penney sat down in the back row and listened to them. After the song, someone stood up and read from the words of Jesus, *"Come unto me all you that are heavy laden and I will give you rest."*[533]

As Penney sat there, God dealt with the heavy bitterness in his heart. He had never gotten over what the church had done to his family. Or what the banks had done to him during the Great Depression. But as the Holy Spirit dealt with his heart, he made the choice to forgive.

Penney would later describe how sitting in that meeting, he felt that, *"A heavy weight seemed lifted from my spirit. A profound sense of inner release came over me. I was amazed at my change, and in the days that followed I regained mental and bodily health."*[534]

In the days that followed, Penney chose to forgive. *"God had helped me to rid myself of the last vestiges of bitterness but more important to me was the feeling of gratitude to God for His power through which I could see it all without resentment."*[535]

Realizing that he had gotten too busy to pray, Penney changed his priorities.

He decided, *"To learn how to give myself over to God's purpose. I became convinced that in order to take my faith seriously, I must find God's will for the use of my talents and experience."*

"Gradually I have come to realize that knowing God's will is not easy, that one must seek it in humility through prayer, and that our prayers are often strained through our own selfish desires and wills."[536]

While his health was recovering, the financial problems were still haunting him. The banks were still coming after him. There were major lawsuits to face.

According to Penney, *"Fighting kept me going on and going on kept me fighting."*[637]

Every day was a battle with the banks to keep his business running. Day after day as he attended court sessions he kept the verse Psalm 91:4 in his pocket. It relaxed him as the pressure grew.

What got him through it was focusing on, *"Thinking more about the power of God and less about the power of money. God alone, not evil, is all-powerful."*[638]

Through it all, his company continued to thrive. Customers kept coming back. Penney financially survived by living on the salary he made from working for his company.

By the time America had climbed out of the Great Depression, Penney had the largest retail chain in the country. Sixteen hundred stores. And through all the turmoil, he had held onto his majority stock ownership.

Keeping that stock ownership restored his wealth. As his stores flourished and America recovered from the Great Depression, Penney's stock portfolio grew again. His wealth returned. This time he was far more careful with his resources.

As Penney learned from his mistakes, he decided to start writing about his experiences to inspire other people. He published a regular newspaper column, describing his walk with God.

In one of his columns he wrote, *"God has blessed me beyond what I deserve. Though I am convinced that there is a Divine purpose at work in the world, man must do his share toward the ultimate achievement of that purpose."*[539]

Penney continued to believe in his employees, opening doors for them to succeed too. He told them that they could also rise to the top of retail if they would work hard and stay focused.

In his own words, Penney would describe his business philosophy, *"We in business must give time and effort to the training of our successors. Do not train men merely to obey orders that they may or may not fully understand."*

"Train them to study the job, to understand what is to be done, then to turn loose upon it fully their understanding, motivation and effort. Encourage them to believe that there is in themselves a mine-pocket full of riches."[540]

Little did Penney know those words would come true.

Penney lived to be ninety-five years old, passing away in 1971. While many people would be inspired by his life, one man in particular would never forget him.

This man started his retail career working as a young assistant manager at an Iowa location of J.C. Penney's. He would treasure the memory of when J.C. Penney himself visited his store and trained him.

Eventually that employee would quit his job, move to Arkansas, and open a little store called Wal-Mart.

17

Getting Paid For Your Work

"God paid a high price for you,
so don't be slaves to anyone else."
1 Corinthians 7:23 (ERV)

While you work hard at your career and deserve to get paid for it, sometimes there might be people who try to take advantage of you. There are bosses who might try to get you to work your primary job for nothing. Why don't they understand that you need your paycheck to pay the bills?

The Bible describes how David had to deal with this problem. David was called to be King of Israel by God. That made Saul, the current King of Israel, want to kill him.

So David had to hide out in the wilderness. Being a strong military leader who had previously been in charge of Saul's army, David knew how to train and lead warriors. So when he was forced to run for his life, he put together a team in the wilderness. *"Then everyone who was in trouble, in debt, or bitter about life joined him, and he became their commander. There were about four hundred men with him."*[541]

David trained these men to become brave warriors which became known for their exploits. But how was David feeding all of them while they were hiding out in the wilderness away from the cities? Especially when the four hundred grew to six hundred men plus their wives and children.

David realized that he had a resource of skilled warriors. The local farmers had a need for protection. The farmers didn't want to plant their crops only to have their harvests stolen by others. So David offered to post his men as protection around the local farmers, if they would help provide him with food for his men.

One of those farmers was Nabal. David's men protected Nabal's shepherds for months until it was time to harvest the food. Then David sent men to ask for something in return for all the work they had done. Yet Nabal was a greedy man, who didn't want to recognize how David had helped him.

He replied, *"Who does this David think he is? That son of Jesse is just one more slave on the run from his master, and there are too many of them these days. What makes you think I would take my bread, my water, and the meat that I've had cooked for my own servants and give it to you?"*[542]

When David's men returned with Nabal's message, David was furious. He had to do something to get food for his men or they might starve in the winter. *"'Everybody get your swords!' David ordered. They all strapped on their swords. Two hundred men stayed behind to guard the camp, but the other four hundred followed David."*[543]

While David was preparing to take the food by force, *"Meanwhile, one of the young shepherds told Abigail, Nabal's wife, what had happened: 'David sent messengers from the backcountry to salute our master, but he tore into them with insults. Yet these men treated us very well. They took nothing from us and didn't take advantage of us all the time we were in the fields.'"*

"'They formed a wall around us, protecting us day and night all the time we were out tending the sheep. Do something quickly because big trouble is ahead for our master and all of us.'"[544]

"Abigail flew into action. She took two hundred loaves of bread, two skins of wine, five sheep dressed out and ready for cooking, a bushel of roasted grain, a hundred raisin cakes, and two hundred fig cakes, and she had it all loaded on some donkeys. Then she said to her young servants, 'Go ahead and pave the way for me. I'm right behind you.' But she said nothing to her husband Nabal."[545]

Abigail took the food and traveled to find David on the road, getting to him just in time. *"As soon as Abigail saw David, she got off her donkey and fell on her knees at his feet, her face to the ground in homage, saying, 'My master, let me take the blame!'"[546]*

David thanked her saying, *"If you had not hurried to meet me, all of Nabal's men would have been dead by morning!"[547]*

"Some ten days later the Lord struck Nabal and he died. When David heard that Nabal had died, he said, 'Praise the Lord! He has taken revenge on Nabal for insulting me and has kept me, his servant, from doing wrong. The Lord has punished Nabal for his evil."[548]

What was the evil that God punished Nabal over? Withholding wages. God cares that you get paid for your career work.

That's why the Bible says, *"What soldiers ever have to pay their own expenses in the army? What farmers do not eat the grapes from their own vineyard? What shepherds do not use the milk from their own sheep? I don't have to limit myself to these everyday examples, because the Law says the same thing."*

"We read in the Law of Moses, 'Do not muzzle an ox when you are using it to thresh grain.' Now, is God concerned about oxen? Didn't he really mean us when he said that? Of course that was written for us. Anyone who plows and anyone who reaps should do their work in the hope of getting a share of the crop."[549]

Everything that affects you is important to God.

In the Bible, God even warned greedy employers that judgment would come on them for cheating their workers out of their wages.

"You refused to pay the people who worked in your fields, and now their unpaid wages are shouting out against you. The Lord All-Powerful has surely heard the cries of the workers who harvested your crops."[550]

Your time is valuable. Stay in control of when and how your time is spent. Invest your time into the best places.

Try not to let people use you. Yes, there will be times when you want to give your time to help others. There will be unpaid things God will ask you to do, but He will reward you in Heaven for them. Even those hours you spend volunteering to help others are earning something. *"God is not unfair. He will not forget the work you did or the love you showed for him in the help you gave and are still giving to other Christians."*[551]

Think About:

"The Lord demands fairness in every business deal.
He established this principle."
Proverbs 16:11 (TLB)

"No," King David told Ornan, "I insist on buying it for the full price. I won't take what is yours for the Lord and offer burnt sacrifices that cost me nothing."
1 Chronicles 21:24 (GW)

"Paying good wages is the
most profitable way of doing business."[552]
-Henry Ford

"In the Lord's good time financial affairs will brighten if we trust Him and keep cheerfully at work doing the next thing."[553]
-A. A. Hyde

18

Sam Walton

"Make good use of every opportunity you have."
Ephesians 5:16a (GNT)

Sam Walton
1918-1992
From Missouri

In 1962, four new discount retailers opened their doors. Experts predicted the success of Kmart, Target, and Woolco. The one store no one thought would make it, was Wal-Mart.

Sam Walton had grown up under the Great Depression. He never forgot what he saw. His father had the difficult job of foreclosing on people's property when they had fallen too far behind in payments. Sometimes Walton went with his father when he had to evict people from their homes. Those experiences made Walton vow to be very careful with money.

In 1936, Walton graduated from high school in Columbia Missouri. Then he worked his way through college by waiting tables and selling magazine subscriptions.

In 1940, he graduated from the University of Missouri with a Bachelor's in Business and two job offers.

Declining the offer from Sears, he chose to work at J.C. Penney's because they gave him the opportunity to train in management.

There he absorbed everything he could learn about running a retail store. He never forgot when J.C. Penney himself visited the store and personally trained him. In those days, plastic grocery bags didn't exist. Instead of bagging customer purchases, clerks wrapped them with paper and string.

Penney showed Walton how to wrap purchases for customers in the most efficient way because, *"You know we don't make a dime out of the merchandise we sell, we only make our profit out of the paper and string we save."*[554]

Walton loved working in retail even though he was not considered the best employee. In fact, the regional manager didn't think that Walton would ever amount to much because he couldn't follow the company procedures. The only thing he was good at was making the customers happy.

Walton later described how his manager told him, *"I'd fire you if you weren't such a good salesman. Maybe you're just not cut out for retail."*[555]

Soon the winds of World War II arrived. Wanting to serve his country, Walton signed up for the military. He was assigned to serve as military police at Fort Douglas (near Salt Lake City). Meanwhile, he fell in love with a beautiful lady named Helen. They married in 1943 and began a family.

After the war, Walton wanted to return to working in retail but this time he wanted to own his own store. That opportunity came in 1945. He was offered the chance to buy into one of the biggest retain chains in the country. For $25,000 Walton could own a Ben Franklin store in a little Arkansas town.

Excited at the opportunity, Walton borrowed the money from his wife's family and dived right in. No one told him that he had just purchased the worst performing Ben Franklin store in the country.

Walton soon discovered that the Ben Franklin Company required all their franchises to follow very specific procedures.

The worst rule was that all store inventory had to be bought from the headquarters of Ben Franklin, even when less expensive items could be purchased elsewhere.

That bothered Walton. How could his store survive if he had to buy merchandise at high prices and then try to sell at even higher prices? Being in the middle between manufacturers and their franchises was giving the Ben Franklin Company a 25% profit on all inventory. Yet that extra overhead was also making it difficult for their franchisers.

Trying to survive, Walton approached manufacturers directly. Most of them refused to deal with him because his one little store could never purchase the big volume that they were selling to major retail chains. Still Walton refused to quit. One by one he continued approaching every manufacturer that he could find until a few began to sell to him. Whatever he could buy from them, he packed into his little station wagon and drove home.

It was hard work and long hours. Walton frequently had to drive several hours out of state to pick up merchandise, only to turn around and drive several hours back. Yet that diligence paid off. Buying at lower prices enabled him to sell at lower prices. Soon his store was packed with customers.

In the first three years, his store did so well that Walton was able to pay back every penny he had borrowed. Within the first five years, he had transformed the worst location into the highest grossing Ben Franklin in the country. Everyone noticed. Especially the Ben Franklin people who were very angry with him.

According to Walton, *"It drove the Ben Franklin folks crazy. Not only were they not getting their percentages, they couldn't compete with the prices I was buying at."*[556]

Walton's one store was making so much money that everyone wanted it. When the property lease came up for renewal, the landlord tried to take over the business.

Walton was backed into a corner. Not having known any better, when he had originally opened the store he had agreed to one of the highest retail rents in America: 5% of sales.

At the time, the business was doing so poorly that five percent was cheap. That all changed once the store became high performing. Now having to pay 5% in rent was raising the overhead too high.

Walton asked the landlord to be reasonable. Maybe they could work out a rent closer to market value. The landlord refused to renew the lease, wanting the store for himself. Running out of options, Walton agreed. He sold the franchise to the landlord for $50,000.

That $50,000 gave Walton the chance to move to another town and open another store.

He chose Bentonville, Arkansas. Population 2,900.

He got involved in the community by attending church, teaching Sunday school and joining the Chamber of Commerce. Everyone knew him and he didn't want it any other way. Choosing small towns overlooked by major retailers would be the secret to his success.

Still loyal to the Ben Franklin Company, Walton opened another franchise but continued to think for himself and try new things.

Once again he was very successful. The money he made enabled him to expand. By 1962, Walton owned sixteen Ben Franklin franchises and wanted to open more. His dream was to have a national chain of discount stores, to help families afford what they needed.

Needing money to launch the stores, he approached Ben Franklin executives with his idea. Suggesting that they lower their profit margin from 25% to 12%, Walton told them that the more ways they could find to lower expenses the more items they could sell and the further they would grow.

The Ben Franklin executives were offended by him. Why should they cut expenses when they were doing just fine?

They were the biggest retailer in the nation. What could Walton possibly know about retail that they didn't? The meeting ended with them telling Walton to mind his own business.

That meeting made Walton determined to open his own store and prove these retailers should not take their customers for granted.

Trying to learn everything he could, Walton went over to Kmart and studied how they did inventory. He pestered the clerks with lots of questions.

Then he got on his hands and knees, crawling around to get a better look. While most people walking by thought that Walton had lost his mind, Don Soderquist saw Walton and realized, he was onto something.

Don just so happened to be an executive at Ben Franklin who knew that Walton was the most successful franchisee in their store history. When Walton asked for his help, Don walked away from everything.

Starting on the ground floor, Don accumulated significant stock holdings. Within twenty years, the value of that stock made Don worth over twenty million dollars.

In the earliest days of Walmart, no one wanted to invest in it. There were so many other highly profitable retail chains. Why should anyone take a chance on a little store in Arkansas?

Fortunately Walton had a family that believed in him. Between their savings and bank loans, the first Wal-Mart opened in Rogers, Arkansas.

Immediately, the Ben Franklin Company sent a team to the store to tell Walton to shut it down or lose the rest of his franchises. Walton graciously greeted the Ben Franklin people but refused to surrender. He would rather cater to the needs of country folks in small towns than bow to the threats of a big corporation. That's how he made his first Wal-Mart store sell over one million dollars of inventory in the very first year.

With those profits, Walton opened another store in a small town. Again he tried to innovate with all kinds of ideas. Not all of his ideas worked. The grand opening of the store was planned with donkey rides for the kids and a gigantic watermelon pile in the parking lot.

No one thought about what the hot Arkansas temperatures would do to the donkeys and watermelons. The watermelons melted in the heat. The donkeys did their thing on the parking lot, leaving deposits everywhere. Crowds of people tracked that all over the parking lot and on every aisle in the store.

By the end of the day, the smell was strong enough to make people cringe. Yet that was what made Walton realize his idea would work. Customers didn't care how dirty or smelly the store was when they were getting a great deal.

According to Walton, *"At the time, people thought that it wouldn't work but there was a lot more business in those towns than people ever thought."*[557]

Realizing that it was time to open more stores meant that Walton had to find good people to help him do it. So he visited other retail stores and watched what they were doing. When he saw a really good manager, he would try to hire him away.

Williard Walker was one of the first people he found. Walton offered him a salary plus part of the store's profits. Walker accepted the offer even though people tried to talk him out of it.

Walker later described how when he quit his job, his boss tried to talk him out of it saying, *"A percentage of nothing is still nothing."*[558]

Walker knew better. Putting everything he had into his store, he worked long hours and sometimes even slept in the back in between shifts. Whatever money he made was invested back into Wal-Mart stock. Owning that stock would make Walker a multi-millionaire.

Another early manager was Bob Bogle. He quit a stable government job to take the risk with Walton. While his wife Marilyn worried about the future, Bob liked the odds.

"I told her you could work for the State of Arkansas forever and never build up any equity, and here was Sam offering me a job and 25% of the profits of the store. The salary was about what I was making, probably $400 a month, and the thing that fascinated me more than the salary was the opportunity to buy an interest in the other stores as we put them in."[559]

As Wal-Mart expanded, Walton continued trying to save money on everything, making his team go without the standard business perks. From the board room to the break room, Walton cut corners. Traveling with him was not easy. He made the team share rooms, sometimes cramming as many as eight men into one motel room.

When they went to New York to buy clothing, they had to walk everywhere because cab rides were too expensive. This made the rest of the retail industry not take them seriously but Walton didn't care. He insisted, *"Every time Wal-Mart spends one dollar foolishly, it comes right out of our customer's pockets. Every time we save them a dollar, that puts us one more step ahead of the competition—which is where we always plan to be."*[560]

Dedicated to the company, Walton worked long hours. However as the company expanded, Walton needed more time in the stores so he tried to reduce the amount of time it took him to travel between stores. Again trying to maximize efficiency by cutting corners, he bought an airplane and learned to fly it himself.

Of course, he bought the cheapest airplane he could find. The first person he asked to fly with him was his brother, Bud Walton. His brother was an experienced combat pilot who had served in World War II. He described how nothing he had seen in the war had scared him as much as flying with Walton.

According to Bud, *"I figured anyone who drove a car like Sam sure didn't need to be in an airplane. I told him no way. I had flown planes before in the war, and I knew the thing wasn't safe. It had a washing machine motor in it, and it would putt-putt, and then miss a lick, then putt-putt again."*

"The old radio was a crank job, and it would have been just as effective to open the cockpit door and use a megaphone to communicate. It was well over a year before I crawled in the plane with him."[561]

Walton's driving was also legendary in Bentonville. Everyone stayed out of his way. The talk of the town was how he had rear ended his own Wal-Mart truck.

One day while driving past a competitor's store, Walton had been too busy counting the cars in the competitor's parking lot to pay attention to the road. He crashed into a Wal-Mart semi truck. The truck driver was thrilled for the chance to meet Sam Walton himself.

Yet as Wal-Mart expanded, Walton worried. His empire was built on borrowed money. What would happen if he couldn't keep up with the loans?

Remembering what he had seen during the Great Depression, Walton decided to get out of debt by taking the company public.

The success of Wal-Mart stock shocked Wall Street. While similar stocks brought in small returns, Wal-Mart would average high returns in its early years.

Forbes declared Walton the richest man in America, because he was the largest owner of Wal-Mart stock.

Walton replied, *"It's just paper. All I own is a pickup truck and a little Wal-Mart stock."*[562]

And Walton was also proud of how many other employees made money on their Wal-Mart stock. *"We've had lots and lots of millionaires in our ranks. Folks who have never had the opportunity to get their hands on the kind of money they've made with their Wal-Mart stock holdings."*[563]

While Walton was frugal with money, he was very generous in giving to others. His wife Helen would manage their charitable giving, carefully screening projects, trying to find the best ways to help the most people. Focusing on investing in education, she launched the program giving college scholarships to Wal-Mart employees and their families.

Walton passed away from bone cancer in 1992.

Helen passed away from heart failure in 2007.

Their money continues to help many people, especially the people in small towns often overlooked by the big charities.

18

Take Your Chances

"The fastest runner does not always win the race,
the strongest soldier does not always win the battle,
the wisest does not always have food,
the smartest does not always become wealthy,
and the talented one does not always receive praise.
Time and chance happen to everyone."
Ecclesiastes 9:11b (NCV)

You don't have to be the most talented person to succeed. God sends opportunities to everyone. We need to make the most of our opportunities even though we may not always be attracted to them.

The Bible tells the story of how Peter was running a fishing business when he met Jesus. As crowds of people swarmed Jesus, He asked Peter to take him out on the lake so He could preach to the crowd.

When Jesus was finished using Peter's boat, Jesus compensated him for it by giving him the chance to catch a lot of fish. Jesus told Peter, *"Push out into the deep water. Let down your nets for some fish."*[564]

That was not what Peter wanted to hear. He had just spent all night fishing. Nothing had been caught. Then he had spent all morning cleaning his nets. Now he was ready for a nap.

Fishing during the day wouldn't work because the fish could see the nets. Besides, he really didn't feel like having to clean those nets all over again. So Peter told Jesus, *"We have worked all night and we have caught nothing. But because You told me to, I will let the net down."*[565]

Notice that Jesus told Peter to use several *"nets"* but Peter chose to use only one *"net."* This caused a big problem. At Jesus' command, great numbers of fish began to swarm Peter's one net.

This was the biggest catch of fish Peter had ever had. One net couldn't possibly hold it all. The net broke, spilling fish everywhere. Hoping not to lose it, Peter had to call to his friends to help him try to salvage what was left. Both of their boats ended up so full of fish that they almost began to sink.

Peter realized that Jesus had given him a great opportunity. He would leave his fishing business to travel with Jesus full time. Maybe that massive catch of fish had been meant to help Peter take care of his family while he was working with Jesus.

God is going to send you some really good opportunities. Try to make the most of all of them, even when they come at inconvenient times and places.

Let the Holy Spirit help you discern the good opportunities from the bad. When the right opportunities come, be willing to take a chance. *"Do good wherever you go. After a while, the good you do will come back to you."*[566]

Think About:

"But there are some things that you cannot be sure of.
You must take a chance.
If you wait for perfect weather,
you will never plant your seeds.
If you are afraid that every cloud will bring rain,
you will never harvest your crops."
Ecclesiastes 11:4 (ERV)

"Never allow your grievances
to overshadow your opportunities."[567]
-Booker T. Washington

"Don't be afraid of taking a chance. Remember that a broken
watch is exactly right at least twice every twenty-four hours."[568]
-Kemmons Wilson

19

Kemmons Wilson & Wallace Johnson

"Two are better off than one,
because together they can work more effectively."
Ecclesiastes 4:9 (GNT)

Kemmons Wilson
1913-2003
From Arkansas

Wallace Johnson
1901-1988
From Mississippi

Kemmons Wilson launched his first successful business right in the middle of the Great Depression. The most surprising thing was that he launched this business at a very young age.

Kemmons was raised by a single mother. After his father died of Lou Gehrig's Disease, his mother struggled to earn a living in a time when very few jobs were available to women.

She worked any job she could find but her career in accounting was never enough to pay the bills. Kemmons tried to help her by getting a job himself, at the tender young age of six.

Kemmon's first job was selling magazines door to door. Housewives who answered the door felt sorry for this small child trying to help his mother and bought subscriptions to the *Ladies Home Journal.*

Then Kemmons heard that he could make more money selling the *Saturday Evening Post.* That paid double the commission rate. Pretty soon Kemmons had recruited a team of other children who were making 20% commission on every sale while Kemmons was paid an extra 10% of their sales.

While his little business thrived, Kemmons attended school. When he grew older he found that he could make more money by building rocking chairs in his living room and selling them in the town.

Everything went well until the neighbors complained about the noise Kemmons was making. Since Kemmons had to attend school during the day, the only time he had to work in his *"factory"* was late at night. The neighbors complained about all the noise, dragging Kemmons to the local courthouse to face the judge. In the courtroom, they complained to the judge that Kemmons was keeping them awake every night.

The judge was impressed. How could he punish a teenager for trying to support his Mom? Instead the judge worked out a schedule where Kemmons could work during certain hours and the neighbors could sleep during other hours. The rocking chair business lasted for a while until Kemmons found other ways to make money.

As he later described, *"I did every odd job you could think of. I was the worst student in the world because I was always tired from working all the time. I had to work. I was hungry. I would go to school and go to sleep."*

"We were always scuffling to have enough money. I can remember not having enough to eat in those days. Streetcar fare was seven cents, but I would always walk to town because I didn't have the seven cents."[569]

Some of his odd jobs included bagging groceries at the corner market and delivering newspapers early in the morning. That job brought his blossoming career to a screeching halt.

One day while Kemmons was working his newspaper delivery route, he was hit by a car. He was completely bedridden for the next year. The doctors said he would never walk again. They would be wrong.

After a full year of laying flat on his back in a full-body cast, he would walk again. He had to. Now he had to catch up on paying all those medical bills.

When the Great Depression came, it took his mother's bookkeeping job. She had a hard time finding another job. Kemmons himself also had a hard time finding a job.

He dropped out of high school to work full-time as a bookkeeper for a financial firm. That's how he realized that he was being paid only one third of what the previous man in his position had been paid. When Kemmons asked for a raise, he was told that because he was a teenager he didn't deserve the same paycheck as a grown man. Hearing that made Kemmons vow to prove them wrong.

During the Great Depression, the movie industry thrived as people tried to forget their troubles by going to the movies.

Kemmons himself loved movies too. One day while walking by the movie theater he noticed something—there was no concession stand selling food to the people. Maybe they would want to buy popcorn to enjoy during their movie.

Kemmons borrowed the money to buy a popcorn machine and set up outside the theatre. Pretty soon he was making more money than the theatre itself. That's when the theatre set up their own concession stand and shut him down. Kemmons didn't complain about it, he just sold the popcorn machine and invested in pinball machines.

This time when Kemmons set up his pinball machines in drug stores, he worked out an agreement to divide the profits with the store managers. Those pinball machines made a good profit and opened new doors for him.

One of those drug store owners was Jack Embry who taught him to fly in a little Aeronica-C3. Once Kemmons became a pilot, he made money on the side by selling tickets to anyone who needed to fly somewhere nearby.

He also got into the business of homebuilding. The first house he built was for his mother.

Kemmons saved up enough money to build the house that his mother had always dreamed about. That experience caused him to realize the potential in the neighborhood real estate market. Maybe other families would like brand new, affordable, comfortable housing.

While Kemmons didn't know much about construction, he didn't need to because he knew this: *"No job is too hard as long as you are smart enough to find someone else to do it for you. You find a fellow who can frame a house, another fellow who can do the plumbing. You just sub everything out."*[570]

Kemmons became a very successful homebuilder, because he always built the homes bigger and better than the competition, but sold them at the same price as the other homebuilders. He did this by negotiating creative financing with the banks.

At the time, the Great Depression had caused so many foreclosures that banks were desperate to sell them. Kemmons negotiated deals where he bought the land with only 10% down. Since he had a real estate license, he made an additional 5% commission on every sale, leaving him only having to borrow 5% to purchase the property.

In the years that followed, Kemmons poured everything he had into real estate. That investment paid off in a big way. By the time that America came out of the Great Depression in 1940, Kemmons owned most of the real estate in Memphis, Tennessee. Having borrowed money to buy it, he had a million dollars worth of mortgages on it.

In 1941, Kemmons married his sweetheart Dorothy. They left on their honeymoon, right when Pearl Harbor happened and America plunged into World War II. Kemmons volunteered for the military. Knowing he might not come back, he sold all of his real estate, paid off the million dollar mortgage and netted a profit of $250,000 cash. That way if worse came to worse, at least his wife would not be left under the heavy burden of the mortgage.

Kemmon's training as a pilot inspired him to try out for the position of fighter pilot. That's how Kemmons learned how little he really knew about flying. When Captain Bud Baron asked Kemmons to demonstrate his flying skills, they almost crashed. Baron had to grab the controls to keep them from plummeting to the ground.

When they finally safely landed after a scary experience in the air, Baron decided that Kemmons had passed the test. He was cleared to be a combat pilot because as Baron described, *"Well, you're sure not much of a pilot, but I don't believe you will kill yourself."*[571]

Kemmons served in the U.S. Air Transport Command. When the Japanese attacked China, cutting off access to the outside world, Kemmons flew in supplies during the famous 1944 *"Hump Airlift."*

After the war, Kemmons returned home to the real estate business. By this time he and his wife had five children and needed a bigger home as soon as possible. Kemmons built it as fast as he could.

Then came a phone call from Wallace Johnson. *"Kemmons, you built your house on the wrong lot."*[572]

Turns out the title deeds had been messed up, resulting in homes being built in the wrong locations. It would take a lot of time and money to solve the problem, but Kemmons had just met the man who would help him the most.

Wallace Johnson was another highly successful homebuilder in Memphis. Born in 1901 to very poor sharecropper parents, he grew up attracted to hammers, nails, and tools. Construction fascinated him.

After marrying his sweetheart Alma in 1924, he worked at the local lumberyard, until the Great Depression laid him off.

When work could not be found anywhere, Wallace sought God for direction and felt guided to launch his own business.

The FHA had just begun offering mortgages for purchasing a home with very low down payments. With home ownership becoming more affordable, Wallace had an idea for building simple and comfortable homes which would be within reach of normal families. As he sketched floorplan designs, he tried to figure where to get the money to launch his business.

Then one day the idea came to him. *"I borrowed $250 on our Ford, which was several years old, and agreed to pay it back at $25 a month. That was the money we had to live on while we got started building."*[573]

The risk he took paid off very well. Within a few years they had grown to hiring a large construction crew, which built house after house.

Wallace explained, *"I felt called to build houses—called by God to my task just as ministers are called to theirs. And as Alma and I started our own business, I felt that our mission was to build for poor folks and help them own their homes. In that way we could help them to live better, happier lives, for homeownership does lift a man to a higher place."*[574]

His wife Alma was very involved in their business. Her interior design skills made those houses look very attractive to buyers. Wallace soon realized it was her skills and simple touches that was selling the homes, *"Often little things like that can make or break a sale. Never overlook the importance of little things."*[575]

The demand for new homes increased as World War II progressed and people moved to the cities to work in manufacturing. With all the men gone at war, Wallace improvised by hiring female construction workers. Yet the more homes they built, the more materials they needed.

Materials were hard to find during the war as things like wood and metal were being rapidly consumed by the military.

Wallace described, *"We couldn't have stood up without the help of the Lord. As was my custom, I made lists of our needs and problems and prayed over them. When desperate for lumber, I asked the Lord to guide me to it. When I needed men, I asked Him to help me find them. When I needed loans, I asked Him to send me to the right bankers. And He did."*[576]

Over the course of the war, Wallace built more than six thousand homes. The U.S. government noticed his productivity and asked for his help.

One day General George Marshall read about Wallace in the *Saturday Evening Post*. He asked for a favor.

Wallace would later tell the story that *"They wanted three thousand homes constructed in ninety days and no questions asked! Just take the subdivision maps they had prepared and go to work."*[577]

Little did they know that those homes were being built to house the scientists who would develop the atomic bomb.

Following the war, Wallace met the other major homebuilder in Memphis Tennessee, Kemmons Wilson. They became close friends. Together they dreamed the ideas that would transform the hotel industry.

In 1951, Kemmons took his wife and five children for a vacation driving across country to see Washington D. C. and stopping to rest in motels along the way. In those days, motels were completely different than they are today. They didn't have air conditioning or TVs. No free ice machines. Swimming pools were rare. Parking was very expensive. Food was inconvenient and repulsive.

What bothered Kemmons the most was having to pay extra for each of his five children to sleep in one already overpriced and cramped room.

Kemmons would change all of that. When President Eisenhower passed the bill to build the paved interstate highway roads, Kemmons realized that the travel industry was about to explode. Thousands of people were going to go on road trips and need good places to stay.

Kemmons called Wallace and asked for help in launching a new chain of motels. That's how they launched a partnership that would last for the rest of their lives. They worked together on every deal, splitting the profits right down the middle. But first they would have to figure out how to dig themselves out of debt.

Both men were so far deep in debt that their local banker would tease them, *"I've heard of men joining their assets to form a partnership, but this is the first time I have heard of two fellows joining their liabilities."*[578]

One year after they started, in 1952, they opened the very first Holiday Inn. It had been built on Kemmon's property that was close to the freeway. While they could have stopped there, Kemmons had a bigger dream. He wanted to franchise the business by building at least four hundred new locations. How could they find people to partner with them?

Kemmons and Wallace put their heads together and figured out that since they were members of the *Homebuilders Association* (Wallace was President of it) they could send out an invitation to the hundreds of other members. Maybe they would be interested in investing in a *Holiday Inn*.

Kemmons and Wallace held a special event for the homebuilders in Memphis. Sixty showed up. They were offered a Holiday Inn franchise for five hundred dollars and five cents per room per night royalties. While that would be the best deal ever offered on a *Holiday Inn,* only three people accepted it.

Years later, Kemmons would look back and be grateful that only a few people had accepted that generous offer. As the years passed by and the value of a franchise rose, the new franchise buyers would pay much more for their franchise.

First Kemmons and Wallace had to build their company into a worldwide corporation. Knowing that there were as a lot of legal issues to address, they hired a lawyer named John Martin. As they launched the company, money was so scarce that they barely stayed afloat.

They couldn't afford to pay their own lawyer so they offered him 10% stock ownership in the company.

These were very difficult years. With lots of interstate franchise law to follow there was always the possibility that they might make a fatal mistake. What if they couldn't keep up with all the money they were borrowing?

Knowing that everything could easily fall apart, the pressure began getting to the lawyer. He asked Kemmons if he was worried. Kemmons replied, *"No. I started off broke. I can't ever be any worse off."*[579]

The pressure of the business continued to eat at the lawyer until he wanted out. One day the lawyer approached Kemmons and asked if he could sell his 10% stock ownership and leave.

Kemmons asked how much he wanted. The lawyer offered to return all his stock for $25,000 cash. Wallace and Kemmons didn't have that kind of cash so they borrowed it.

The lawyer returned to his private law practice. Little did he know that thirty years later, the stock that he had sold would be worth $111,000,000.

Kemmons hired a new corporate attorney named Bill Walton who was a man of prayer. When Bill joined the firm he knew there was a major learning curve. This business was trying to think outside the box. They needed him to keep them on track with all the risks they were taking.

With the weight of this pressure on him, Bill turned to God for help, saying, *"Lord, You and I both know I don't know the first thing about franchising, protecting the name of a company, or putting together a corporation that can go public. If this is something You want me to do, You will have to show me the way."*[580]

In the years that followed Bill would figure out very creative ways of copyrighting their innovations. He also held onto his stock ownership as the value rapidly increased.

There was one aspect of the company that he had a lot of trouble with: flying in the company airplane. While their business required frequent travel and Bill was a veteran of the Air Force, he was terrified by Kemmon's flying skills.

When Kemmons got tired he would turn on the autopilot and take a nap, thinking that he had taught Wallace enough that Wallace would know how to fly the plane for him.

Then there were the times that Kemmons and Wallace would get completely distracted by looking at the real estate below. *"And if we didn't watch ourselves, we'd get so excited we'd forget we were flying a plane. In fact, we forgot completely one day and went into a spin. Down and around and around we went, and Kemmons had to use all his skill to get us out of it,"*[581] Wallace described.

Holiday Inn was growing. More franchise owners came, many of which were doctors and lawyers.

Kemmons carefully selected sites for new locations, staying close to major freeways. He also invested in a new computer system, pioneering the concept of electronic reservations. Quality was always kept as the main priority.

By 1972, Holiday Inn had reached a major milestone. They were feeding and housing more people than anyone else in America.[582] The money that Kemmons and Wallace made was reinvested into all sorts of other businesses. Some succeeded. Some failed.

When Kemmons was asked what he had learned through it all he replied, *"The only people that don't make mistakes are the people that don't do anything."*[583]

Kemmons never slowed down, until he had a heart attack at age sixty-six. When he recovered he retired from managing Holiday Inn. (Wallace also retired that same year at age seventy-seven.) Kemmons quickly became bored in his retirement and got involved in another business. He would serve on the board of a bank in Arkansas, which introduced him to Sam Walton. Together they played tennis after business meetings.

Wallace Johnson went home to Heaven in 1988 after suffering a heart attack at age eighty-six.

Kemmons lived on until 2003 when he died peacefully at home at age ninety. By then Kemmons had created lots of jobs and donated enough to charity to keep food on the table for many other families.

His principles are still taught at the University of Memphis Hospitality School that bears his name. And his words are never forgotten.

"I feel I must give thanks everyday for the many blessings I have received throughout my life," Kemmons wrote at age eighty-three. *"For without God, nothing is possible."*[584]

19

Working Together

"Don't forget your own friends or your father's friends. If you have a problem, go to your neighbor for help. It is better to ask a neighbor who is near than a brother who is far away."
Proverbs 27:10 (ERV)

Our lives are so busy that it can be challenging to make enough time for our friends. Yet we need them as much as they need us.

We learn and grow through our relationships. *"Just as iron sharpens iron, friends sharpen the minds of each other."*[585]

While sometimes relationships don't work out, leaving us with emotional hurts, we cannot allow ourselves to be alone.

No matter how many bad people there are in the world, there are still far more good people that we can connect with.

It's much worse for us to withdraw into isolation than to take the risk of opening ourselves back up to relationships.

That's why the Bible warns about the danger of isolation being *"pointless and a terrible tragedy."*[586]

God has something better for you.

"God places lonely people in families."[587] Together you can get more done than you could ever get done by yourself.

When God gave you a destiny, He also prepared people to help you accomplish what you were born to do. Build those relationships.

Together you and they can do far more than could ever be done alone. Remember that the time you spend investing into your friend-ships is very important because it's your friends that will be there for you when you need help.

If you lose your job, it's more likely that you will find another job through the people you know.

"If you fall, your friend can help you up. But if you fall without having a friend nearby, you are really in trouble."[588]

Life is meant to be enjoyed. With others through healthy relation-ships. Just be careful to choose good friends.

"Be friends with those who are wise, and you will become wise. Choose fools to be your friends, and you will have trouble."[589]

Think About:

"Jesus continued, 'I'm telling you that although wealth
is often used in dishonest ways,
you should use it to make friends for yourselves.'"
Luke 16:9a (GW)

"The unity in the Body of Christ for which our Savior prayed
can only come as we overlook our little differences
and obey His command to 'Love one another.'"[590]
-A. A. Hyde

"Just as Helen and I were raised in the church, we felt
that our kids would benefit from a church upbringing.
Church is an important part of society, especially in small
towns. Whether it's the contacts and associations you
make or the contributions you might make toward helping
other folks, it all sort of ties in together."[591]
-Sam Walton

20

Mary Kay

"This is too much work for you. You can't do it alone!"
Exodus 18:18b (GW)

Mary Kay Ash
1918-2001
From Texas

When your accountant and lawyer tell you that your business idea will fail, most people give up. Not Mary Kay. While she listened carefully to her financial advisors and read the government report on the frequent failure of cosmetic companies, sent by her attorney, she believed her idea would work, because it would make women feel better about themselves. Putting her entire life savings on the line, she launched her dream.

Her dream of financial independence had begun long before her business. When she was seven years old, her father became bedridden from tuberculosis. Her mother worked fourteen hour long shifts as a waitress, leaving her to take care of her siblings.

At seven years old, Mary Kay cooked full meals, got her siblings ready for school and took the bus by herself to go grocery shopping.

After raising herself and her siblings, when she became an adult, she fell in love and got married, hoping to live happily ever after.

Then came World War II. Her husband joined the military and went overseas, leaving her to again run a household by herself. She looked forward to when the war would end and he would come home.

When the war ended, her husband came home and wanted a divorce. As she would later describe she was left as *"The sole support of those kids in the days before day care."*[592]

Life was hard for her. There were very few career opportunities open to women and even fewer that would give her the flexibility to be at home when the children needed her. She ended up selling other people's multi-level marketing products during the day, while the children were in school. Then she would rush home to be there when they came home.

There never were enough hours in the day. The harder she worked, the more it felt like she was falling behind. Coming home from work, felt like her second job began with meals to cook and a house to clean. She thought that if she could afford a housekeeper then she could have more time with her children. Mary Kay thought about it and decided to find a way to make the extra money. Taking a leap of faith, she put an ad in the paper for a housekeeper. Then she interviewed several ladies, found the right one and hired her.

She still didn't have any money to pay that lady but knew that she had two weeks to sell enough extra products to get the money before she would have to issue the first paycheck.

Mary Kay worked furiously, selling as much as she could. By the end of the two weeks she had made enough to cover both her bills and the housekeeper. That made her realize she had a gift for sales. Mary Kay quickly rose to the top in sales at that company.

Yet no matter how much money she made for the company, they refused to promote her because she was a woman.

When she asked for a raise, the company leaders made excuses for keeping her salary low. Adding insult to injury, they asked her to train all the new salesmen who would be quickly promoted to better positions with higher salaries.

She wrote, *"Several times I would take a man out on the road for training, and after I'd been teaching him the business for six months, he'd come back to Dallas and end up being my superior at twice my salary."*

"What really angered me was when I was told that these men earned more because they had families to support. I had a family to support, too."[593]

For twenty-five years she worked for other people while saying to herself, *"I can't believe that God intended for a woman's work to receive only fifty cents on the dollar."*[594]

Yet as long as her company refused to pay women what they were worth, maybe the only way she could get ahead was to start her own company.

Doing that required finding the right product to sell. Mary Kay looked at all kinds of different products, trying to find something that everyone would want to buy.

One day while she was doing a house party in a new city, she noticed all the ladies there had very beautiful skin. Turned out that they were all using products made by a friend who was the daughter of a tanner.

This tanner had noticed that some of the ingredients involved in the tanning process made the skin on his hands look really good. He had experimented with different formulas until he had developed his own skin care line.

His daughter had been successfully marketing his products but Mary Kay noticed that the packaging was simple and unattractive. Seeing the potential in the product, she bought the product formula and patents to begin developing them for mass market distribution.

Beauty by Mary Kay was launched in 1963. That was the idea that her attorney and accountant tried to discourage. While they couldn't see the possibility of her success, her family could.

Her three children, now grown and starting families of their own, told her: *"If you could be successful working for someone else, we know that you can do even better working for yourself."*[595]

Together they worked day and night, telling everyone about their new company. Many people were interested and signed up to sell her products.

There was a man who wanted to work for her too. Mary Kay liked his enthusiasm and energy but felt something was wrong. She declined his application. He was furious with her.

Pretty soon he had copied all her ideas and launched his own network marketing company, which was what he had planned to do all along. However, he didn't know as much about the industry as she did. Within a few years, his company was bankrupt while her company continued flourishing.

Unlike many startup companies, her company became profitable in its first year. As she helped many other ladies achieve their own financial independence, her company grew way beyond what she had ever imagined.

In 1981, more ladies were making $50,000 a year at Mary Kay than any other American company.[596] She never hesitated to tell everyone that they were successful *"Because the first thing we did was to take God as our partner."*[597]

By 1993, her fortune had reached $320,000,000 and Mary Kay's words were inspiring people to realize that *"Often it's the little, daily decisions that mean the difference between success and failure. And I feel that God put His protective arm around us and guided us to the right path."*[598]

Meanwhile the company that had once held her back from promotion realized their mistake in losing the best employee they had ever had.

Someone told them how Mary Kay often talked about her time working with them. She talked about how they used to offer prizes to the top salespeople. In her first year there, the prize had been an expensive alligator purse. She had hoped to sell enough products to win that alligator purse but that year had been difficult and she hadn't made it.

Thirty years later, she got it. The company sent one of their top executives to present her with the purse.

He honored her achievements by saying, *"Mary Kay considers this handbag to be the prize that got away. We consider the prize that got away was Mary Kay."*[599]

20

Putting Your Team Together

"Do the right thing for those who work for you."
Ephesians 6:9 (NLV)

Do you ever feel like there are just not enough hours in the day? You're right. What God has called you to do is bigger than you can do by yourself.

The Bible tells many stories of how leaders tried to do everything themselves only to wear themselves out. When Moses tried to govern the Israelites all by himself, he couldn't do it.

He had to be reminded by those closest to him that he needed a support staff. *"That will make it easier for you, as they share your burden. If you do this, as God commands, you will not wear yourself out."*[600]

In Proverbs 31, the Bible describes how a godly woman doesn't do everything by herself. She has an entire support staff to help her.

"She gets up before daylight to prepare food for her family and to tell her servant women what to do."[601]

While we all have a different destiny to accomplish, we will need other people to help us get it done. As good as we can be at one thing we don't have enough time to be the best at everything.

We need help from our dishwasher, toaster, microwave and dryer. Plus we need people like doctors, lawyers, accountants and other professionals to advise us. As we grow and progress in our destiny we will come to the point of needing to assemble a team to get it done.

Working together with that team, we will be able to accomplish far more than we could ever do on our own.

Think About:

"Better to be a nobody and yet have a servant than pretend to be somebody and have no food."
Proverbs 12:9 (NIV)

"Most people waste many hours everyday on tasks that could be streamlined, delegated, or just eliminated."[602]
-Wallace Johnson

"The ability to deal with people is as purchasable a commodity as sugar or coffee, and I pay more for that ability than for any other under the sun."[603]
-John D. Rockefeller Sr.

21

Colonel Harland Sanders

"Those who work hard will be put in charge of others."
Proverbs 12:24a (ERV)

Colonel Harland Sanders
1890-1980
From Indiana

Day after day, millions of people eat Kentucky Fried Chicken. Yet many people have no idea that Colonel Harland Sanders was a real person born in 1890. And his greatest success only came after he was a sixty-five year old senior citizen struggling on social security.

Sanders started his first job at only age ten. His father had passed away and his mother couldn't feed three children with sharecropping and sewing jobs. Trying to make ends meet, she sent him down to a neighbor to work on the farm for two dollars a month.

His first assignment was to go pull tree stumps but he couldn't concentrate on the work. He was just a child. How could he hold down a job? He kept getting distracted by looking at the nature around him, watching the squirrels scamper and birds flutter.

Watching him, the farmer got upset that very little work was being done and fired him. Giving him his two dollar paycheck, the farmer said something Sanders would never forget. *"Now son, you had better go on back to your Mama. You ain't worth a doggone to me. I can't even feed you for the amount of work you do."*[604]

Ten year old Sanders was humiliated. When he got home, his mother was furious. She berated him for getting fired. Her harsh words cut him deeply and would haunt him for many years.

From that point on, Sanders vowed never to suffer that humiliation again. He went back out looking for work and found another farm job for four dollars a month. This time he worked as hard as possible, vowing never to let anyone cut him down again.

Meanwhile, his mother fell in love and married again. Broaddus, the new stepfather, took control of the home with an iron fist. Sanders rebelled. Having a mind of his own, he questioned why Broaddus demanded so many chores from him and his siblings.

Broaddus answered by raising his fists. Sanders fought back. Then he ran away. He would have to survive on his own at twelve years old.

Sanders dropped out of school in the sixth grade. There was no time for studying when he had to find another job. He continued working farming jobs while trying to find an easier way to make a living.

Sanders asked his uncle to help him find a different job. The uncle found him a job working on a trolley type street car.

Sanders loved this new job. All he had to do was dress up in a nice suit and punch tickets all day long. While working this job, he talked to the passengers, which is how he met two army recruiters who convinced him to join the military. He did. Eager to serve his country, he lied about his age and got into the military at only sixteen.

Sanders figured that by serving his country he would get to see the world. However, after finishing basic training, the first thing he saw was dozens of mules. Even in the military, his agriculture skills got assigned him to farm labor.

When President Roosevelt sent U.S. troops to Cuba to protect people's ability to vote in the elections, Sanders went along on the ship with the assignment of caring for all the mules on board. Working with these animals broke his health.

By the time they got to Cuba, Sanders had dropped over twenty pounds and his commanding officer had discovered his real age. He was promptly dismissed from the military.

Sanders went home and once again asked his family for help finding a job. He ended up working for the local railroad. His strong work ethic helped him learn how to run railroad steam engines and work his way up to a better paying job. By seventeen years old, Sanders was operating the train himself—firing up the heavy steam engines.

Now he could afford a family. He fell in love with a beautiful local girl named Josephine who he had met while going to the movies with friends. They quickly married and had two girls and a boy. Sanders was a proud father, happy to spend everything he made on them.

Meanwhile, he was getting in trouble at work. Sanders had a mind of his own. He believed in standing up for what was right. When one of his co-workers was fired and blacklisted for the wrong reasons, Sanders stood up for him, getting him reinstated with a year's back pay. The railroad didn't like that. They fired him.

He found another job working at a different railroad. This job didn't last very long either.

Working on the railroad, Sanders saw how they were covering up big problems. In those days, laws requiring better safety measures were routinely ignored. Accidents were common. When passengers were hurt and had major medical bills, the railroads tried to avoid taking responsibility by getting injured passengers to settle for very little.

Watching all this happen, Sanders decided to stand up for the passengers. When accidents happened and railroad lawyers approached injured passengers with paperwork to sign away their rights, Sanders approached the passengers with a different opportunity. Handing them a power of attorney form, Sanders offered to negotiate their claims with the railroad. Then he vigorously fought for their rights, demanding reasonable settlements that could actually cover their medical bills.

He was very successful. The people he represented received much higher personal injury settlements, paying him a percentage. That made the railroads look for a way to get rid of Sanders. Once again he was fired.

This whole experience inspired Sanders to pursue a career in law. He moved to Arkansas where small claims courts allowed people to practice law without passing the bar exam. Here he was able to make a living representing the claims of regular people in court, standing up for those who needed it the most. Working with these people, Sanders found new ways to help them.

One time he successfully lobbied the Arkansas state legislature to pass laws protecting people from the excessive interest rates charged by loan sharks.

Sanders became the person no one wanted to face in court. No matter what happened, he never backed down. Bringing his hot temper to court, he never hesitated to tell the judge or opposing counsel exactly what he thought of him.

That resulted in fights breaking out in the middle of the courtroom. According to eyewitnesses, when the fight started, Sanders held his own, even breaking a chair over the opposing counsel just before the bailiffs dragged both of them out of the courtroom.

Sanders fiery legal career helped many people. Then it suddenly ended when the state of Arkansas changed the laws. Anyone representing clients in court was required to have a license to practice law, putting Sanders out of his job.

Looking for a new career, Sanders decided to open a barber shop. His brother Clarence was trying to recover from alcohol addiction and needed a job to stay busy.

Neither one of them knew how to cut hair.

Sanders told him, *"When those woolly old farmers come in, just start cutting the best you can and be sure to end up by dousing them with this good smelling stuff. When they get home, their women folks will be so thrilled with the way they smell, they won't even notice how their hair was cut."*[605]

Sanders was right. The women loved it. The men kept coming back. The barber shop was a success. However, Sanders soon tired of it and wanted to try something else. He became a door-to-door life insurance salesmen. Selling came so natural to him that soon he had broken many of the company's sales records. At one point he actually turned the worst performing territory into the highest grossing area.

Until he lost his job again. The insurance company found out that Sanders was breaking the rules. The rules were that salesmen had to wait five months from the time they sold the policy until getting paid for it, just in case the customer changed their mind and cancelled the policy.

Sanders couldn't provide for his family that way. Instead, each time he sold a policy he required that the customer pay a year's premiums in advance. Then he kept his commission and turned in the rest of the money. They fired him for it.

Sanders moved back to Kentucky and started his own business. Noticing that the town had very limited public transportation, Sanders raised the funds to buy a ferry. Passengers loved the comfort of his new ferry. When he got tired of this business, he sold it for twenty-thousand dollars.

Then he started another business marketing a new type of lighting. While Sanders did everything he could to try to sell it, he couldn't compete with the less expensive versions available. Once again, he ended up broke and having to start over again.

Michelin offered him a job selling tires. All he had to do was make a certain quota and he would have steady income. He did. Month after month, he easily posted the numbers they wanted. He made enough money that by the time his son turned fourteen years old and wanted a car, Sanders was able to buy one.

He purchased a Model A Ford so that his son, Harland Jr, could drive his sisters Margaret and Mildred, to school.

On a cold November morning, the car wouldn't start. Sanders decided to tow it into town by hooking it up to his own car. Carefully attaching both cars together, Sanders began driving to town. Everything was fine until he crossed the Hickman Creek bridge. It suddenly collapsed.

Both cars plunged forty feet down to land upside down. Sanders was badly hurt. His scalp was ripped open with blood pouring out. While people tried to call for a doctor, Sanders begged them to leave him alone. *"I don't need a doctor sewing me up with his needle and thread. All I have to do now is let this blood harden real good and it will hold everything in place until my head heals."*[606]

His sixteen year old daughter Margaret never forgot watching him *"Stretching his scalp until the edges of his wound met, he held it in place until the blood coagulated into a thick crust."*[607]

While his son managed to walk away from the crash without a scratch, he still died before his twenty-first birthday. Undergoing a medical operation to remove his tonsils, resulted in a severe infection that took his life. Losing his son devastated Sanders. He would bury the pain deep inside by once again immersing himself in his work.

Except that now he didn't have a car to get him to work. How could he sell tires without being able to drive around to talk to customers? Amazingly, he still found a way to make his quota that month.

Taking the bus, he went to a dealership and managed to make one sale that was enough to fulfill his quota. With one last paycheck secured, he quit that job and focused on recovering from his injuries. Weeks later when his body had healed from his injuries he still didn't have a car. But he figured out how to look for work. He hitchhiked.

That's how he ended up in the right place at the right time. One day while he was hitchhiking, he met the man in charge of every Standard Oil station in the entire state of Kentucky.

The man was impressed by how hard Sanders was trying to find a job. Would he like to become his own boss, managing a gas station?

Sanders said yes and moved his family to Nicholasville. There he took over the gas station. The deal was that Sanders made two cents on every gallon sold. So how could he attract more customers to buy more gas? He started by opening the station at 5AM, which was two hours before any other station opened in town.

When customers came by, he pumped their gas, inflated their tires, washed their windows and swept their floorboard. Seven days a week, working from dawn to dusk, he never slowed down. Soon he was selling more gas than all the other local stations combined.

Money poured in. Until the Great Depression came and people couldn't afford gas. Things got so bad, farmers had to sell their cattle because they couldn't afford to feed them. As demand for gas plummeted, Sanders had to sell the gas station.

Just when he didn't know what to do, Shell Oil called him.

Would he like to run their gas station in Corbin, Kentucky? They offered free rent and the freedom to run it as he wanted. It was the perfect opportunity.

Working at this gas station, Sanders tried to think of how to increase sales. Some of his customers traveled long distances. Would they like to purchase a home cooked meal before getting back on the road?

"I got to thinking about it, and it came to me that one thing I always could do was cook, and I figured I couldn't do worse than these people running these places around town."

He explained, *"I didn't have any money to buy furnishings, so I just brought out the dining room table and chairs and put them out there, in that room. And I started serving meals to anyone who wanted them."*[608]

Sanders was a very talented chef. Word soon spread throughout Kentucky about how good the food was at his gas station. With his station right off Interstate 25, customers kept coming. Soon he was selling lots and lots of fried chicken.

There was a problem. While people loved his fried chicken, they didn't have time to wait for it. While Sanders like to cook each batch from scratch, it took too long to prepare. Customers would get restless and leave.

Trying to speed up the process, he began experimenting with cooking chicken in a pressure cooker. The chicken came out perfect. Knowing he had something, Sanders quickly patented his idea.

Meanwhile, he had another idea.

Families traveling down the highway on vacation had very few affordable places to stay. Maybe he could build a nice motel on his property. Knowing that he needed to get the attention of potential customers, he figured out a creative way to do it.

Anyone who needed to use the bathroom at his gas station had to walk through part of his motel to get to the restroom. That way they noticed how nice the rooms looked. His advertising worked. The motel became so successful that even when a fire broke out and it burned down, he rebuilt it and people kept coming.

Sanders began to receive offers to buy his business. He didn't want to sell. Even when they offered $164,000, he turned it down.

Then a new highway was built. Traffic was rerouted way far around his place. Sales dropped. His only option was selling out for whatever he could get. When someone offered $75,000 he took the money, even though it could barely pay off all his bills. Once again, he had to start over from scratch

By then he was sixty-five years old and had no idea what to do. All he had was a social security check and a house.

He thought about all the different types of work he had done and realized what he did best. He made the best fried chicken.

Maybe he could find a new way to market it. Franchising his idea would enable him to make money without having to work so hard.

Not sure if his idea would work or not Colonel Sanders prayed, *"You've helped me in the past, and I need Your help now, God."*

"And I promise You, if this idea of franchising works out because of Your blessing, You'll get Your share."[609]

Then he walked out the door and tried to sell his idea.

While running his own restaurant at the gas station he had gotten involved in the national restaurant association, even serving on the board at one point. Through this organization he had become friends with many other restaurant owners from around the country. Maybe some of them would like to sell his chicken.

Loading up his car with thirty-five hundred brochures, he drove to the national restaurant convention. His daughter Margaret came along to help. Together they offered everyone the deal of a lifetime. They could have a franchise for free if they purchased Sander's eleven herbs and spices mixture and paid royalties of four cents on each piece of chicken sold.

Margaret described, *"I strategically positioned myself and handed out brochures as restaurateurs left the registration desk to enter the exhibit hall. Father stood just inside the entrance, introduced himself and spoke to anyone he spotted looking at the brochures."*[610]

Most of the people they approached turned it down.

Sanders described, *"At first, a lot of people weren't interested. Didn't think chicken could be a big item and didn't want to be bothered with it. Or some thought they knew more'n me about cooking."*[611]

One of those people who regretted missing this opportunity was Don Towles. He described how Colonel Sanders tried to recruit him by saying, *"I'm getting ready to start franchising. It's going to catch on like wildfire. Come to work for me, and we'll make a fortune."*

"I didn't take him seriously. It was just old Sanders, up to one of his wild schemes. We told him, 'No thanks,' and he said 'All right, you're going to miss out.' By George, he was right."[612]

Some people were interested. The few that signed up got to have Colonel Sanders himself come and teach their chefs.

Sanders would make trip after trip, while not even having enough money to afford a motel room. He slept in his car, washed up in the public restroom, put on his suit and served the people. And many of the people who became his earliest franchisors also became multi-millionaires.

One was Dave Thomas who started out working as a busboy in an early one of Sanders' franchises. When Sanders saw his work ethic he remarked, *"That young man is going to amount to something someday."*[613]

Dave Thomas asked Sanders for a franchise. Then he poured everything into it, making so much money from it that he would have the finances to launch his dream for Wendy's.

Another person who listened to Sanders was Pete Harman. When he opened his franchise he plastered large advertisements for it all over his hometown of Salt Lake City. Once he had made the entire state of Utah fall in love with fried chicken, Colonel Sanders gave him exclusivity to that state.

More than ever, money poured in enabling Sanders to help many other people. While he had always been generous, now he could really make a difference. He was able to benefit many different orphanages, churches and charities. His generous heart found different ways to share, yet it also got him in trouble.

Sanders didn't like to use contracts. He believed in shaking hands and trusting people's words. So when he had a chance to sell the business for two million dollars he decided to take it.

Not knowing enough about stock he turned down the opportunity to own the stock and just settled for two million dollars and a salary to appear in commercials.

Yet he appreciated being freed from the mundane details of running a business to enjoy being the face of the business. And many of his low level employees would become millionaires, when he sold the company and they kept the stock that they owned.

However, he ended up clashing with the new owners. He protested any way that they tried to change his ideas.

As a perfectionist he would visit local franchises to inspect his food. If he didn't like it, he would yell at the staff.

One time a New York reporter overheard Sanders berating a clerk and printed his words in the newspaper, *"What the hell have you done to my gravy? This damn stuff tastes like wallpaper paste!"*[614] Surprisingly his outburst actually boosted sales.

Sanders committed his life to the Lord at the age of seventy-nine. He passed away at age ninety in 1980, leaving a powerful legacy.

In his own words, Sanders described, *"That's my story. And I pray to God Almighty it will encourage you also to commit your life to Jesus. If you will, no matter what hard times you may go through—if you keep turning to Him acknowledging Him, and honoring Him in all you do—He'll help you through."*[615]

21

Persistence Pays

"Whatever you do, work at it with all your heart,
as though you were working for the Lord
and not for people."
Colossians 3:23 (GNT)

Colonel Sanders is one of the best examples of how a strong work ethic mixed with creativity and perseverance can bring success.

We admire how he overcame such a difficult childhood and many other failures in order to achieve his dreams. How he never gave up even though it took many years for his dreams to come true.

That same work ethic can also help you achieve your dreams.

Did you know that when you go to work, you are fulfilling a very important part of God's plan for your life? Work pleases God.

While many things that you do at work may go unnoticed by your boss, God sees your efforts. He is pleased when you try your best.

"Christ is the one you are really serving, and you know that he will reward you."[616]

Work is the way that we fulfill our destiny. Without it, nothing can be done.

Since God can only bless us according to the effort we put into making our dreams happen, the Bible warns us to avoid laziness.

"Lazy people will cause their own destruction because they refuse to work."[617]

Keep working hard at what God has called you to do and enjoy the fruits of your labors.

Think About:

"As you serve the Lord, work hard and don't be lazy.
Be excited about serving Him!"
Romans 12:11 (ERV)

"Work is the master key
that opens the door to all opportunities."[618]
-Kemmons Wilson

"I believe in push. We must push ourselves."[619]
-Madam CJ Walker

22

Orville & Wilbur Wright

"Put everything to the test. Accept what is good."
1 Thessalonians 5:21 (CEV)

Orville Wright
1871-1948

Wilbur Wright
1867-1912
From Ohio

Milton and Susan Wright had five children: Reuchlin, Lorin, Otis, Ida, and Katharine, plus two more sons who would be remembered as the Wright Brothers—Orville and Wilbur.

Milton Wright felt called by God as a preacher, so he quit a comfortable career as a schoolteacher and began preparing for the ministry. He was ordained in 1856. By 1859, he had fallen in love and married the woman of his dreams, Susan. Then he left to volunteer for one of the hardest jobs in the old west.

In 1862, Congress passed the Homestead Act, giving families the chance to obtain their own farm. Any person could move out west, claim 160 acres of federal land, homestead it for five years, then pay a small filing fee and that would become their private property. This was a huge opportunity for many struggling families to escape high rents through building a future of property ownership.

There was a massive migration of families moving to the western frontier, causing small towns to spring up almost overnight. Many of these towns were too small and too remote to have their own churches. Most credentialed pastors didn't want to leave the comfort of the big cities to pastor some little church in the middle of nowhere. Yet there were a few brave men willing to travel hundreds of miles across the wilderness to minister to the spiritual needs of these small towns. They rode regular routes, preaching in a different town every week. Milton Wright was one of those circuit riding preachers.

It was a hard life. Traveling in the 1800's was uncomfortable at best and mostly miserable. Transportation by horse left little protection from the icy cold, heavy rain, and dirty filth of the road. Yet what kept Milton on the road was his desire to fulfill the call of God on his life and his heart for ministering to people. So he stayed in the ministry through the loneliness of missing his family and the harshness of constant travel.

Day after day, year after year, while Milton was on the road, he always thought about his family. Whenever he could, he wrote letters home wondering how Susan and the children were doing. Fortunately he was able to provide for them because he had been ordained through the United Brethren denomination, which paid him a small salary.

Everywhere he traveled, he looked for gifts and toys to bring home to his children. Little did he know that the toy he bought in 1878 would change the world.

One day Milton noticed a tiny toy helicopter. Pulling a string caused it to lift off the ground. That seemed like a fun way to learn about science. Milton bought it and brought it home as a surprise.

Seven year old Orville and eleven year old Wilbur were fascinated by this toy. They played with it for hours, until it broke. Then they rebuilt the entire toy and played with it even more.

Inspired by the toy, Wilbur and Orville began to dream of building a real airplane. Together they built a small airplane, but it couldn't fly like the little helicopter did.

That puzzled them for days. and got Orville in trouble at school. Instead of paying attention to the teacher, he was trying to build a model size airplane at his desk. For that the teacher punished him. But when he went home and told his parents, they understood his dream. They suggested that he take a few days off from school.

For weeks Orville and Wilbur kept trying and failing at building their little airplane.

Years passed before they discovered *"That a machine having only twice the linear dimensions of another would require eight times the power."*[20]

Life moved on.

Orville and Wilbur went back to school and stayed active, playing with the other children. As they grew into their teens, Wilbur suffered a severe injury. He had been playing hockey with friends at the local lake, when he was hit with a hockey stick, knocking out several teeth.

With no medical care available, the wound became infected. Wilbur became seriously sick. The only treatment available was to stay home for several months, rest and try to recover. Wilbur's dream of attending college and becoming a teacher was shattered. He sank into a dark depression, feeling like he would never amount to anything.

Meanwhile, their mother Susan became very ill and was bedridden. Wilbur served as her primary caretaker, until she died at the young age of fifty-eight.

Orville was eighteen and Wilbur was twenty-two when they lost their mother. With their father still traveling extensively, they helped raise their siblings as best as they could.

For the rest of his life, Milton grieved the woman he had deeply loved, even visiting her grave with flowers every year on their anniversary. Yet he never got angry at God. He continued serving in the ministry until retiring at age seventy-seven.

Meanwhile, Orville dropped out of high school because he felt he wasn't learning much. Instead he decided to launch his own business.

Having grown up with a love of reading, both Orville and Wilbur liked the idea of starting their own newspaper.

Launching the *West Side News* they wrote the news with their own style of humor. As subscriptions only cost ten cents for six weeks, their newspaper quickly became very popular in the town. Publishing it made the Wright brothers stay in touch with national news.

That's how they heard about some engineer in Detroit, named Henry Ford, who had built a car in his garage only to realize that it couldn't fit through the door. He had to knock out an entire wall just to take his first test drive.

Reading that made Orville and Wilbur think about trying to build a car too, but Wilbur decided, *"To try to build one that would be any account, you'd be tackling the impossible. Why, it would be easier to build a flying machine!"*[621]

As their newspaper business expanded, Orville built his own printing press. It worked so well that soon he had a side business of printing books and pamphlets for people. The church denomination that employed his father, also hired him to print their books and publications. Within a few short years, they had become successful businessmen.

As bicycles became very popular, the Wright brothers opened their own bicycle shop in 1892. They sold, rented, and even built bicycles. As Wilbur described in a letter to their father, *"Selling new wheels is about done for this year, but the repairing business is good and we are getting about $20 a month from the rent of three wheels."*

"We get $8 a month for one, $6.50 for another and the third we rent by the hour or day. We have done so well renting them, that we have held on to them instead of disposing of them at once, although we really need the money invested in them."[622]

The other Wright Brothers, Reuchlin and Lorin, married and raised families. Their children loved visiting their uncles.

Their niece Ivonette remembered, *"When my mother had an errand taking her downtown, we were dropped off at the bicycle shop, and either Orville or Wilbur, or both, babysat us. They were never too busy to entertain us. If {Orville} ran out of games he would make candy. If he happened to be busy with something else, he would make caramel, which was easier to make and the kind children couldn't eat fast."*

"If he had time, he made fudge with a long thermometer to test how long it should be boiled. It was delicious."[623]

Ivonette noticed how much her uncles loved to play with toys. *"When we were old enough to get toys, Uncle Orv and Uncle Will had a habit of playing with them until they were broken, then repairing them so that they were better than when they were bought."*[624]

Another nephew, Leotine, also recalled happy family memories at his Grandpa Milton's house. *"Grandpa Wright's house was a favorite place. He and my Aunt Katharine and my Uncles Wilbur and Orville spent many days entertaining us there. Sometimes there was picture taking, fascinating candy making, good reading sessions, and good games indoors and out."*[625]

Meanwhile, people were still trying to figure out how to fly. Various people built all sorts of flying machines, but most only crashed. A few people were able to build gliders which could briefly float on the wind, but no one could control the take off or landing.

In France, Otto Lilienthal had set a record for being able to glide on the wind longer than anyone else. He would jump off a hill and float until gravity pulled him down. But being unable to control his glider caused him to die in a crash in 1896.

Lilienthal's obituary caught the attention of the Wright brothers. They had enjoyed writing about his flying experiments and grieved the loss of this inventor. Wilbur wrote articles in their paper to honor Lilienthal's achievements *"In really comprehending that balancing was the first, instead of the last of the great problems with human flight."*[626]

Thinking about this, rekindled their interest in trying to invent the airplane. While people still considered it to be impossible, the Wright brothers began studying it.

They started by writing to the Smithsonian Institute, requesting any published information on experiments with flying.

The Smithsonian responded by sending them hundreds of pages. The Wright brothers closely studied all of the research, trying to understand the scientific data that had been recorded about flying.

Wilbur was surprised by the info. Many inventors such as Alexander Graham Bell and Thomas Edison had tried and failed at flying.

According to Wilbur, *"At that time there was no flying skill, but only a flying problem. Thousands of men had thought about flying machines and a few had even built machines, which they called flying machines, but these were guilty of almost everything except flying. We found that even the highest ranked professional scientists and inventors had attempted to solve the problem, but one by one, they had been compelled to give up. In studying their failures we found many interesting points."*

"Thousands of pages had been written on the so-called science of flying, but most of the ideas, like the designs for machines, were only guessing and probably ninety per cent was false. Things which seemed reasonable were often found to be untrue, and things which seemed unreasonable were sometimes true. Under these conditions, we paid very little attention to things that we hadn't personally tested."[627]

Complicating matters even more was the religious tradition against flying. At the time many Christians believed it couldn't be God's will. Religious leader Roger Bacon taught: *"It is not necessarily impossible for human beings to fly, but it so happens that God did not give them the knowledge of how to do it. It follows, therefore, that anyone who claims that he can fly must have sought the aid of the devil. To attempt to fly is therefore sinful."*[628]

Orville disagreed. *"Isn't it wonderful that all these secrets have been preserved for so many years just so that we could discover them?"*[629]

Discovering those secrets required testing what they read about flying to figure out if it actually worked. To do these experiments, the Wright brothers built a biplane kite. Then they played with it to learn about how the wind affected flight. Each experiment was carefully written down in hopes that they could discover the mathematical formula of how much power it would take to lift off the ground.

Meanwhile, the neighbors wondered why two grown men were playing with toys. Someone who watched them remarked, *"I felt sorry for them. They seemed like well-meaning, decent young men. Yet there they were, neglecting their business to waste their time day after day on that ridiculous flying machine."*[630]

After weeks of working with the kite, the Wright brothers built a life size glider to test out their theories. Then they looked for a new place to conduct experiments. Where could they find lots of wind to lift them off the ground, soft sand to keep them from getting hurt if they crashed and as much privacy as possible? They wrote to the U.S. Weather Bureau and were told to go to Kitty Hawk, North Carolina.

Taking several weeks off from their business, the Wright brothers packed up their glider and went to Kitty Hawk. There they camped on the beach, pitching tents. They had no idea what was coming.

Mosquitoes were waiting for them. Heavy winds blew sand in their face. The first several experiments ended with the glider crashing hard. Everything came to a screeching halt as it took several days to repair the glider.

When they were finally able to resume flying, they ended up very frustrated. No matter how hard they tried, they could only float for a few minutes on the wind. Soon they gave up and went home.

As Wilbur later described, *"When we left Kitty Hawk at the end of 1901, we doubted that we would ever resume our experiments. Although we had broken the record for distance in gliding, yet when we looked at the time and money which we had spent, we considered our experiments a failure. At that time, I predicted that someday men would fly, but not within our lifetime."*[631]

Something was wrong. It was how they had relied on theories and math equations from other people. Even Lilienthal, whom they greatly admired, had passed down math that wasn't adding up. Wilbur realized, *"Lilienthal is very unfair to the plane. He greatly under describes its lifting power, and exaggerates its drift."*[632]

The Wrights had to figure it out for themselves. They went back home and built a wind tunnel to study how wind pressure affected wings on a small scale. It took a long time but eventually they discovered the math equations which are still used today by modern pilots in multi-million dollar aircraft.

The breakthrough came when they remembered something they had learned from their bicycle business. Bicycle riding required controlling two dimensions: balance and sideways movement.

Realizing that adding a vertical dimension of control was the secret to flight, they invented the tri-dimensional control system, which is still used today in modern aircraft.

Another important discovery they made was wing warping. Think about an ice cube tray. You take it out from the freezer and twist it one way, and then another to release the ice into the glass. This is the same type of movement that they used to invent wings to twist against the wind, stabilizing and controlling the flight.

Meanwhile, trouble was brewing in the church. Milton had been elected to Bishop in 1877, yet there were rival factions determined to remove him from leadership. They knew Milton was a man of principal who wouldn't allow them to seize control. Somehow they had to get him out of the way.

Someone came into the church organization and got himself elected to oversee the church's funds.

Milton had a bad feeling about this guy and asked Wilbur to audit the church accounts. The audit revealed $6,800 was missing.

Milton was furious. He tried to bring criminal charges against the man but the church disagreed. They just replaced the trustee. Instead of punishing the man who had stolen the money, the church leadership punished Milton, reassigning him to the far away western territory and cutting his salary by twenty-five percent.

Wilbur didn't like it. Putting flying experiments on hold, he wrote pamphlets on proper money management in the church. Then he went to confront the church leaders.

They listened to him. Policies changed. Better trustees came into authority.

While it would take years to repair the damage, the battle was won and Wilbur reported, "*We won a complete victory; turned every one of the rascals out of office, and put friends of my father in their places. It will be a relief to have that matter off my mind hereafter.*"[633]

Now they could go back to Kitty Hawk and try again. Thousands of experiments later, they could accurately calculate the scientific laws of lift. All they needed was an engine and they would be able to control flight. However, airplane engines had not yet been invented so they couldn't just go buy one. They would have to build their own.

December 17, 1903: Milton received an urgent telegram. Orville and Wilbur had made history. For the first time, an airplane heavier than air had flown completely controlled by the pilot, not at the mercy of the wind. They had the pictures to prove it. Now they knew what had to be done.

Once they were finished, they applied for a patent on their airplane. It was declined. They applied again and were again rejected. No one would believe that they could actually fly. The Wright brothers would just have to prove what they knew.

To protect their ability to get a patent, they carefully guarded their secrets. They knew that once everyone saw their machine, everyone would try to copy it.

So they patiently waited until the patent was approved on May 22, 1906. Then they could show their plane to the world.

Writing to their local Congressman, the Wright brothers asked if the U.S. Government would like to see their new invention. Not only can it fly, it also *"Lands without being wrecked."*[634]

They were rudely rejected. Government officials refused to believe that anyone could fly. Congress had already paid Samuel Langley fifty thousand dollars to invent an airplane. He had literally crashed and burned, resulting in a congressional investigation into what went wrong. After that fiasco, Congress wasn't interested in anyone else who thought they could fly.

With the door slammed shut in their face, Wilbur worried, *"We have done our full share toward making this an American invention."*

"We knocked hard on the U.S. Defense Department's door. But seeing no way to change the attitude of our own government, we made a formal proposal to the British government."[635]

They had no choice. Their only way to succeed in America would be through marketing to Europe. The British were interested, but still very skeptical. If the Wrights could fly, why didn't they do it publicly? Thousands of dollars of prize money was available to anyone who could publicly demonstrate a flying machine, yet Orville and Wilbur weren't interested. Instead Wilbur felt, *"We do not fear any serious competition until after we show our machine."*[636]

The French wanted to talk to them and asked to see them demonstrate flying. The Wrights refused. No one was allowed to see the aircraft, until a contract was signed and money deposited. Sitting on the knowledge of aerodynamics, fame and fortune was waiting. Yet Orville and Wilbur wouldn't budge. They turned down offer after offer, explaining, *"I know of only one bird, the parrot, that talks, and he can't fly very high."*[637]

Public opinion never frightened them. While their credibility was challenged, they trusted that truth would prevail. So they waited until they had what they wanted—America's attention.

One day President Theodore Roosevelt read an article in the newspaper about the Wright Brothers. Did they actually know how to fly? Why wasn't the government listening to them?

He immediately sent an official down to meet with them. In the end, the Wright Brothers would offer America a huge discount.

The airplane they had offered to Europe for $200,000, they sold to America for $25,000.

It was 1908. The Wrights returned to the air for the first time in three years. Crowds were stunned to watch them do what was still considered impossible.

Becoming instant celebrities, they were awarded the Congressional Medal of Honor. Ivy League schools, including Harvard and Yale, granted honorary degrees to them.

Awards and honors poured in from all sides. Never again would they have to work for a living. Now they would have enough time and money to work on whatever they needed.

They worked with flight crews to teach the military how to use their equipment. That's when something went really wrong. One day Orville was scheduled to demonstrate flying for the U.S. Army at a base in Fort Myer. Crowds of people gathered to watch the air show.

Recognizing Orville, they swarmed him, asking all sorts of questions. Orville tried to greet as many people as he could, trusting that his crew was completing the pre-flight maintenance. But something that was supposed to be checked before flying, didn't get done.

When Orville climbed into his airplane with his passenger Thomas Selfridge, everything seemed normal. They took off and began circling over the crowds. Then Orville heard an unusual noise. The propellers gave out, sending them into a nose dive.

It was the first fatal airplane crash. Thomas Selfridge died on impact. Orville was seriously injured. For the rest of his life, he would suffer from the injuries.

Wilbur felt guilty. If he had been there to check the plane, maybe it wouldn't have happened.

Orville insisted, *"The only thing I'm afraid of is that I can't get well soon enough to finish those tests next year."*[638]

Eventually he would recover enough to return to flying and fulfill their contract with the military.

Never again would Orville try to fly without having personally checked his equipment first. Plus, he began working on developing safety features. He invented the automatic pilot system and the flight simulator to train pilots on potential emergencies.

Orville also became a consultant to the military, helping them develop new technology that would result in major progress in aviation between World War I and World War II.

Meanwhile, family of the Wright brothers would also serve in the military. Three of them became combat pilots. One courageously died in battle just after shooting down two enemy aircraft.

Wilbur Wright died of typhoid fever at age forty-five in 1912. The world mourned losing him. Twenty-five thousand people attended his funeral.

Orville lived on to age seventy-six. He never stopped inventing. He designed his own dream home from the ground up. Every room displayed different aspects of his creativity like air conditioning, a record player that could change songs by itself and his own version of a washing machine.

The only thing he couldn't figure out was the typewriter. Buying a typewriter, he took it apart to see how it worked. Then he couldn't figure out how to put it back together.

When a repairman was summoned to his home, not even the repairman could figure out how to put it back together, he just brought a new typewriter to Orville.

Meanwhile, Orville sent the world's first airplane to the Smithsonian Institute. There it sits, reminding everyone of the old joke that two wrongs don't make a right, but two Wrights can sure make an airplane!

Wright Brothers Photos

Orville flying with Katherine

The Wright Brother's Bicycle Shop

First successful flight at Kitty Hawk

Wilbur flying

Wilbur and Orville Wright

Wright Brothers getting the airplane ready for the military

Wilbur timing the flights

Orville being rescued after an airplane accident

ORVILLE WRIGHT   WILBUR WRIGHT   KATHERINE WRIGHT   E M HAWLEY

Orville, Wilbur, and Katherine Wright

Milton Wright and family

22

Truth vs. Tradition

"Your ear tests the words it hears."
Job 34:3b (ERV)

The Wright brothers had to test the scientific data to discover the real laws of aerodynamics instead of just accepting everything they heard.

When you eat a nice steak dinner, you cut away the gristle and bone to enjoy the meat. In the same way, when we hear sermons in church we need to enjoy the meat of God's Word while cutting away human opinions added to it that disagree with the Bible.

The Bible warns us, *"Dear friends, do not believe everyone who claims to speak by the Spirit. You must test them to see if the spirit they have comes from God. For there are many false prophets in the world."*[639]

In the Bible, the Apostle Paul was impressed when he went to one town and found the people checked everything he preached with the Word of God. *"They listened to the message with great eagerness, and every day they studied the Scriptures to see if what Paul said was really true."*[640]

You will hear very popular Christian doctrines that sound spiritual and religious. Before you accept them, check the Bible.

Take the Apostle Paul's advice: *"We will not be influenced by every new teaching we hear."*[641]

The Bible warns us to discern between tradition and Scripture.

"Be careful not to let anyone rob you of this faith through a shallow and misleading philosophy. Such a person follows human traditions and the world's way of doing things rather than following Christ."[642]

Let's take a quick look at some common doctrines.

Myth #1: Money is the root of all evil.

> *"For the love of money is the root of all kinds of evil.*
> *By craving it, some have wandered away from the faith*
> *and pierced themselves with many sorrows."*
> 1Tim 6:10 (BSB)

The Bible warns us that the *love* of money (covetousness) is the problem.

"Keep your lives free from the love of money and be content with what you have, for God has said, 'Never will I leave you, never will I forsake you.'"[646]

Thus, dangerous times will come in the last days when people

"Love only themselves and their money. They will be boastful and proud, scoffing at God."[644]

God hates covetousness (Psalms 10:3). That's why in the Bible, David prayed that God would give him a heart for God's laws instead of covetousness (Psalms 119:36).

"Labor not to be rich, cease from your own wisdom."[643]

When God gave the Ten Commandments He warned us:

"Thou shalt not covet."[645]

In the Old Testament, the Biblical requirements for leaders was that they must *"fear God"* and *"hate covetousness."*[647]

In the New Testament, again the requirement for church leaders was that they must be *"not greedy"* and *"not covetous."*[648]

Do we love God or do we love money?

Our love for God is proven by our obedience to God. Do we serve money by chasing it above all else? Or do we make our money serve the Lord by seeking His kingdom first and letting everything else be added to us? (Matt 6:32).

Think about how you have a trash can in your kitchen. Do you serve the trash can or use it? Can you have the trash can without craving it?

Money is a tool just like that trash can. Another good example is the gasoline in your car. You need it to travel. Can you use gasoline without serving it? Of course.

The Bible warns us against serving money. Jesus taught us:

"You cannot serve two masters at the same time. You will hate one and love the other, or you will be loyal to one and not care about the other. You cannot serve God and Money at the same time."[649]

Look at that verse very closely. Since you cannot serve two masters at once, if you are obeying God, then you are automatically not serving the money that you have.

You can make your money serve the Lord just like LeTourneau, Crowell and many other people in this book. Think about it. Seventy years after Henry Crowell died, his money is still serving the Lord because he set up a living trust to control it from beyond the grave.

You can pursue the career that you love while keeping God first in your life just as Jesus said, *"Put God's work first, and these things will be yours as well."*[650]

Myth #2: Money will always corrupt you. Only poverty will bring you closer to God.

What the Bible actually teaches us is that since money can corrupt, therefore it's our responsibility to not allow it to corrupt us.

"Make sure that when you eat and are satisfied, build pleasant houses and settle in, see your herds and flocks flourish and more and more money come in, watch your standard of living going up and up—make sure you don't become so full of yourself and your things that you forget God."[651]

And the Bible warns us NOT to be fools because *"The prosperity of fools shall destroy them."*[652]

When your money grows, you have a choice. *"You must decide who you will serve."*[653] That's the same choice you have when you're broke. Will you let money change your heart? Or when your bank account expands will you make the money serve the Lord with you?

Money is important enough that Jesus actually thought about it *while He was hanging on the cross!* He made sure that His mother would be financially provided for after His death by asking his friend John to take care of her. *"And from then on this disciple took her into his home."*[654]

The Bible helps us understand how God feels about money.

"Tell those who have the riches of this world not to be arrogant and not to place their confidence in anything as uncertain as riches. Instead, they should place their confidence in God who richly provides us with everything to enjoy."[655]

That verse was written by the Apostle Paul, who also wrote most of the New Testament while he was locked up in prison for preaching the gospel. While Paul was in prison, the Roman Governor Felix *"hoped Paul would pay him a bribe, so he sent for Paul often and talked with him."*[656]

Think about how the Governor was hoping Paul would pay him off, because he knew Paul had enough money to afford a bribe!

Of course, Paul refused to pay any bribes, instead preferring to follow legal procedure by appealing his case directly to the Roman Emperor.

This took a long time and involved him having to relocate to Rome where he *"Stayed two full years in his own rented house. He welcomed all the people who came and visited him."*[657]

Renting his own house (while being under house arrest) was a lot more expensive than sitting in a jail cell but was easier for him to write the New Testament. He was also able to continue ministering to people and have visitors at that house. The Apostle Paul used money as a tool to serve the Lord. Maybe that's why he wrote, *"Now follow the example of the correct teaching I gave you, and let the faith and love of Christ Jesus be your model."*[658]

Myth #3: All of us need to follow the instructions that Jesus gave to the rich young ruler to sell everything he owned and give it to the poor.

While Jesus traveled and ministered to the people, He had a team of women traveling with Him. *"These women used their own money to help Jesus and his apostles."*[659]

Did Jesus ever tell these women to sell everything and give it to the poor? Nope. He honored their decision to make their money serve God and even rebuked those who criticized it.

As we saw in an earlier chapter, when the woman with the very expensive alabaster box, poured it all out on Jesus, then Judas complained that it should have been sold and given to the poor.

Jesus actually rebuked him for saying that! Instead, Jesus honored the woman's personal decision on how to spend her own money by prophesying that her story would be told around the world. When people quote those words of Judas, instead remember what Jesus said.

Now back to the story of the rich young ruler. This wealthy young man came to Jesus to ask a question. *"Good teacher, what must I do to receive eternal life?"*[660]

Notice that the conversation was focusing on how to get into Heaven.

"Why do you call me good?" Jesus asked him. *"No one is good except God alone."*[661]

Then Jesus begins to talk about the Ten Commandments. *"If you want to enter eternal life, keep the commandments."[662]*

Remember the Tenth Command is to avoid covetousness.

Jesus is making the point to this man that covetousness is blocking him from following Christ.

The rich young ruler replies that he's kept the commandments since he was young.

Then Jesus says, *"There is still one thing you need to do. Go and sell everything you have. Give the money to those who are poor, and you will have riches in heaven. Then come and follow me."[663]*

This is an opportunity for the young man to take a step of faith. To move away from trusting in his own righteousness and learn a whole new way of doing things by following in the footsteps of Christ. How does he respond?

"When the man heard this, gloom spread over his face, and he went away sad, because he was very rich. Jesus looked around at his disciples and said to them, 'How hard it will be for rich people to enter the Kingdom of God!'"[664]

The disciples were completely shocked. They asked Jesus, *"Who then can be saved?"[665]* Why would the disciples be so shocked? If they were poor then they would have been happy. Instead, they were shocked because they were men of substance. Now they're worried about whether or not they can get into Heaven too.

Jesus clarifies His point by adding, *"How hard it is for them that <u>TRUST</u> in riches to enter the kingdom of God. It is easier for a camel to go through the eye of a needle than for a rich man to enter the kingdom of God."[666]*

That worries the disciples even more. Now they are *"Astonished out of measure."[667]*

Jesus continues, *"With men it is impossible but not with God for with God all things are possible."[668]* Once again Jesus is pointing us towards trusting in God instead of ourselves.

At this point Peter has to speak up. Having left a successful fishing business to follow Jesus, he reminds Jesus that they have forsaken everything for Him.

Jesus responds with another really important point—everyone who has given up their home, family, lands, *"For my sake and the gospel"* will *"Receive an hundred fold now in this time."*[669]

The promised reward includes financial substance *"houses and lands"* and *"in the world to come, eternal life."*[670]

So if the rich young ruler had obeyed Jesus' personal instructions to him to give up everything, God would have blessed him by restoring his financial assets in greater measure. Plus, he would have received the eternal life that he was seeking.

The moral of the story is that no one is good enough to get into Heaven by doing good works. Jesus made that very clear. He also showed us that while we will sacrifice for God, in the end, God's will is to bless us even more. Letting go of these religious myths is necessary for us to discover the good things that God has for us.

Think About:

"For the wisdom of this world is foolishness with God."
1 Corinthians 3:19a (KJV)

"Never let the world's wisdom rule your heart."[671]
-William Tyndale

"Ignore the conventional wisdom.
I always prided myself on breaking everybody else's rules,
and I always favored the mavericks
who challenged my rules."[672]
-Sam Walton

23

John D.
Rockefeller Sr.

*"God lifts up the poor from the dirt and raises up the needy from the
garbage pile to seat them with leaders."*
Psalm 113:7-8a (CEB)

John D. Rockefeller Sr.
1839-1937
From New York

The most financially successful person in American history is John
D. Rockefeller. Starting from scratch, he built some of the largest companies in the world, pioneering the oil industry long before automobiles
and airplanes were available to use the oil. Yet even when his personal
fortune reached the modern day equivalent of $600,000,000,000, he
never forgot the source of his success.

He always insisted, *"God gave me my money."*[673]

John D. Rockefeller was one of six children born to William &
Eliza Rockefeller. His childhood was hard. Most of the time his father
was gone.

William Rockefeller made a living by traveling from town to town, selling all sorts of questionable medical potions that supposedly could cure any sickness.

From time to time, William brought money home to help Eliza with the children but it was never enough. She bought groceries from the local store on credit, promising that whenever William got back he would pay the bill. Sometimes he did come back and pay the bill. Most of the time he didn't. They fell further and further behind. Eventually, Eliza's frugality couldn't keep up with William's extravagance.

By 1850, their home had been seized to pay William's debts. They left town completely humiliated. Yet even with all the disappointments, John Rockefeller still deeply loved his father. What little time they had together was deeply treasured. Unlike his father, Rockefeller saved whatever money he could.

Starting very young, Rockefeller was a hard worker. He found ways to earn money by doing chores for neighbors. He did everything from pulling weeds to milking cows and chopping wood. One time he worked all summer harvesting crops for thirty-seven cents a day. He made enough money to both help his mother and still save up fifty dollars.

The neighbors were impressed that a young child could save up fifty dollars. One farmer asked to borrow the fifty dollars. One year later, the farmer repaid the entire fifty dollars plus seven percent interest. That $3.50 of interest was the easiest money Rockefeller had ever made.

That whole experience made him began to realize that there were easier ways of making money than the heavy physical labor on the farm. He decided, *"To let the money be my slave and not make myself a slave to money."*[674]

When someone asked him what he was going to do when he grew up, he dreamed, *"Someday, I'll be worth a hundred thousand dollars."*[675]

Meanwhile, his dad was cheating on his mom. When his dad finally left his mom for another woman, Rockefeller dropped out of high school to help his mom with the bills.

At sixteen years old he found an accounting job that would pay him sixteen dollars a month.

Within three months, he was doing such a good job for them that they raised his wages to twenty-five dollars a month ($300/yr).

He enjoyed the work. Keeping track of their finances taught him all sorts of things about business like calculating shipping costs and finding the profits in buying and selling produce.

Rockefeller remembered, *"They owned houses, warehouses, and office buildings which were rented for a variety of uses and I had to collect the rents. They shipped by railroad, canal, and lake. I was in close touch with all the many different kinds of negotiations and transactions going on."*[676]

Yet even while the business was prospering, the bosses continued paying low salaries to the workers. Rockefeller noticed this as he kept the books. The first two years, he was given no salary raise at all. Then the third year they offered to raise his salary to $700/yr.

Rockefeller declined. By keeping their books he knew they were making a lot more money. He asked for $800/yr. They refused. That was the last straw. Believing that he could do better working for himself, Rockefeller quit his job and launched his own firm.

Living frugally, he had saved up a thousand dollars. That money opened a lot of doors but wasn't enough to start the whole business. So he borrowed another thousand from his dad and two thousand from a new business partner named Maurice Clark. With total starting capital of four thousand, he launched a new business buying and selling train loads of groceries.

The idea was to approach local farmers, offering to buy their entire harvest. This gave farmers a guaranteed income and gave Rockefeller a product he could sell to grocery stores.

The business was an overnight success. Rockefeller described, *"To our great surprise, business came in upon us so fast that we hardly knew how to take care of it. In the first year we sold half a million dollars."*[677]

After expenses were deducted from their gross sales of $500,000, there was only a small profit left of several thousand dollars.

Yet this was still more than he had made working for someone else. Rockefeller realized, *"It was a great thing to be my own employer."*[678]

While building his business, Rockefeller also invested in his walk with God.

Throughout his life he was a devout Christian, attending services every week at the Erie Street Baptist Church. There he volunteered as general trustee, cleaning and prepping before services.

When he started helping with the offerings, he realized that the church was way behind on its bills. The offerings had declined until there wasn't enough money to pay the mortgage. When the Pastor told him that the church was about to lose their building to foreclosure, Rockefeller took matters into his own hands.

He began standing at the door of the church after the services so he could talk to all the members on their way out. He asked them to help save the church from foreclosure. Within nine months, he had raised enough money to pay off the entire two thousand dollar mortgage.

Meanwhile, he found the love of his life. Laura Spelman had grown up helping her family run their dry goods store. Their store was also a thriving station on the Underground Railroad, providing food and shelter. When the economy crashed in 1851, their store went bankrupt. Forced to start over, they moved to Cleveland, Ohio. Laura enrolled in high school and met the handsome young Rockefeller.

They married just as Rockefeller's business began to take off. He would later admit that her advice had been a major part of his financial success, *"Without her keen advice, I would be a poor man."*[679] Just as they began their life together, a new opportunity came their way.

In 1859, Edwin Drake figured out how to pump oil from the ground. This was a major technological achievement. At the time the only way that raw petroleum could be extracted from the ground was when it had bubbled up by itself. Lack of technology had kept petroleum too expensive for most people to afford. The standard oil used for lamps was whale oil.

Edwin Drake's invention opened the door for many people to make a living pumping oil out of the ground.

As news of his invention spread, there was a huge rush of people moving to Pennsylvania, buying up land and drilling. Many overnight fortunes were made.

News quickly spread. People wondered if petroleum could be the new fuel source.

One of those people was a member of Rockefeller's church named Samuel Andrews. Utilizing his scientific training and knowledge of chemistry, Andrews worked on ways to process petroleum into kerosene for lamps. Pretty soon he had invented a much more efficient method of refining the petroleum. Believing that building a refinery would ride the wave of the future, he approached Rockefeller for the money to do it.

Rockefeller invested four thousand dollars into this idea because he believed the newly discovered oil was part of God's plan. It must be needed for something.

Rockefeller believed that the greatest wealth lay in developing a new product, instead of just selling the same thing as everyone else. *"I saw a marvelous future for our country and wanted to participate in the work of making our country great."*[680]

As more and more oil was pumped out of the ground, Rockefeller's new refinery processed it, marketed it and soon his oil was in kerosene lamps everywhere in America. As business grew, other people jumped into it as well.

Refineries sprang up everywhere. Without knowing what they were doing, many people were quickly overwhelmed. At that time very little was known about the oil industry. Accidents were frequent. Costs were high. Machinery was outdated. Inefficient methods increased costs, but demand for oil was so high that it kept selling as people began switching to kerosene to light their home lamps.

According to Rockefeller, *"The Oil industry was considered a very hazardous undertaking. I well remember my distinguished friend Rev. Thomas W. Armitage, for some forty years the Pastor of a great New York church, warning me that it was worse than folly to extend our plants and operations."*

"He was sure we were running unwarranted risks, that our oil supply would probably fail, the demand would decline, and he, with many others— sometimes I thought almost everybody—prophesied ruin. None of us ever dreamed of the expansion that was coming."[681]

Then the Civil War ended. Demand for oil dropped overnight.

Yet people continued pumping oil out of the ground, resulting in too much supply and no customers to buy it. Unsold barrels of oil began piling up in warehouses. Prices fell lower and lower. Refineries began going bankrupt. Rockefeller realized something had to change, before everything collapsed. Shutting down his produce company, he focused everything on his oil refinery. His new company was Standard Oil.

Looking at the big picture, Rockefeller realized that he had to find new products to use the oil. Costs had to be cut to bring the price of oil down to where people could afford it. If someone could consolidate the oil industry, then higher volume would enable them to lower costs even further.

Rockefeller prayed about it until *"I had our plan clearly in mind. As a matter of conscience, it was right between me and my God."*[682]

Rockefeller could have just sat back and waited until all of his competitors had gone bankrupt. At the time his business was doing so well that he was selling oil at a profit for a price way below what it cost his competitors to produce the same barrel of oil. But Rockefeller believed that the right way of doing things was to give his competition a fair chance.

So he approached them with an offer to buy their companies for fair market value. He offered to pay them in either cash or stock in his own company. If they took the stock then they would be able to sit back and relax, getting paid for the rest of their lives from stock dividends while Rockefeller did all the work.

As he later described, *"It was unprecedented for the strongest company in the industry to turn to its competitors who had been losing money and could not last much longer and say, 'Come with us. We will save you from being wrecked and give you a return on your capital.'"*[683]

Rockefeller's grandson David described, *"Standard Oil offered not only an honest, but often a generous price for competing refineries—so generous, in fact, that competitors often re-entered the business simply for the opportunity to be bought out again. Grandfather's partners complained bitterly about this persistent pattern of 'blackmail,' but he continued to buy in order to complete his plan."*[684]

Rockefeller described, *"Most of them took the stock—very wisely, as it turned out. In some cases where the sellers were not very well up in business matters we persuaded them that it would be better for them to take at least part of their payment in stock because this would be more profitable for them in the end."*[685]

Over the next few decades the value of stock in Standard Oil grew remarkably well. Those that had traded their companies for stock became some of the wealthiest people in America. Those that had turned down Rockefeller's offer became some of his most bitter critics.

Meanwhile, Rockefeller never stopped working on trying to find new markets for oil. He sent oil to help young inventors like Henry Ford and the Wright Brothers during their early experiments. As their products were developed into entire new industries, the demand for oil skyrocketed. Eventually by being in the right business at the right time, Rockefeller ended up controlling ninety percent of the oil industry, making him the first self-made billionaire in American history.

Yet Rockefeller tried to help people by keeping the cost of oil down as low as possible. He didn't even want his company stock to be traded on the stock market for fear it would drive up the price of oil.[686]

All the money he made never changed his love for God. To Rockefeller, managing wealth was just another part of his walk with God. When reporters asked him for an interview, he would often talk about his relationship with God.

One time he told a reporter this story. *"I remember clearly when the financial plan of my life was formed. It was out in Ohio, under a dear old minister, who preached, 'Get money; get it honestly and then give it wisely.' I wrote it down and have tried ever since."*[687]

Rockefeller still attended church regularly. For many years he even taught a Sunday School class for adults where he shared his heart that *"Nothing can satisfy but Christ. We can never learn too much of His will towards us, too much of His messages and His advice."*[688]

When people asked him for the secret of his success he liked to say, *"I believe the power to make money is a gift from God—just as are the instincts for art, music, literature, the doctor's talent, the nurse's, yours—to be developed and used to the best of our ability for the good of mankind."*

"Having been endowed with the gift I possess, I believe it is my duty to make money and still more money, and to use the money I make for the good of my fellow man according to the dictates of my conscience."[689]

In 1911, the Supreme Court ordered Standard Oil to be broken up into several different companies. This was exciting news for the critics of Rockefeller who had hoped he would be punished for having too much. Little did they know that he would actually make more money on this. When his company was broken up into smaller companies, it actually increased costs, resulting in higher fuel prices and higher profits.

In the end, Rockefeller would set the record for charitable giving. By the time he passed away in 1937, at age ninety-seven, he had given away half a billion dollars. Yet he still had so much money left that he was able to give a six hundred million dollar inheritance to take care of his family.[690]

Today Rockefeller's original Standard Oil enterprise lives on as some of the biggest companies in the world including Exxon-Mobil, Chevron, Amoco, & Pennzoil.[691]

Rockefeller Photos

Rockefeller's team leaving the courthouse

Rockefeller with his son

23

Make Your Money Serve God

*"If God makes what grows in the field so beautiful, what
do you think he will do for you? It's just grass—one day it's
alive, and the next day someone throws it into a fire.
But God cares enough to make it beautiful.
Surely he will do much more for you.
Your faith is so small!"*
Matthew 6:30 (ERV)

If you live on more than $2 per day, then you are considered rich by millions of people living on less in other countries around the world.

If you have indoor plumbing and can get water by turning a handle in the wall, then you are considered rich by people who have to walk long distances to get water and then carry that water on their back all the way home.

If you have electricity that works 24 hours a day, then you are envied by people who only get electricity for some hours per day and then the electricity shuts off from time to time.

If you have a car, then there are lots of people riding the bus right now who wish they were as rich as you.

If you only have a bicycle, there are still lots of other people who envy you because they have to walk everywhere and carry things on their shoulders while you get to rest a little and have an easier time carrying things on the bicycle.

Think about this for a minute. What is the definition of *"rich"*? What we consider to be poor in America would seem like luxury in other places where people are living without electricity, running water or air conditioning.

There is no exact definition of *"rich."* Everyone has a different idea of what *"rich"* is. We look at other people and if they have more than us—then we think they are rich and we are poor. Yet there are other people in the world who would think of us as rich because we have electricity and running water while they don't.

The goal of our life is not to pursue money but to obey God. Yet there is always the temptation to want more stuff than we have. Ponzi schemes are designed to trap people by offering them what they don't have. So resisting the temptation to crave more stuff, actually protects us.

Now Jesus warned us about the temptation of greed. *"Watch out! Guard yourselves against every form of greed, for one's life does not consist in the abundance of his possessions."*[692]

The Apostle Paul agreed writing, *"Don't be greedy, which is the same as worshiping idols."*[693]

Greed is a relentless master who pushes us to get more and more and more. It allows no rest, as it drives us to focus on what we don't have. It steals our enjoyment of what we do have—by helping us feel sorry for ourselves because someone else has more than we do. Yet we could spend our whole lives trying to get rich and someone else would still have more than we do.

Jesus warned us, *"What shall it profit a man, if he shall gain the whole world, and lose his own soul?"*[694]

Proverbs says, *"Better is a poor man who walks in his integrity than a rich man who is crooked in his ways."*[695]

Jesus warned us how greed would try to choke God's Word in our lives. In the parable of the sower, the farmer goes out and sows seed on various types of soil (Mark 4:1-20). Some of it falls on thorny ground. The thorns spring up and choke it.

Jesus explained how some people *"Hear the word and the cares of this world, the deceitfulness of riches and the lusts of other things enter in and choke the word, and it becomes unfruitful."*[696]

Covetousness is the *"lust for other things"* that *"chokes"* God's Word in our lives. Covetousness is when we choose to disobey God to get more stuff.

> Never allow what someone else has to make you ungrateful for what you have.

Can money deceive people? Absolutely. The world serves money. They do whatever they have to do to get it. In the parable, some people allowed—craving more stuff—to steal God's word from them. There were other people in the parable who heard the Word and brought forth fruit. That raises the question—will we serve money or make our money serve God?

The real test of our love for God is what we do with our money.

- Do we give God what belongs to Him as Jesus taught us in Matthew 22:21?
- Do we complain about what we don't have or are we grateful?
- Do we pity ourselves because other people have more than us?
- Do we obey God or follow the world's desires first in our lives?

The money itself is not the problem. It's how we handle it.

"He that trusts in his riches shall fall."[697]

We can overcome that temptation by making our money serve God.

Jesus told us to *"Go into all the world and preach the gospel."*[698] How could we try to do that without finances? Especially when the Bible warns us: *"The poor man's wisdom is despised, and his words are not heard."*[699]

If we accept the religious tradition that giving up everything to become poor will please God, we could miss the good things that God has for us.

God has something much better for you. *"I will abundantly bless."*[700] God's perfect will is for you to have more than enough for your own needs and plenty left over to help others. *"And God is able to give you more than you need, so that you will always have all you need for yourselves and more than enough for every good cause."*[701]

Jesus explained how this was supposed to work in our lives when He told us to seek God first ahead of everything else—instead of seeking money first like the world does. Then after we seek God first, we can seek other things second, third, and fourth like building a career and raising a family.

By putting God first in our lives, we are opening ourselves up to God's ability to bless us with those material goods that we need as Jesus said, *"So do not start worrying: 'Where will my food come from? Or my drink? Or my clothes?' For the Gentiles seek after all these things, and your heavenly Father knows that you need them all. But seek first the kingdom of God and his righteousness, and all these things will be added to you."*[702]

Is it God's will for us to be destroyed by poverty? If so, then let's get rid of our cars, houses, computers, furniture, etc. Hmmmm....wonder why the people who preach this—don't seem to follow through on it?

The Bible actually warns against poverty because *"the destruction of the poor is their poverty."*[703] There's a reason the Bible tells us to repeat over and over that God *"takes pleasure in the prosperity of His servant."*[704]

So then why do some people say that it's wrong to have too much? Who gets to define what having too much is? Why are some people so critical of your success?

Is it sinful for us to have a couch? Dining room table? How much must we sacrifice for people to stop criticizing us for having too much in resources?

No matter how much we have, there will always be someone who thinks that it's wrong for us to have it. Yet the irony is how many of those critical people are holding onto material things, even while teaching you how having material things is sinful.

The truth is that God wants you to have material things because you actually need them. There's no other way to accomplish your destiny. Whatever God has called you to do will require resources.

In Matthew 25:14-30, Jesus tells the Parable of the Three Servants and how resources were given to each person. Why would God give out resources if having resources is wrong?

In that parable, they were held accountable for what they did with what they were given. That's another thought to ponder. Each of us was born into different circumstances. Some people have been given more than others.

Yet God only holds us accountable for what we do with what we have. Not what others did or didn't do with their portion. That's why Jesus said, *"To whom much is given, much shall be required."*[705] In that parable, the two servants that were rewarded were the ones who did something with what they were given.

What God wants for you is revealed in the promise of Psalm 23. *"The Lord is my shepherd. I am never in need."*[706]

Now the key that unlocks all of God's goodness is faith. *"Be like those who believe and are patient, and so receive what God has promised."*[707]

Through faith and patience we obtain God's promises (Hebrews 6:12). *"This is the victory that overcomes the world even our faith."*[708] Yet things don't just happen automatically. We have to step out according to our level of faith, moving towards our goals.

Regardless of how little or how much we have, we must keep our hearts open to allow God to guide us into His dream for us.

That's a process that unfolds over a period of time. God tests us in the little things before He can trust us with the big things (Luke 16:10). Step by step we can progress into the good things that God has, as we move according to our level of faith (Romans 12:3).

Part of God's process in our lives will include experiencing some very difficult seasons. God will test our hearts just like the Bible describes how the Israelites passed through a time of testing in the wilderness. After that season ended, Moses reminded them that this had all been part of God's plan. *"So he could humble you, testing you to find out what was in your heart: whether you would keep his commandments or not."*[709]

Then God brought the Israelites into *"a wonderful land"* where they had no more shortage and they lacked nothing.[710]

The suffering according to the will of God that we will experience is only supposed to last for a period of time. The Apostle Paul described, *"Our suffering is light and temporary and is producing for us an eternal glory that is greater than anything we can imagine."*[711]

Notice that the Apostle Paul referred to the suffering as *"temporary."* We can move through that temporary situation into the good things God has waiting for us.

In the darkest moments of our lives, will we have more confidence in the goodness of God than the harshness of our circumstances?

Will we believe God can bring us into the place of abundance that He has for us?

As the Bible describes, *"We went through fire and through water; but you brought us out into a wealthy place."*[712]

Remember that God's dream for you is: *"Beloved, I wish above all things that you may prosper and be in health, even as your soul prospers."*[713]

Think About:

"Remember that it is the Lord your God who gives you the power to become rich. He does this because He is still faithful today to the covenant that He made with your ancestors."
Deuteronomy 8:18 (GNT)

"I wasn't interested in making money as much as in being the first to invent something society needed.
If you do that, the money comes in.
But if you find the market fades away,
get into something else."[714]
-Thomas Edison

"People say that religion and business won't mix. Well, they used to say that oil and water won't mix either, but in our manu- facturing plants we use thousands of gallons of oil, water, and a third ingredient that causes the oil and water to mix for cooling tools as they run at high speed. Religion and business will mix when the Lord Jesus enters the human heart."[715]
-Robert LeTourneau

24

Albert Pujols

"Whatever you do, do everything to the glory of God."
1 Corinthians 10:31b (GW)

Albert Pujols
1980-
From Santo Domingo, Dominican Republic

In 1998, at age twenty-one, Deidre gave birth to a beautiful baby girl with Down Syndrome. She was worried. Even with a degree from Kansas State University, her secretary's salary didn't go very far. How could a young single mother care for this precious little bundle? As she wondered about the future, God's voice interrupted her worried thoughts. *"Trust Me."* She did. In the hospital, Deidre recommitted her life to the Lord. Things were about to change.

Several weeks later, her friends took her out dancing. She needed the break and the fun. There she met a tall, handsome stranger who spoke very little English. She spoke no Spanish. Still, they connected. Before long they were seriously dating. On New Year's Day 2000, they were married. Albert Pujols had fallen in love with Deidre and her daughter, Isabella.

Albert Pujols was barely eighteen years old when he first met Deidre. Up until the age of sixteen, before his family had moved to the United States, he had grown up in the Dominican Republic. There he had happily played baseball without either a bat or a ball. Limes and sticks had taken their place. They had used cardboard cartons to catch the balls (limes) in the absence of mitts.

Pujols was part of a large family that included his grandmother, his father, and his father's eleven siblings, many of whom still lived at home. Pujol's mother had left the family, divorcing his father and disappearing from his life. Still his family, with his grandmother at its helm, was a happy one. There was lots of love to go around. Although electricity and running water were luxuries they lived without, they were able to eat every day. He never felt that his family was poor.

His father, Bienveniedo, was a well known baseball pitcher, but it did not pay well, so he had a second job as a painter. Finding work was hard. At times he would be away from his family for months, working to earn just a little money for their large family.

By the time Pujols was sixteen, his family had relocated to the United States, settling in New York. But the violence that they encountered there frightened his grandmother. One day, as Pujols ran an errand to a grocery store, he witnessed a shooting. Although he safely escaped harm, his terrified grandmother was finished with New York. The family quickly moved to the Midwest.

Teenage Pujols enrolled at Fort Osage High School in Missouri. One morning Coach Dave Fry heard the powerful sound of a bat striking a ball. "*What in the world?*" he thought. He went to see who was in the batting cage and found Pujols there hitting line drive after line drive. He was impressed with what he saw. "*He was a man among boys. I never saw a kid swing so hard on every pitch. Not just once in a while, but every pitch.*"[16]

For the next two and a half years, Fry worked with Pujols. At times it wasn't easy. He was learning English, but still didn't understand enough. Fry coached by acting things out. He had to address some things Pujols had never been taught, like proper throwing technique. It worked. Pujols stunned the high school world with his ability to swing.

It got to where opposing teams refused to pitch to him. He got walked more than any player. Some pitchers would try to injure him by hitting him with the ball, when he stepped up to the plate. Pujols didn't flinch. He just stared them down.

As his baseball skills advanced, his English held him back. At eighteen years old, he was only a high school junior, ineligible for the draft. Staying in high school would deny him the ability to bat, with pitchers who refused to face him. He was advised to find a community college. Pujols found Maple Woods, enrolling in 1999.

Once again, he turned heads. In the very first game, he pulled off the most difficult play in baseball: the unassisted triple play. If that wasn't enough, he finished the same game with a grand slam.

Coach Marty Kilgore noticed, *"He had baseball instincts that just couldn't be taught. The way he would run the bases, going from second to third when a third baseman came up throwing across...just knowing how much to get off so they wouldn't throw behind him....just the little things you can't teach that made him a special player. He was the best athlete I've ever seen with the baseball skills and power."*[17]

By the end of his first year in college, the Cardinals had snapped him up into their minor league. Now he had a $125/week league salary to give Deidre. Pujols kept up his non-stop intense focus on becoming the best. Day in and day out, he practiced.

When the 2001 Cardinal's Spring training camp came along, Mark McGwire sat with Tony La Russa, watching the players practice. Already Pujols had surprised La Russa, by practicing even on his day off. He was a machine that wouldn't stop. La Russa tested him physically, pushing Pujols to the limit. Still, La Russa wasn't sure if Pujols was ready for the big leagues.

Watching him hit a ninth inning home run, McGwire poked La Russa and blurted out, *"Did you see that? How are you not going to take him?"*[18]

La Russa took the risk to put Pujols in the lineup. It turned out to be a record breaking season. His batting average would lead the team. When the season ended, Pujols had become one of the few to earn Rookie of the Year by unanimous vote.

To the sports journalists, Pujols explained, *"God gave me this natural ability. But it's even better when you work hard and you put those two things together. The main thing is I can read a pitcher. I can make adjustments. People wonder how I am able to do that. I don't know. I can't explain. I try to see the ball and have a plan."*[19]

The Cardinals wanted to sign him, but Pujols was a tough negotiator. Back and forth it went. Finally they offered one hundred million for seven years. He would earn every penny, even helping them win the World Series in 2006.

The following year, tragedy struck the Cardinals. Pitcher Josh Hancock died in a car accident after getting behind the wheel while intoxicated. For Pujols, it brought back painful memories of a childhood under an alcoholic father.

Pujols had loved growing up watching his father play baseball, but after most games his father would get drunk. Pujols would have to help his father stagger home even when Pujols was only nine years old and his father was two hundred and thirty-five pounds of weight leaning on him. *"And every night I did it, I kept thinking to myself, 'I can never do this to my son when I grow up.' There's no way a kid should have to go through that."* Pujols remembered, *"Can you imagine what that's like, man? I'm a kid, you know, and I'm dragging him home and putting him to bed drunk."*[20]

While Pujols loved his father, he would grow up determined to avoid substance abuse. That included steroids as Pujols emphasized in an interview, *"I fear God too much to do any stupid thing like that."*[21]

When the 2011 World Series came, once again Pujols would make history. The Cardinals weren't supposed to even be in the 2011 World Series. Not coming out of a season with only eighty-three wins and being one strike away from losing everything.

As Pujols described, *"We're supposed to be home, watching the World Series. Now we're world champions."*[22]

Struggling through games one and two, Pujols couldn't get a hit. He was hit by a pitch and then allowed a run to score by error. Then came game three where Pujols put in what sport writers called, *"The greatest individual hitting performance in World Series history."*[23]

In just one game he achieved five hits, three home runs, and six RBIs. What Pujols had always dreamed.

After that game Pujols began receiving offers from other sports teams. He would accept a deal from the Angels for two hundred fifty-four million over ten years. It would make another one of his dreams come true, giving him the funds to help many other people.

Throughout his career, Albert and Deidre Pujols have opened their hearts and wallets. Many times they have returned to the Dominican Republic, bringing doctors, medicine, supplies, even mattresses, and lots of love. It made a difference in places where there was little to no access to medical care. They built baseball diamonds with nice sports equipment. Pujols also took the time to play baseball with the children for hours. *"That was me twenty-five years ago. I was one of those little boys with no hope, just a dream. This is my passion, and I believe this is what God is calling me to do. Baseball has given me a platform to give back to the community and put a smile on kid's faces."*[24]

So where is Pujols headed now? *"Over the last decade my life has radically changed. I went from being a kid with a dream in the Dominican Republic, to playing professional baseball, Rookie of the Year, National League Most Valuable Player, and winning a Gold Glove and World Championship!"*

"What has not changed is my love for Jesus Christ. If it weren't for Jesus, I would not be where I am today and my life would be without purpose. I've heard kids say they want to be just like me when they grow up. They should know—I want to be just like Jesus."[25]

[After many years together, Albert and Deidre are now divorced and raising their children together.]

24

Becoming Yourself

"God has given each of you a gift.
Use it to help each other."
1 Peter 4:10a (NLV)

One of the most important things we can do as Christians is to be ourselves. To develop the gifts and talents that God has given us. To stay on the pathway toward God's dreams for our life.

While we work towards those goals, sometimes we might feel as though the work we are doing is insignificant. We will be tempted to compare ourselves to other people and feel we are not doing enough for God.

The truth is that God has called different people to do different things. The call of God on one person's life will be completely different than another person's.

We don't have to try to be like anyone else. We just have to develop what God gave us. By focusing on being ourselves, we will do much greater things than if we try to fulfill someone else's calling.

Maybe you're still trying to figure out what your destiny is. If that's where you are, then try not to stress over it. Remember that life is a journey. God has given you the time you need to do what you are called to do. As you continue on that journey, think about these things.

Listen to the desire of your heart. Jesus told us that we don't have to look over here or over there, *"Because the Kingdom of God is within you."*[726]

God has planted certain desires in your heart, which will cause you to be drawn to certain directions in life. Listen to those desires. Try not to be afraid of them. Yes, we all have flesh inside of us, pulling us towards carnal desires. But we also have the Holy Spirit inside of us, drawing us toward God's desires for our lives.

"For God is working in you, giving you the desire and the power to do what pleases him."[727] God has given us the Holy Spirit to help us discern between the desires of our spirit and flesh.

"Let the Holy Spirit guide your lives. Then you won't be doing what your sinful nature craves....The Spirit gives us desires that are the opposite of what the sinful nature desires."[728]

Think about what you do the best. This gifting comes so naturally to you that you might not even notice it. It's the thing that you are drawn to. What you find yourself doing in your free time. What people often complement you for doing. That's the talent God gave you.

People need you to function in that area as the Bible says,

"In his grace, God has given us different gifts for doing certain things well. So if God has given you the ability to prophesy, speak out with as much faith as God has given you. If your gift is serving others, serve them well. If you are a teacher, teach well. If your gift is to encourage others, be encouraging."

"If it is giving, give generously. If God has given you leadership ability, take the responsibility seriously. And if you have a gift for showing kindness to others, do it gladly."[729]

Look at what is available to you. There's a story in 2Kings 4:1-7 of the widow woman who went to Elisha for help.

What was the first thing that Elisha asked her? *"What do you have in the house?"*[30] The miracle came to her through the resources available to her.

God has already given us, *"Everything we need to live a life that pleases God."*[31] The plan of God for your life is right in front of you.

It's available to you. You don't have to look for complicated, difficult things. Find what is available to you right now. Also, keep in mind that God will not reveal every part of your destiny to you immediately.

God waits for you to take the first step. To do what you can with what you have right now.

As you take one step and another step and another step, God will show you what the next step is. Over a period of time, you will find out the rest of the plan after you've taken those early steps.

Stay active. Jesus said to *"Ask, seek, and knock."*[32] To research, study, explore, investigate, and find out things. To take the initiative to study the possibilities that you have right now.

Take a moment and think about your resources. Remember the parable that Jesus told of the three servants. (Matthew 25:15-30)

The servants that pleased God were the ones that went out and did something with the talents they had. While they might have made mistakes, God never got upset at them for making mistakes. God only got upset at the one servant who did nothing with his talent. The one servant who buried his talent in the ground.

You are smarter than that. By staying active it's easier for you to find the God-given opportunities.

Live one day at a time. God's plan for you will unfold over a period of several years. Try not to feel pressured to rush into anything. You don't have to run out and save the world overnight.

Take the time to develop into what God has for you. Make the most of your opportunities and let the rest fall into place.

Try not to wait for signs. Because you love the Lord and want to find His plan for your life, sometimes we can be tempted to wait around, hoping that God will send us a sign of which way to go.

Yet Jesus warned us against looking for signs. (Matthew 16:1-4) Instead of hoping for God to write his plan in the sky or speak to you through the supernatural, you can step out in faith.

Follow the inner guidance of the Holy Spirit in your heart. Don't be afraid of making a mistake. Have more confidence in God's ability to get you back on track than in our own human weakness.

Be yourself. Serve the Lord in the way that comes naturally to you. If you're an introverted personality, then be the best introvert for God. You don't have to become an extrovert. Instead of trying to fit into someone else's mold, find ways to serve God that feel most natural to you while staying grounded in God's Word, letting it light your path.

Be realistic. Thousands of people have moved to California, dreaming of becoming a movie star. While they have strong hopes and dreams, that's not enough to actually achieve their dreams.

We must be realistic about our real potential and humble enough to pursue our real skills. We cannot just blindly chase hopes and dreams. We cannot put our faith in faith. Our faith must always be rooted in God's Word. We must guard against putting our faith in anything other than God's promises.

Look at the big picture. Your destiny is a part of God's plan. While how we fulfill it will vary from person to person, all of us were created by God for reasons such as:

- For relationship with God---------------1 Cor. 1:9 & 2 Cor. 13:14
- To worship God----------------------------John 4:23 & Luke 4:8
- To glorify God-------------------------Matthew 5:16 & John 15:8
- To share the Gospel-----------------------Mark 16:15 & Acts 1:8

Rest in the comfort of knowing that you are fulfilling your destiny when you love God, obey God, love people and share the Gospel within your own personal circle of influence.

As you walk towards your destiny, don't listen to the devil. Because the call of God on your life matters, the devil will do anything to try to convince you to take your own life.

Fight back. Resist the devil. No matter what has happened to you, God still has a great future for you. As long as you are still breathing, you are defeating the devil's plan to destroy you. Everything the devil tells you is a lie. You do have hope. You do have options. God has wonderful things planned for you. Just keep moving towards it.

No matter how many mistakes you have made, God's mercies are new every morning (Lamentations 3:23).

Maybe you are reading this while sitting in a jail cell. You are not alone. God is with you. God has not forgotten you.

You can be a mighty prayer warrior who accomplishes great things for God in prayer, right where you are in that cell (James 5:16).

As you begin to discover your destiny, try not to feel discouraged if it isn't what you thought it would be. Avoid comparing yourself with others. At church we often hear more about the calling to the ministry than any other calling. This can cause us to feel like the only way we can please God is to quit our job and enter the ministry. But the truth is that God gives out all sorts of different callings. The most important calling for you is the one that God gave you.

As we saw earlier, Pujols is touching more lives by playing baseball than he would have by entering the ministry. We also studied how R. G. LeTourneau was called to be a mechanic.

Think about all the machinery he invented that helped so many people because he stayed in his calling. The things that God has called you to do are just as important.

God has called plumbers, police officers, doctors, nurses, soldiers, writers, firefighters, teachers, electricians, engineers, truck drivers, graphic designers, etc. and the work they do helps the rest of us do what we are supposed to do.

"Whatever your hand finds to do, do it with all your strength."[733]

If you're a mechanic, be the best mechanic.

If you're a truck driver, work with all your heart, knowing your work helps people.

Called to the military? Prove your strength by *"Enduring hardness as a good soldier of Jesus Christ."[734]*

If you're a wife and mother, enjoy what God has given you. Know your work is building the future. Remember that society could not exist without mothers. The whole future of society is birthed by mothers.

Make life easier for yourself by focusing on your own calling. As Jesus said, *"Occupy until I come."[735]*

> Remember what Jesus said, *"I am coming soon.*
> *So hold firmly to what you have,*
> *and no one will take away the crown*
> *that you will be given as your reward."[736]*

Think About:

"But God has put all the parts into the body
just as He wants to have them."
1 Corinthians 12:18 (NLV)

"God didn't have time to make a nobody. Every one of us is
important and necessary to God's plan."[737]
-Mary Kay

"In fulfilling our own calling,
there is more happiness than we could dream."[738]
-J.C. Penney

25

Adam Brown

"Don't laugh at me, my enemies. Although I've fallen, I will get up.
Although I sit in the dark, the Lord is my light."
Micah 7:8 (GW)

Adam Brown
1974-2010
From Hot Springs, Arkansas

Even when we get off track from our pathway in life, God gives us
second chances. This story is about how people can change. How even
a drug addict can become a Navy SEAL.

Growing up, Adam Brown was the type of child that had to be
watched closely. He was often practicing the skills of climbing, jump-
ing, and falling.

While his thirst for adventure kept him on the edge of danger, when
things went wrong, a high pain tolerance got him through multiple
broken bones.

He didn't realize how those skills could come in handy until he
saw the movie *Navy Seals* in high school and discovered what he was
born to do.

As soon as he graduated high school, he wanted to join the military. People talked him out of it, telling him to go to college first. So he enrolled in college and worked in his family's electrical business.

Somehow he got involved with the wrong crowd. One particular girlfriend pulled him away from the straight and narrow. The more time he spent with her, the more he sank into addiction.

No longer did he show up on time for work. He began stealing to fund his habit.

One by one he used his friends and family, testing the limits of their patience until they were left with no choice but to cut all ties with him.

Eventually the law caught up to him. Adam was arrested.

His family showed tough love, refusing to bail him out of jail until he was willing to enter drug rehab. That motivated him to enter a program at Teen Challenge.

After completing one year of treatment, he was clean. It was time to move back home.

There he met Kelley. They were in love at first sight and started seeing each other.

Meanwhile, the drugs never quit calling his name. Adam relapsed.

No one knew where he had disappeared. Kelley hunted him down. Determined to find him, she searched through every inch of the town.

Finally, she found him and dragged him away while insisting, *"You are so much better than this!"*[739]

Adam found a job as a waiter and enrolled in college classes again. Kelley kept him busy. Or so she thought. Behind her back, Adam was still using.

When his parents found out, they warned Kelley that Adam couldn't seem to stay clean long enough to make it. She remembers, *"Everyone was telling me to run away from him."*[740]

Kelley thought long and hard about what she wanted in life. *"The more I prayed about it, God told me to stay."*

"I did question the fact, though, whether this was God really wanting me to stay or if maybe it was my own selfish desires, my own desire to get things the way I wanted them."[741]

Adam went back to rehab at Teen Challenge for another month. Then he came home and tried to stay clean.

He didn't last long. Once again Adam disappeared. Again he stole from his parents. Again Kelley hunted him down.

As Kelley drove around town looking for Adam, she had no idea that Adam was watching her. As he saw her go from one place to another, he began to worry that she would get hurt, by putting herself in the wrong place at the wrong time.

From a distance, Adam secretly followed Kelley, making sure she was safe, until she gave up looking for him and went home.

That night, as she drifted off to sleep she decided, *"I need to quit trying to be in control of this, because there is nothing I can do that is going to make him stop. He's got to want it on his own."*[42]

Little did she know that Adam was thinking the same thing. After watching from a distance to make sure she reached home safely, as he drove away that night, he had a long talk with God. He really was in love with Kelley. Hating himself for causing her to suffer and feeling like he didn't deserve her anyway, Adam left town.

Trying to start over, he went to Texas to stay with a friend named Jeff Buschmann. They had known each other since grade school.

In high school Adam had saved Jeff's life after he was stabbed in a fight. Now it was Jeff's turn to help Adam. Together they talked about the future. Adam decided, *"I want to join the military. This is what I wanted to do a long time ago before I lost my direction."*[43]

Jeff questioned if Adam could make it in the military. Adam didn't seem to stick to anything. But the more they talked, Adam decided he was going to try again.

The plan was to move back home and ask Kelley to marry him. Then he would start preparing to meet the strict military qualifications. There was a lot he would have to change if he was going to make it there but he was determined. *"This is what I need to do. I can feel it in my heart."*[44]

Adam flew back home. Kelley said yes. They got married the very next day at the local courthouse. Now the problem was how could a convicted felon be accepted by the Navy?

Adam went down to the local recruiting office and told the truth about his eleven felonies.

The recruiter was not impressed. Getting into the military with one felony was hard enough.

Adam responded by pointing to the picture of Captain Roger Buschmann on the wall. Could the recruiter ask him for a character reference on Adam? The recruiter's eyebrows went up. Captain Buschmann was one of the highest ranking recruiting officers in the Navy. Did he really know Adam?

Turns out that he was the father of Jeff Buschmann and deeply grateful to Adam for having saved Jeff's life many years prior. Returning the favor, he put in a good word for Adam and the paperwork was started.

While waiting for the paperwork to clear, Adam began heavy physical training. All day long as Kelley worked at a local travel agency, he pounded out endless pushups, pull-ups and crunches. He ran miles and swam laps. Soon the paperwork cleared and Adam was notified to report for basic training. Kelley quit her job and moved with him.

Her love kept him on track, from boot camp to BUDs school (Basic Underwater Demolition/Seal training). Knowing that the cells of Adam's body would always crave the high—that having too much downtime or money in his pocket might be too much temptation, she kept a sharp eye on him.

Kelley drove him to and from work, making sure that Adam was never alone. She set boundaries and wouldn't back down. Every dollar was monitored. Every moment was occupied. And Adam loved it. He was living his dream with a whole new set of friends.

Fulfilling his dream to serve in the military, he excelled under tough conditions. Impressing even the harshest critics, he became one of the best of the best.

By the time Adam was accepted to join SEAL Team Six, he had also started a family with Kelley. They had two beautiful children: Nathan and Savannah. Kelley took care of them while he served deployment after deployment.

Adam became known in the military for being totally fearless. Always willing to try the hardest things, he told Kelley, *"I'm not afraid. God gave me this gift—I don't feel fear."*[45]

Adam was also known for never turning down a dare. One time while training in Mississippi, his team noticed a massive red anthill.

Someone got a bright idea. Twenty dollars to the first person who could lay naked on it for thirty seconds. No one volunteered. But as more and more men continued gathering around the anthill, they kept adding money to the betting pool. When the betting pool reached six hundred dollars, Adam stripped down. Lying directly on top of the anthill, he screamed bloody murder as the ants brutally attacked.

Four hundred insect bites later, someone called time and he waddled away. As soon as he was released from medical treatment, he dashed to the local jewelry store. Kelley had been wanting a diamond necklace that they couldn't afford. With that wad of cash, Adam surprised Kelley with the birthday present she couldn't believe.

When September 11, 2001 came, Adam told Kelley he finally knew why God had called him into the military.

Proud of his Arkansas heritage, he loved showing up for work with his military ID stuffed into a *"Welcome to Wal-Mart"* badge. He tucked the Arkansas flag underneath his shirt to remind him what he was fighting for.

Serving in Afghanistan, Adam had a big heart to help people. He kept noticing little children running barefoot on rugged terrain in the bitter cold.

He told Kelley, *"Don't send anything more for me. Just get children's socks and shoes."*[46] She recruited their entire church to send care packages.

Once again, Adam impressed his team. According to an anonymous team guy, *"Here's Adam, in the middle of the war zone, passing out shoes to these kids. It's unbelievable. You know, the military is not the easiest place to live out your faith. But Adam was the guy that everyone looked up to—he would not only talk the talk, but walk the walk."*[47]

The work was still very dangerous. At one point, Adam lost four fingers when his vehicle crashed and rolled.

Using the fingers he had left, he rescued a badly injured teammate. He wouldn't allow the medic to touch him until everyone else was treated.

It took long procedures and the best of surgeons to reattach the fingers to his right hand. This injury made Adam worry about whether he would be able to stay in the military.

Disability retirement was offered. Adam rejected it, preferring to remain with his team. He would continue to suffer severe injuries. One time he lost his right eye when a training operation went wrong. Again he was offered disability retirement. Again he declined. He returned to help his team work in the most dangerous places.

On March 17, 2010, his ten year old son Nathan had a feeling of what was about to happen. Then came the knock at the door, dreaded by every military family.

"The minute I saw Daddy's friends there, they didn't have to tell me what happened," Nathan recalled, *"God had been telling me all day."*[748]

Hunting a high ranking Taliban officer, Adam's team had gone into a part of Afghanistan where no American had been before.

One particular enemy leader was responsible for numerous American deaths. Adam's team wasn't coming back until they caught him.

Entering his heavily fortified compound, the team encountered heavy fire. Worrying about the safety of nearby civilians, the team decided against blowing the whole building. Instead they tried to pick off the hidden shooters one at a time.

Adam saw where the main shooter was crouching but couldn't get an angle to take him down. Someone had to advance forward.

Adam volunteered. Getting into position, Adam was hit while protecting his team from the hail of bullets. As they were carrying him out, hoping to get him to the hospital before it was too late, his last words were, *"I'm okay."*[749]

Years later, what happened that night was described by one of Adam's team guys on the Shawn Ryan Podcast #94 (January 29, 2024).

Dom Rasso had gotten to know Adam while they served together on Seal Team Six. *"We started in sniper school. We went through green team together. We sparred together."*

Dom was impressed by Adam's deep faith and love for his family. *"There were times when I'm like, 'Hey Adam, we're going to the bar.'"*

"He's like: 'I've got a ball game with my son or I'm doing something else with my children.'"

Dom said, *"He poured his heart out. I went to a couple dinners with his wife and him. He talked about his children. Of course Christ was a part of his life. You could tell there was something different there. He was bringing guys to the faith."*

"Adam was a go getter. He would always put himself in bad positions to protect and help everyone else. That was one of those nights."

"The guys were above a room and above a structure that was getting shot through. That's when Craig got shot in the arm. So Adam jumped into action and tried to flank wherever that (shooter) position was."

"In pure Adam Brown fashion, he shimmied up a tree and then wedged himself between a tree and the wall and tried to get in the best position to get an angle in there. Right at the time he was getting to the top of his position, someone came out and just sprayed the wall (with bullets) and he got hit in the side."

"I would not have expected anything less from Adam to find the one spot he could shimmy up and try to get an angle on."

"What I want people to know is that Adam was like—I'm going to try and help my brothers, I'm going to pour my heart into this because it will make the guys better. I'm going to try to get in the best position possible and I'm going to go and do what I need to do. He went out fighting. That's what he did with everything in his life. He's like, where can I ambush the bad guy? Where can I go out in front of everyone else and try to get in the best position possible?"

"I wish I had the level of faith Adam did to trust in God's plan. Because we don't stick to Biblical principles, because we don't get in the Bible everyday, because we don't recognize the love of Christ in our lives, we veer away from the truth of what we are supposed to be doing but he had that spark in him."

The funeral was held at Adam's church in Hot Springs, Arkansas.

As his pictures were shown on the video screen, his kids Nathan and Savannah started crying.

Adam's teammates came over to hug them, whispering, *"When you lost one father, you gained twenty new fathers."*[50]

Adam's team comforted Kelley with the remembrance of what Adam had accomplished.

His friend John Faas told Kelley, *"Adam died a hero, protecting his teammates. Tomorrow, we avenge him."*[51]

Almost one year later, Faas and the rest of Adam's team would invite Kelley to come celebrate with them after they had taken down Osama Bin Laden.

25

Second Chances

"Anyone who belongs to Christ is a new person.
The past is forgotten, and everything is new."
2Corinthians 5:17(CEV)

Note to readers: please don't try this at home. Even though Kelley succeeded in helping Adam transform his life, it's not always possible to rescue people. Thinking that if you just try hard enough, you can change someone else is very dangerous.

The truth is that no matter how hard you try or how much you sacrifice—you can't change other people. You can be the perfect spouse and yet still feel the pain of watching your mate choose evil. That's not your fault. Each person is responsible for their own decisions.

If your mate has chosen to walk the path of evil, be careful about hoping they will change. Be honest with yourself, recognizing when that person is causing tremendous damage.

Understand when something needs to be done to protect yourself from the consequences of their bad choices. Don't wait around too long for them to change.

Recognize that some people will never change—even if you sacrifice your whole life trying to help them.

There comes a point when you have to move on and stop sacrificing to help them if they are still refusing to change themselves.

There will be people in your life that you have to walk away from. There will be times that you have to leave to protect yourself. Never be afraid to let go. Remember there's only so much you can do for others.

Think about how God handles these situations. Even God sets limits on how long He will help us. While God does love us unconditionally, He only gives us a limited time to repent before the judgment comes. Thus the Bible warns us, *"Seek the Lord while he may be found."*[52]

The story of Adam Brown is about repentance. Saying sorry wasn't enough. Repentance wasn't just asking for forgiveness. Real repentance meant turning around and going in the other direction. That's what Adam did.

Adam's powerful story of redemption was included to encourage all of us that even though we have made mistakes, God will send us second chances.

We begin our journey with God by believing in Jesus and how He died on the cross and rose for our sins. Then we asked God to forgive our sins. If it's been a long time since you asked God for forgiveness, take a moment to do that right now.

We walk with God by turning away from the pleasures of the world to obey Christ. By following Christ. Studying His words. Trying to become more like Him. Doing what He told us to do. Believing the words of Christ over anyone else. Staying faithful to God no matter how much pressure the world puts on us to walk away.

Committing your life to God can feel like getting on a rollercoaster. Once you've made the decision to get on the rollercoaster, just relax and enjoy it. You can't control everything that happens but as long as you hold onto God, God will hold onto you.

Enjoy the ride as it carries you to your destination—Jesus' promise: *"And I give them eternal life. They will never be lost, and no one will tear them away from Me."*[53]

The greatest day of your life is yet to come.

Someday you'll close your eyes on earth and open them in Heaven. Family and friends will greet you with open arms. All those things you did for God that seemed unnoticed on Earth will be recognized in Heaven.

The scars that you suffered here will be your medals of honor there.

And Jesus will be looking at you saying, *"Well done, you good and faithful servant; you have been faithful over a few things, I will make you ruler over many things—enter into the joy of your Lord."*[754]

Think About:

"For to me, living means living for Christ,
and dying is even better."
Philippians 1:21 (NLT)

"It is the inward, not the outward noise that keeps people from hearing the voice of God, and the will of God for them. Before you can hear, you must be willing to listen."[755]
-James Kraft

"God took me by the hand from my poor log cabin and put me at the head of the greatest nation. Yet as we must all die, may God grant me the honor to die for my nation."[756]
-President Abraham Lincoln
June 9, 1864

26

Quotes to Remember

"Then God, who gives peace,
will soon crush Satan under your feet."
Romans 16:20a (CEV)

"Love, not fear, must be our guide."[757]
-Rosa Parks

"Fear no one. Fear is the cause of all idolatry."[758]
-William Tyndale

"God made you for victory and not defeat. To have dominion is your
mission. Therefore, work, read, think, meditate, commune with
the Source of wisdom, seeking Him to guide your plans."[759]
-J.C. Penney

"Before doing anything else, seek God's will and put your trust in Him. If I were able, I would blot out every scrap of my life not devoted to the Lord and to His cause."[760]

-William Colgate

"Never cut short your time with God, no matter how much pressure you feel."[761]

-Henry Crowell

"God's plan is the only safe plan. Through it, He leads us far beyond our own human dreams."[762]

-Merrell Vories

"Long ago, when the Lord told me 'Go, free My people,' I felt like Moses. I said, 'No, I can't. Get some better educated person.' But He told me, 'I want you.' Then I decided that as long as I live, I would do what He told me to do."[763]

-Harriet Tubman

"There is literally nothing that I ever wanted to do that I asked the Creator to help me to do, that I have not been able to accomplish. The secret lies right in the promises of God. Those promises are real, but so few people believe that they are real. They are infinitely more solid and substantial than the table beside you. If you would only believe."[764]

-Dr. George Washington Carver

"Do the best you can, where you are, with what you have today."[765]
-Henry Heinz

"It has seemed as if I was favored and got increase because the Lord knew
that I was going to turn around and give it back."[766]
-John D. Rockefeller Sr.

"The moral out of my life is don't quit at age sixty-five.
Maybe your boat hasn't come in yet. Mine hadn't."[767]
-Colonel Harland Sanders

"Keep going when everyone else quits. That's how I designed machinery.
The bright idea you start with seems to grow dim as you squirm through
the maze of problems looking for a solution.
After you've tried a hundred things that didn't work,
keep on beating out your brains until you find the answer.
For the answer that you'll get then will be different
than anyone ever thought of before, giving you the unique advantage."[768]
-R. G. LeTourneau

"The one thing I learned from all my camping trips with Thomas Edison
and Henry Ford was this advice—Go it alone.
Never fail to try because someone has already tried and failed."[769]
-Harvey Firestone

"I had to make my own living and my own opportunity. But I made it! Don't sit down and wait for the opportunities to come. Get up and make them."[770]
-Madam CJ Walker

"Swim upstream. If everybody else is doing it one way, there's a good chance you can find your niche by going in exactly the opposite direction."[771]
-Sam Walton

"Don't worry. You can't change the past, but you sure can ruin the present by worrying over the future. Remember that half the things we worry about never happen and the other half are going to happen anyway."[772]
-Kemmons Wilson

"Do not let yourself be forced into anything before you are ready."[773]
-Wilbur Wright

"You doubtless will make some mistakes, just as we do, and just as everybody else does."[774]
-Orville Wright

"If God can forgive us for our sins and errors—and He can and does when we ask Him to—then surely we can forgive ourselves."[775]
-Wallace Johnson

"No matter how many failures you make in other directions, do not fail to find a few minutes to study or read your Bible."[776]
-Booker T. Washington

"I have always been thankful that I had a mother who revered the Bible. It was her daily food, and she never let a Sunday go by without reading some portion of it, and in her humble way explained it to me.
What she instilled in me as a boy helped me to keep my feet on the ground when the going was tough."[777]
-Milton Hershey

"A daily reading and meditation on the Word of God is of utmost importance in our Christian life
that we may learn to know God and His will toward us."[778]
-A. A. Hyde

"Read the Scriptures for yourself. Find out what God really requires of you. Never just follow along what your leaders tell you."[779]
-Susan Schmidt

"Learn to love yourself. Get your own identity back."[780]
-Irene Spencer

"There is no safer reliance than upon the God of our fathers who will not forsake us so long as we obey His commandments and walk humbly in His footsteps."[781]
-President William McKinley

"I believe that our Heavenly Father invented man because He was disappointed with the monkey."[782]
-Mark Twain

"The Almighty has His plans, and will work them out; and, whether we see it or not, they will be the best for us. I seek His counsel, lay my plans before Him, and never begin proceeding in a new direction without being assured, as far as I could be, of His approval."[783]
-President Abraham Lincoln

"I've found that when you just let go and place yourself in God's hands, everything in your life goes right. When you try to do everything alone and rely on yourself, you begin to make major errors."[784]
-Mary Kay

"My life is not mostly dedicated to the Lord, it is 100% committed to Jesus Christ and His will. Baseball is simply my platform to elevate Jesus Christ."[785]
-Albert Pujols

"Just know that God can perform miracles."[786]
-Kelley Brown

"If you will cultivate first the listening mind and heart—if you will hear the will of God for you—nothing can keep you from triumphant success in life. Nothing can keep you from developing your own full potential."[787]
-James Kraft

"Our people defeated Satan because of the blood of the Lamb and the message of God. They were willing to give up their lives."
Revelations 12:11 (CEV)

Jesus promised, *"To those who win the victory I will give the right to sit beside Me on My throne, just as I have been victorious and now sit by my Father on His throne."* Revelation 3:21 (GNT)

Author's Note:
Throughout this book you've read about how people overcame everything that the world did to them.
They fulfilled their destiny.
You have a destiny too.
People need you to fulfill it.
My dream is that these stories will inspire you to:

Let your love for God burn stronger than the pain you feel.

Forget about the past. God can give you more than you lost.

Focus on what the Holy Spirit is telling you.

Do what Jesus said to do: *"Ask, Seek, Knock"* and do research until you find your destiny.

Move towards God's dreams for you.

27

Bonus Story: Tommy Ratzlaff

"The road the righteous travel is like the sunrise, getting brighter and brighter until daylight has come."
Proverbs 4:18 (GNT)

Photo of Tommy looking at the sunrise is courtesy of the Ratzlaff family

Tommy Ratzlaff
1977-2011
From: Green Forest, Arkansas

With close to two decades in the Navy SEALs Tommy Ratzlaff had worked his way up to being a Senior Chief Petty Officer. Carefully, he led men through one dangerous mission after another and he started each one with prayer.

Growing up in Green Forest, Arkansas, Tommy had always dreamed of the day he would become a SEAL. Getting to high school, he played football as a linebacker while the town of twenty-seven hundred people cheered him on. His coach, Jim Atkinson, would remember, *"Failure was not an option with Tommy. If he wasn't successful the first time, he got up, dusted himself off and said, 'Let's do it again.'"*[788]

Falling in love, Tommy married his sweetheart. In fourteen years together they had two sons and a daughter. Right after high school he volunteered for the military where he would serve around the world. His service would be recognized with many honors. For saving the lives of Canadian soldiers in Afghanistan, he received the Star of Military Valor. He also earned multiple Bronze Stars, National Defense Service Medals, and even the Enlisted Surface Warfare Specialist. Yet he didn't talk much about it or any of his other awards. Everyone knew him as a humble warrior.

On SEAL Team Six, Tommy Ratzlaff and Adam Brown worked together. Impressed by his testimony, Tommy became the driving force behind getting Adam's story told. When writer Eric Blehm began researching to write a biography on Adam's life, Tommy volunteered to meet with Eric to tell the powerful story of Adam's transformation. He brought other team guys who knew Adam and were able to give Eric the details of what Adam had achieved.

As the years passed by, Ratzlaff served twelve deployments. Every time he climbed into a helicopter, he would quietly say the Lord's Prayer and intercede for his team.[789]

In his own words he would describe, *"Then I move straight into thinking about what I'm about to do—the target, the map study, making sure I know which way's north so I can call out things correctly on the target."*[790]

On August 6, 2011, Tommy met Jesus face to face and Adam gave him a bear hug. Some of our bravest walked through the Pearly Gates in Heaven together after their helicopter was shot down over Afghanistan.

His home state of Arkansas would honor Tommy by flying all flags at half staff when his body came home. At his funeral, those who loved him the most would celebrate his life. His nephew, Jeff Adams, would say, *"He was a hero to our family. He did what he loved and died defending those he loved and those who loved him."*[791]

His sister Julie Adams, described, *"Tommy would have been grateful for the outpouring of love, support and prayers for his family, but would want the focus to remain on the cause for which he made this sacrifice, not the sacrifice itself."*[792]

Bibliography

Abbe, Truman, and Hubert Howson. *Robert Colgate, The Immigrant; a Genealogy of the New York Colgates.* New Haven, CT: Tuttle, Moorehouse & Taylor, 1941.

"About Adam Brown." Adam Brown Legacy Fund. 2013. www.adamslegacy.com.

Abrams, Garry. "Ervil LeBaron Said God Told Him to Kill......" *Los Angeles Times,* September 20, 1992.

Abrams, Dennis. *Albert Pujols.* New York: Chelsea House, 2008.

Adams, John, Abigail Adams, and Charles F. Adams. *Familiar Letters of John Adams and His Wife Abigail Adams,* Boston: Houghton, Mifflin, 1875. Kindle Edition.

Allen, Gov. Henry. "Trying to Get His Debt All Paid Off." In *YMCA Association Men,* 676-706. Vol. 44. North America: Young Man's Christian Association, 1919. Google Books.

American Experience: The Wright Stuff. Directed by Nancy Porter. WGBH Educational Foundation, 1996. DVD.

"American President: William McKinley." Miller Center. 2013.

"Angels Reach Agreement In Principle With Albert Pujols." MLB.com. December 8, 2011.

Arber, Edward. *The Story of the Pilgrim Fathers, 1606-1623 A.D.: As Told by Themselves, Their Friends, and Their Enemies.* London: Ward and Downey, 1897. Google Books.

Ash, Mary Kay. *Mary Kay.* New York: Harper & Row, 1981.

Ash, Mary Kay. *Mary Kay, You Can Have It All: Lifetime Wisdom from America's Foremost Woman Entrepreneur.* Rocklin, CA: Prima Pub., 1995.

Associated Press. "Fugitive Daughter of Polygamist Ervil LeBaron Arrested." DeseretNews.com. May 14, 2010.

Associated Press. "Portraits of Navy SEALs Killed In Helicopter Crash." The Seattle Times. August 11, 2011.

Bancroft, George. *History of the United States.* Vol. 1. New York: Appleton, 1888. Google Books.

Bancroft, George. *History of the United States.* Vol. 6. Boston: Routledge & Warne, 1861. Google Books.

Benson, Tom. "Orville Wright's Biography." & "Wilbur Wright's Biography." National Aeronautics and Space Administration. NASA. April 26, 2010.

"Biography of Vories." Omni 8. Web. 2012.

Blehm, Eric. *Fearless: The Undaunted Courage and Ultimate Sacrifice of Navy SEAL Team Six Operator Adam Brown.* Colorado Springs, CO: WaterBrook Press, 2012.

Blehm, Eric. "The Navy SEALS' Dying Words." Time Magazine Website Article. August 6, 2012.

Bradford, William, and Charles F. Adams. *History of Plymouth Plantation.* Vol. 1-2. Boston: Massachusetts Historical Society, 1912. Google Books.

Bragg, Melvyn. *The Book of Books: The Radical Impact of the King James Bible, 1611-2011.* Berkeley, CA: Counterpoint, 2011.

Bradlee, Ben, and Dale Van Atta. *Prophet of Blood: The Untold Story of Ervil LeBaron and the Lambs of God.* New York: Putnam, 1981.

Brodie, James Michael. *Created Equal: The Lives and Ideas of Black American Innovators.* New York: W. Morrow, 1993.

Bronstein, Phil. "The Man Who Killed Osama Bin Laden... Is Screwed." Esquire Website Article. February 11, 2013.

Brown, Frank. *A Sunday School Tour of the Orient, by a Commission Authorized by the World's Sunday School Association.* Garden City, NY: Doubleday & Page, 1914. Google Books.

Bobrick, Benson. *Wide as the Waters: The Story of the English Bible and the Revolution It Inspired.* New York: Simon & Schuster, 2001.

Booker T Washington Society. New York Times Obituary, "On The Death of Booker T. Washington." November 15, 1915.

Bradford, Sarah. *Harriet Tubman, the Moses of Her People.* New York: Lockwood, 1886. Archive.org.

Bradford, Sarah. *Scenes in the Life of Harriet Tubman.* Auburn: W. J. Moses Printer, 1869. Archive.org

Bridges, George. *The Oxford Reformers and English Church Principles: Their Rise, Trial, and Triumph.* London: E. Stock, 1908. Google Books.

Brown, Marcus Monroe. *A Study of John D. Rockefeller.* Cleveland, 1905. Google Books.

"Bryan Burwell Article." Gateway Redbirds. May 6, 2007.

Bundles, A'Lelia Perry. www.madamcjwalker.com. 2012. Web. *A'Lelia is the Great-Great-Granddaughter of Madam CJ Walker.*

Bundles, A'Lelia Perry. *On Her Own Ground: The Life and Times of Madam C.J. Walker.* New York: Scribner, 2001.

Burford, Betty, and Loren Chantland. *Chocolate by Hershey: A Story about Milton S. Hershey.* Minneapolis: Carolrhoda Books, 1994.

Burroughs, John. *Under the Maples,* Boston: Houghton Mifflin, 1921.

Carey, Charles W. *American Inventors, Entrepreneurs, and Business Visionaries.* New York: Facts on File, 2002.

Chernow, Ron. *Titan: The Life of John D. Rockefeller, Sr.* New York: Random House, 1998.

Christian, Ralph J. *American Association for State and Local History: Historic Landmarks Project.* June 1977. U.S. National Park Service: National Register of Historic Places Inventory Nomination Form, Kemmerer, Wyoming.

Clinton, Hillary. "Senator Clinton Secures Funding to Repay Harriet Tubman Civil War Pension." HARRIET TUBMAN. October 29, 2003.

Clark, Glenn. *The Man Who Talks With the Flowers; the Intimate Life Story of Dr. George Washington Carver.* Saint Paul, MN: Macalester Park, 1939.

Clarke, Francis. *The Life of William Tyndale.* London: W. Swan Sonnenschein, 1883. Google Books.

"The Code of 1650: Being A Compilation of the Earliest Laws and Orders," Hartford: S. Andrus, 1822. www.openlibrary.org.

Collins, Mary. "I Have Today Seen Wilbur Wright and His Great White Bird." Air and Space Magazine. March 2003.

"1979 Colonel Sanders Interview." Interview by Coleman McDuff. Youtube Video. Posted March 10, 2011.

Criswell, W. A. "Christ and This Crucial Hour." Church Service, First Baptist Church of Dallas, Dallas, March 6, 1979.

Crouch, Tom D. *The Bishop's Boys: A Life of Wilbur and Orville Wright.* New York: W.W. Norton, 1989.

Crowell Trust. *The Henry Parsons Crowell and Susan Coleman Crowell Trust Founders Directive.* Colorado Springs, CO: Board of Trustees, 1927. www.crowelltrust.org.

Crump, Steve. "Passage from Polygamy." Banderas News. April 26, 2006.

Curry, Mary E. "J. C. Penney Biographical Sketch." In *American National Biography.* Vol. 17. New York: Oxford University Press, 1997.

Daniell, David. *The Bible in English: Its History and Influence.* New Haven: Yale University Press, 2003.

Daniell, David. *William Tyndale: A Biography.* New Haven: Yale University Press, 1994.

Daniell, David. *Tyndale's New Testament.* New Haven: Yale University Press, 1989.

D'Antonio, Michael. *Hershey: Milton S. Hershey's Extraordinary Life of Wealth, Empire, and Utopian Dreams*. New York: Simon & Schuster, 2006.

Day, Richard. *A Christian in Big Business; the Life Story of Henry Parsons Crowell*. Chicago: Moody Press, 1946.

"Dedication of the Harriet Tubman Home." HARRIET TUBMAN. June 24, 1908.

Della Cava, Marco R. "George Lucas' 'Red Tails' Salutes Tuskegee Airmen." *USA Today*, January 5, 2012.

Demaus, R., and Richard Lovett. *William Tyndale, a Biography; a Contribution to the Early History of the English Bible*. London: Religious Tract Society, 1886. Google Books.

Denawa, Mai. "The Great Kanto Earthquake of 1923." Brown University. 2005.

Denger, Mark J. "California's Story of Flight . . . A Historical Perspective." California Aviation History. Accessed January 08, 2013. www.Militarymuseum.org.

Depew, Chauncey. *1795-1895. One Hundred Years of American Commerce*. New York: D.O. Haynes, 1895. 422-28. Google Books.

Dick, John and Anne Richardson. *William Tyndale and the Law*. Kirksville, MO: Sixteenth Century Journal Publishers, 1994.

DiGiovanna, Mike. "The Angel As Guardian: Albert Pujols' Charitable Commitment." Los Angeles Times. February 13, 2012.

Drew, Benjamin. *A Northside View of Slavery*. Boston: J.P. Jewett, 1856. Google Books.

"Dynamic and Destructive." Transcript. In *Fearless (Day 1 of 3) Guest Kelley Brown*. Family Life Today Radio. November 7, 2012.

Duke, Alan. "'I Wouldn't Wish This On Anyone.' Navy SEAL Widow Says." CNN. August 8, 2011.

Durham, Ken. "Robert Gilmour LeTourneau." Texas State Historical Association. 2012.

Ecenbarger, William. "Milton Hershey School Begins Its 100th Year." *The Inquirer* (Pennsylvania), July 7, 2011.

Edes, Gordon. "One That Got Away." Boston.com. October 11, 2006.

Edwards, Ethel. *Carver of Tuskegee.* Self-Published, 1976.

Elliott, Alan C. "Mary Kay Does a Beautiful Thing." *Texas Ingenuity: Inventions, Inventors & Innovators.* Dallas, TX: Atriad, 2010. 76-80.

Ellis, James Joseph. *William Tyndale.* New York: Thomas Whittaker, 1890. Google Books.

"Ervil LeBaron, Utah Polygamist Is Found Dead in His Prison Cell." *New York Times,* August 17, 1981.

"Escaping Polygamy." Interview by Carrie Seim. Betty Confidential. March 30, 2009.

Everts, W. W. *William Colgate: The Christian Layman.* Philadelphia: American Baptist Publication Society, 1881.

Farris, Michael. *From Tyndale to Madison: How the Death of an English Martyr Led to the American Bill of Rights.* Nashville, TN: B & H Pub. Group, 2007.

Federer, William. *America's God and Country: Encyclopedia of Quotations.* Coppell, TX: Fame, 1994.

Federer, William. *George Washington Carver: His Life & Faith in His Own Words.* St. Louis, MO: Amerisearch, 2002.

Ferrell, John. *Fruits of Creation: A Look at Global Sustainability as Seen Through the Eyes of George Washington Carver.* Shakopee, MN: Macalester Park, 1995.

"Final Mission." Transcript. In *Fearless (Day 3 of 3) Guest Kelley Brown.* Family Life Today Radio. November 9, 2012.

"Financier's Fortune in Oil Amassed In Industrial Era of Rugged Individualism." *NY Times* May 24, 1937.

Fineberg, Gail. "'Let There Be Light' Exhibition Spotlights William Tyndale, English Martyr." *Library of Congress* 56, no. 12 (July 1997). www.loc.gov

Firestone, Harvey and Samuel Crowther. *Men and Rubber; the Story of Business,* Garden City, NY: Doubleday & Page, 1926.

Fisher, Isaac. "The Funeral of Booker T. Washington." Booker T. Washington Society. November 18, 1915.

Fletcher, Grace. *The Bridge of Love.* New York: Dutton, 1967.

"The Flight Forebears." Smithsonian Education - Stories of the Wrights' Flight. 2013.

Flynn, John T. *God's Gold; the Story of Rockefeller and His Times,.* New York: Harcourt, Brace, 1932.

Forbes, B. C. *Men Who Are Making America.* New York: B.C. Forbes, 1917. 296-309. Google Books.

"*Fortune 500 2012: Annual Ranking of America's Largest Corporations from Fortune Magazine.*" CNNMoney. May 21, 2012.

Foraker, Joseph Benson. *Tributes to Wm. McKinley.* Cincinnati: [s.n.], 1901. PDF. www.hathitrust.org.

Frere, Walter Howard, Charles Edward Douglas, John Field, W. T, and Thomas Cartwright. *Puritan Manifestoes. A Study of the Origin of the Puritan Revolt.* London: www.openlibrary.org.

Fowler, Glenn. "Obituaries: Wallace E. Johnson, Co Founder of Holiday Inns Chain in 1950's." *NY Times,* April 29, 1988.

Foxe, John. *The Acts and Monuments of John Foxe: A New and Complete Edition.* Edited by Stephen Cattley. Vol. 5. London: R.B. Seeley and W. Burnside, 1837. Google Books.

Funk, Isaac K., Wilfred J. Funk, William B. Woods, and Arthur S. Draper. "Queen of Gotham's Colored 400." *Literary Digest.* By Edward J. Wheeler. Vol. 55. 1917. 75-79. Google Books.

Gammon, Roland. *Faith Is a Star,* New York: Dutton, 1963.

Gates, Henry Louis. *Life upon These Shores: Looking at African American History, 1513-2008.* New York: Alfred A. Knopf, 2011.

Gee, Henry, and William Harvey, eds. "*First Act of Succession: 1534.*" In Documents Illustrative of English Church History, 232-33. London: Macmillan, 1914. Luminarium: Encyclopedia Project.

Gokhman, Jennifer. "A Secret Life." Lodi News Sentinel. 2006.

Gorski, Eric. "Mormons Launch Campaign to Put Distance between Themselves and Polygamists." USATODAY.com. June 26, 2008.

Government, U.S., U.S. Army, and Central Intelligence Agency. Spies and Spying in the Civil War. 2012 ed. Kindle Edition.

Gross, Daniel. *Forbes Greatest Business Stories of All Time.* New York: J. Wiley & Sons, 1996. 262-83.

Hallett, Anthony, and Diane Hallett. *Entrepreneur Magazine: Encyclopedia of Entrepreneurs.* New York: Wiley, 1997.

Hammer, Joshua. "The Great Japan Earthquake of 1923." Smithsonian Magazine. May 2011.

Hansell, George. *Reminiscences of Baptist Churches and Baptist Leaders in New York City and Vicinity; from 1835-1898.* Philadelphia: American Baptist Publication Society, 1899. Print. Google Books.

Hardin, Shields. *The Colgate Story.* New York: Vantage, 1959.

HARRIET TUBMAN. Web. www.harriettubman.com

"Harvey S. Firestone and Henry Ford: Joining Rubber to Rims." Firestone100.com. February 10, 2000.

"Harvey Samuel Firestone." Gale Encyclopedia of U.S. Economic History, 1999.

Hartman, Emory. *"God's Little Workshop." Altoona Mirror* (Pennsylvania), July 23, 1943.

Hayes, Thomas C. "Sam Walton Is Dead at 74; The Founder of Wal-Mart Stores." *New York Times.* April 6, 1992.

Hendricks, Nancy. "Charles Kemmons Wilson (1913-2003)." Encyclopedia of Arkansas. February 22, 2013.

Heinz, Henry J. *Henry J. Heinz: Founder & President, H.J. Heinz Company.* Pittsburgh, PA: Company, 1919.

"Heinz John Heinz: A Man of Uncommon Vision." & "Heinz Ketchup: A 135-Year History of Innovation." Heinz Corporate History. 2012. Web.

Hill, Harvey. *He Heard God's Whisper,* Minneapolis, MN: Jorgenson Press, 1943.

Hinkle, Marla. "Behind the Chocolate Curtain." The Morning News. Bentonville, Arkansas. February 8, 2004.

"H. J. Heinz Is Victim of Pneumonia." Carnegie Library of Pittsburgh. May 14, 1919.

Hogan, Dr. John. "20 Steps for Success." Hospitality Net. October 22, 2010.

Howard, Fred. *Wilbur and Orville: A Biography of the Wright Brothers.* New York: Knopf, 1987.

Holt, Rackham. *George Washington Carver: An American Biography.* Garden City, NY: Doubleday, Doran and, 1943.

Holt, Rosa Belle, DR. "A Heroine In Ebony." In *The Chautauquan: A Weekly Newsmagazine.* 459-62. Chautauqua, NY: Chautauqua Press, 1896. Google Books.

Hume, David. *History of England from the Invasion of Julius Caesar.* Vol. 4. London: Frederick Warne &, 1884. Google Books.

Huffman, Lambert. *Not of This World.* Canton, OH: Self-Published, 1951.

Humes, James. "Bishop's Sons Helped Give Mankind Wings." December 11, 2011.

Hunt, Gaillard. *The History of the Seal of the United States.* Washington, D.C.: United States Dept. of State, 1909. Google Books.

Hyde, A. A. "The Modern Man and His Money." In *Rural Manhood,* 20-23. Vol. 4. New York: International YMCA, 1913. Google Books.

Hyde, John. "A Balm in Gilead." *Kansas History: A Journal of the Central Plains.* 9 (1987): 150-63. Kansas State Historical Society.

Ingham, John N. *Biographical Dictionary of American Business Leaders.* Westport, CT: Greenwood, 1983.

"Irene Spencer Speaks." Just One Wife. 2008.

Irving, George. *Master of Money: A.A. Hyde of Wichita.* London: Fleming H. Revell Company, 1936.

James, Charles. "The 1923 Tokyo Earthquake and Fire." University of California Berkely. October 8, 2002.

"John D. Rockefeller Dies at 97 in His Florida Home; Funeral to Be Held Here." *NY Times* May 24, 1937.

Johnson, Wallace E., and Eldon Roark. *Together We Build: The Life and Faith of Wallace E. Johnson.* New York: Hawthorn Books, 1978.

Jarman, Rufus. "LeTourneau: America's Most Spectacular Maker of Earth-Moving Machines Is 'In Partnership With God.'" *Life Magazine,* October 16, 1944, 49-59.

Jenness, Mary. *The Man Who Asked God Questions: Dr. George Washington Carver.* New York: Friendship Press, 1946.

Johnson, Jamica. "Arkansas Navy SEAL Remembered." Navy.mil. August 17, 2011.

Johnson, William. *Abraham Lincoln the Christian.* New York: Eaton & Mains, 1913. Google Books.

Johnson, William. *George Washington the Christian.* New York: Abington Press, 1919. Google Books.

"Kelley Brown: A Fearless Widow." In *700 Club.* CBN. Accessed December 27, 2012.

Kelly, Fred C. *The Wright Brothers: The Authorized Biography of Two Americans Whose Inventive Genius Changed The World.* New York: Ballantine's Books, 1950.

"Kemmons Wilson School of Hospitality and Resort Management." University of Memphis. December 20, 2012.

Kingseed, Wyatt. "President William McKinley: Assassinated by an Anarchist." American History Magazine. October 1, 2001.

Klepper, Michael and Robert Gunther. *The Wealthy 100: From Benjamin Franklin to Bill Gates—a Ranking of the Richest Americans, Past and Present.* Secaucus, NJ: Carol Pub. Group, 1996.

Knox, Andrew. "Albert Pujols: A Hero's Worship." Albert Pujols: A Hero's Worship. 2012.

Kraft, James L. "Face Up To Fear." *The Guideposts Anthology,.* Pawling, NY: Guideposts Associates, 1953. 236-38.

Kraft, James L. "Face Up To Fear." *Spokane Daily Chronicle,* February 26, 1953.

Kraft, James L. *Like Unto; a Philosophical Review of a Vacation Journey on Strange Waters,* 1939.

Kraft, James L. "A Message of Inspiring Faith From James L. Kraft." *Miami News,* February 16, 1951.

Kraft, James L. "Pattern For Prosperity." *New Guideposts,* New York: Prentice-Hall, 1951. 186-190.

Kraft, James L. "Pattern for Prosperity." *St. Petersburg Times,* February 16, 1951.

Kraft, James L. *Adventure in Jade.* New York: H. Holt, 1947.

Kreydatus, Beth. "Enriching Women's Lives: The Mary Kay Approach to Beauty, Business, and Feminism." *Business and Economic History Online* 3 (2005): 1-35. www.thebhc.org.

Lagace, Martha. "Beauty Entrepreneur Madam Walker." *Harvard Business School Cases* (June 25, 2007). *Harvard Business School.*

Lamb, Scott, and Tim Ellsworth. *Pujols: More than the Game.* Nashville, TN: Thomas Nelson, 2011.

Larner, Robert M. "The President's Bible and the Important Part It Has Played in Many Historic Inaugurations." *Saturday Evening Post* 177, no. 3 (January 7, 1905): 15. Google Books.

Latham, Charles. "Madam CJ Walker Biographical Sketch." Indiana Historical Society. June 1, 2004.

Layman's Missionary Movement. "Speech By A. A. Hyde." In *Proceedings of the Men's Missionary Congress of the U.S.A May 3-6, 1910,* 358-62. Chicago, IL: Layman's Missionary Movement, 1910. Google Books.

LDS Church. "Do Mormons Practice Polygamy?" Mormons and Polygamy. Web. 2008.

Leach, Matthew. "Pujol's 3 Home Runs Answer Critics." Major League Baseball, October 23, 2011. Web.

Leech, Margaret. *In the Days of McKinley.* New York: Harper, 1959.

Leslie, Eliza. *Miss Leslie's Lady's House-Book,* Phil.: A. Hart, 1850. Google Books.

LeTourneau, Robert Gilmour. *Mover of Men and Mountains: The Autobiography of R.G. LeTourneau.* Moody, 1967. Kindle Edition.

LeTourneau Christian Center. "R.G. LeTourneau—God's Businessman." 2009.

Levy, Andrew. *The First Emancipator: The Forgotten Story of Robert Carter, The Founding Father Who Freed His Slaves.* New York: Random House, 2005.

"Lights Out in the City of Light" - Anarchy and Assassination at the Pan-American Exposition - PUBLIC OPINION - Volume XXXI, Number I2, Thursday, 19 September, 1901, P.355-361. Editorial. September 19, 1901.

Lief, Alfred. *The Firestone Story: A History of the Firestone Tire & Rubber Company.* New York: Whittlesey House, 1951.

Lief, Alfred. *Harvey Firestone: Free Man of Enterprise.* New York: McGraw-Hill, 1951.

Lincoln, Abraham. *Complete Project Gutenberg Abraham Lincoln Writings.* Ed. Arthur B. Lapsley. Vol. 1-7. Project Gutenberg, Kindle Edition.

Livingstone, Seth, Bob Nightengale, and Mel Antonen. "Focus of Cardinals First Baseman Pujols: Higher Power." USA Today, April 1, 2009.

Lowry, Beverly. *Her Dream of Dreams: The Rise and Triumph of Madam C.J. Walker.* New York: Alfred A. Knopf, 2003.

Lyon, William. *An American in Japan: William Merrell Vories: 1905-1964.*

Lyon, William. "Planting the Mustard Seed." *Journal of Arizona History,* 38, no. 3 (1997): 257-82.

Lorimer, Albert. *God Runs My Business; the Story of R.G. LeTourneau,* New York, Fleming H. Revell Company, 1941.

Marlowe, Michael. "The American Bible Union Version." www.bible-researcher.com. 2012.

Manber, David. *Wizard of Tuskegee; the Life of George Washington Carver.* New York: Crowell-Collier Press, 1967.

Mathews, Anna. "Green Forest SEAL Killed in Afghanistan." Carroll County News. August 8, 2011.

Mattern, Joanne. *Milton Hershey: Hershey's Chocolate Creator*. Edina, MN: ABDO Pub., 2011.

Miller, Scott. *The President and the Assassin: McKinley, Terror, and Empire at the Dawn of the American Century*. New York: Random House, 2011.

Marshall, Peter, and David Manuel. *The Light and the Glory*. Old Tappan, NJ: Revell, 1977.

Maryland Dept of Natural Resources. "Harriet Tubman Underground Railroad State Park." 2013.

"Mayor Bloomberg Signs Legislation Renaming 67 Thoroughfares and Public Places Throughout the City." December 20, 2010.

McCafferty, E. D. *Henry J. Heinz; a Biography,* New York: B. Orr Press, 1923.

McGrath, Alister. *In the Beginning: The Story of the King James Bible*. New York: Doubleday, 2001.

"Mr. McKinley at Tuskegee." *NY Times,* December 17, 1898.

McIlwain, Charles Howard, and King James, I. *The Political Works of James I.* Cambridge [Mass.: Harvard University Press, 1918.

McMillen, Wheeler. *Too Many Farmers; the Story of What Is Here and Ahead in Agriculture,* New York: W. Morrow, 1929.

McMillen, Wheeler. "Great Creator, I Said 'Why Did You Make the Peanut?'" *Farm and Fireside,* Nov. 1928: 8.

"Memorial Service for H.J. Heinz In Tokyo." *American Lutheran Survey Publishing Company* 10 (September 24, 1919): 694. Google Books.

"Memorial to Harriet Tubman to Be Unveiled." *The Advertiser,* 1914. June 12, 1914.

Mendham, Joseph. *The Life and Pontificate of Saint Pius V.* London: Duncan, 1832. Google Books.

Mennem, Kent. "My Name Is William Heber LeBaron: Federal Prisoner Number 22254-077." *Hell on Earth,* August 10, 2011. Blog.

"Mentholatum Story." Rohto. 2009. www.rohto.co.uk.

Miller, Ivonette Wright. *Wright Reminiscences*. Self-Published. Miller, 1978.

Miller, Scott. *The President and the Assassin: McKinley, Terror, and Empire.* New York: Random House 2011.

Miklasz, Bernie. "'60 Minutes' Story on Pujols Is Refreshing." St Louis Today, April 11, 2011.

"60 Minutes: The Incredible Albert Pujols." Interview by Bob Simon. CBSNews. April 10, 2011.

Montreal Gazette. "Holiday Inn Will Send 2,000 to This Year's Convention." June 15, 1965.

Moody, William. *The Life of Dwight L. Moody,.* New York: Fleming H. Revell, 1900. Google Books.

Muhlenberg, Henry. *The Life of Major-General Peter Muhlenberg, of the Revolutionary Army.* Philadelphia: Carey and Hart, 1849. Google Books.

Musser, Joe. *The Cereal Tycoon: Henry Parsons Crowell.* Chicago: Moody Press, 1997. Kindle Edition.

New England Freedmen's Aid Society. *Freedmen's Record.* Richmond, 1865. Google Books.

Nevins, Allan. *John D. Rockefeller.* New York: Scribner, 1959.

Newton, James. *Uncommon Friends: Life with Thomas Edison, Henry Ford, Harvey Firestone, Alexis Carrel & Charles Lindbergh.* San Diego, CA: Harcourt Brace Jovanovich, 1987.

Nightengale, Bob. "How Pujol's $254 Million Deal Got Done." USA Today, December 9, 2011.

Niles, Hezekiah. *Principles and Acts of the Revolution in America,* Baltimore: W.O. Niles, 1822. Google Books.

Northrop, Stephen Abbott. *A Cloud of Witnesses,* Fort Wayne, Ind: Mason Long, 1894. Google Books.

Norton, David. *The King James Bible: A Short History from Tyndale to Today.* Cambridge: Cambridge Univ. Press, 2011.

NY Times. "How The Deed Was Done." Newspaper. September 6, 1901.

NY Times. "McKinley Visits Tuskegee." Newspaper. December 17, 1898.

NY Times. "Wealthiest Negress Dead." Newspaper. May 26, 1919.

NY Times. "Wealthiest Negro Woman's Suburban Mansion." Newspaper. November 4, 1917.

"Obituaries: Kemmons Wilson, 90; Holiday Inn Chain's Founder." *LA Times*, February 14, 2003.

O'Halloran, Robert M., PhD. "Kemmons Wilson: An American Original." *Journal of Hospitality & Tourism Education* 15, no. 4 (2004): 5-18.

O'Reilly, Joseph. "1919-2009: Celebrating 90 Years in Ship By Truck." Inbound Logistics.

"Overcoming Adversity." Transcript. In *Fearless (Day 2 of 3) Guest Kelley Brown.* Family Life Today Radio. November 8, 2012.

Owen, Mark, and Kevin Maurer. *No Hero: The Evolution of a Navy SEAL.* New York: Penguin Group, 2014.

Paine, Thomas. *Common Sense,* Philadelphia: W. and T. Bradford, 1776. Kindle Edition.

Parks, Rosa, and Gregory Reed. *Quiet Strength: The Faith, the Hope, and the Heart of a Woman Who Changed a Nation.* Grand Rapids, MI: Zondervan Pub. House, 1994.

Patterson, Bryan E. *The "Beach People" Take Flight: Inventing the Airplane and Modernizing the Outer Banks of North Carolina, 1900-1932.* Connecticut College History Department. May 1, 2008.

Pearce, John Ed. *The Colonel: The Captivating Biography of the Dynamic Founder of a Fast-food Empire.* Garden City, NY: Doubleday, 1982.

Pendleton, Chris. "Into the Wild: The Camping Adventures of Edison, Ford and Friends." Edison & Ford Winter Estates Blog. July 22, 2012.

Penney, J. C. *Fifty Years with the Golden Rule.* New York: Harper, 1950.

Penney, J. C. *Lines of a Layman.* Great Neck, NY: Channel Press, 1956.

Penney, J. C. *View From the Ninth Decade; Jottings from a Merchant's Daybook.* New York: T. Nelson, 1960.

Perry, John. *Unshakable Faith: Booker T. Washington & George Washington Carver: A Biography.* Multnomah Publishers, 1999.

Pond, Enoch. *Lives of the Chief Fathers of New England.* Vol. 5. Boston: Massachusetts Sabbath School Society, 1870. Google Books.

Porter, Eduardo. "Helen Walton, Matriarch of Wal-Mart Family, Dies at 87." *New York Times.* April 20, 2007.

Press, Associated. "Cardinals Reliever Hancock Killed In Car Crash." ESPN. April 29, 2007. Web.

Pujols, Albert. "Albert Pujols: 'Giving Back Means Everything'" USATODAY. November 29, 2010.

Pujols, Albert. "My Testimony." *Pujols Family Foundation.* 2012.

"Radio Interview with Milton Hershey." Transcript. In *It Can Be Done.* CBS. June 8, 1938. www.protecthersheychildren.org.

Rains, Rob. *Albert the Great: The Albert Pujols Story.* Champaign, IL: Sports Pub. L.L.C., 2005.

Rasuli, Daryl. "James B. Parker Revisited." University of Buffalo Digital Collections. 2001. https://digital.lib.buffalo.edu.

Rauchway, Eric. *Murdering McKinley: The Making of Theodore Roosevelt's America.* New York: Hill and Wang, 2004.

Rawsthorn, Alice. "An Icon, Despite Itself." Editorial. *NY Times,* April 12, 2009.

Redmond, George. *Financial Giants of America,* Vol. 1-2. Boston, MA: Stratford Company, 1922. www.openlibrary.org.

Reilly, Corinne, and Kate Wiltrout. "Fallen Navy SEALs, Sailor Came From Many Walks of Life." *Virginian Pilot.* Norfolk Virginia, August 8, 2011.

Renstrom, George. *Chronology Commemorating the Hundredth Anniversary of the Birth of Orville Wright.* U.S. Centennial of Flight Commission. NASA. July 4, 2003.

Rhoads, Mark. "Illinois Hall of Fame: James L. Kraft." 'Illinois Review' November 10, 2006.

Richardson, James D. *A Compilation of the Messages and Papers of the Presidents.* Published by Authority of Congress, 1902. Kindle Edition.

Richmond, Dean. "Founded 75 Years Ago as a Matter of Survival, Metholatum Co Is Still Run By Hyde Family." *Buffalo Evening News,* October 31, 1964. www.forgot-tenbuffalo.com.

Rockefeller, David. *Memoirs.* New York: Random House, 2002.

Rockefeller, John D. *Random Reminiscences of Men and Events,.* New York: Double-day, Page &, 1909. Kindle Edition.

"Rockefeller Sees No Portent of Disaster." *New York Times,* October 20, 1907: Web.

Roosevelt, President Theodore. "A Tribute to Booker T. Washington." Booker T. Washington Society. August 28, 1916. Web.

Ryan, Shawn and Dom Rasso, Shawn Ryan Podcast #94: Dom Rasso. Shawn Ryan Show, January 29, 2024.

"Sacred Text: Tyndale New Testament." British Library Online Gallery. www.bl.uk.

Safer, Morley. "60 Minutes Original Interview 1979: Making Millions the Mary Kay Way." 60 Minutes Overtime on CBS News. October 28, 1979. Web.

Sanders, Harland. *The Incredible Colonel.* Carol Stream, IL: Creation House, 1974.

Sanders, Margaret. *The Colonel's Secret: Eleven Herbs and A Spicy Daughter.* Welling-ton, FL: M. Sanders, 1996.

Santella, Andrew. *The Wright Brothers: Inventors and Aviators.* Chanhassen, MN: Child's World, 2003.

Savage, Cynthia. "Escaping Four Generations of Polygamy." *CBN.* N.p., n.d. Web.

Scheeres, Julia. "Killing for God." Crime Library on TruTV.com. 2013.

Scherder, Jay. "Memorial Service Honors Navy SEAL in Green Forest." KY3. August 16, 2011.

Schlesing, Amy. "Fallen SEAL Died a Hero, Mourners Told." *Arkansas Democrat Gazette*, March 25, 2010.

Schmidt, Susan Ray. *Favorite Wife: Escape from Polygamy*. Guilford, CT: Lyons Pr., 2009.

Schmidt, Susan Ray. "From Polygamy to Jesus: The Testimony of Susan Ray Schmidt." YouTube. September 27, 2010.

Schmidt, Susan. "Life After Being A Sister Wife." Interview by Rachel Ray. *www.rachelrayshow.com*. Rachel Ray, January 3, 2011.

Schraff, Anne. *Harriet Tubman: Moses of the Underground Railroad*. Berkeley Heights, NJ: Enslow Pub., 2001.

"Senior Chief Thomas Arthur Ratzlaff-Special Warfare Operator." Carroll County News. August 16, 2011.

Serwer, Andy. "The Waltons: Inside America's Richest Family." CNNMoney. November 15, 2004.

Seward, Jack. *Strange but True Stories from Japan*. Boston, MA: Tuttle, 1999.

Shook, Robert L. *Heart & Soul: Five American Companies That Are Making the World a better Place*. Dallas, TX: BenBella, 2010. Kindle Edition.

Shurtleff, Nathaniel Bradstreet, ed. *Records of the Governor and Company of the Massachusetts Bay in New England. Printed by Order of the Legislature*. Vol. 2. Boston: W. White, Printer to the Commonwealth, 1853. Archive.org.

Singler, Shelley. "Irene Spencer, Daughter Speak of Hardships of Polygamy." Daily Vidette Reporter: Illinois State University. March 16, 2011.

Sidey, Hugh. "William McKinley: 1897-1901." In *The Presidents of the United States of America*, by Michael Beschloss. Washington, D.C.: White House Historical Association, with the Cooperation of the National Geographic Society, 2009.

Siebert, Wilbur. *The Underground Railroad from Slavery to Freedom*. New York: Macmillan, 1898. www.archive.org.

Smedley, R. C., *History of the Underground Railroad in Chester and the Neighboring Counties of Pennsylvania*. Lancaster, PA: John A. Hiestand, 1883. Google Books.

Smith, Jessie Carney. "Madam CJ Walker: Entrepreneur, Philanthropist." *Black Heroes of the 20th Century*. Detroit, MI: Visible Ink, 1998. 625-30.

Smith, Marcia C. "Pujols Has Been an Angel for Long Time." *The Orange County Register*, December 13, 2011.

Snavely, Joseph Richard. *An Intimate Story of Milton S. Hershey*. Hershey, PA: Printed Privately, 1957.

"Society of Entrepreneurs - Bios: Wallace E. Johnson." Memphis Society of Entrepreneurs, Business Leaders, Owners, Executives. 2009.

Solomon, Dorothy Allred. *Predators, Prey, and Other Kinfolk: Growing up in Polygamy*. New York: W.W. Norton &, 2003.

Spencer, Irene. *Cult Insanity: A Memoir of Polygamy, Prophets, and Blood Atonement*. New York: Center Street, 2009.

Spencer, Irene. "All We Knew Was Polygamy." Interview by Rebecca Kimbel. Part 1 & 2. Youtube. July 28, 2011.

Spencer, Irene. "Secrets of Polygamy Revealed." The Christian Broadcasting Network. 2013.

Spencer, Irene. *Shattered Dreams: My Life as a Polygamist's Wife*. New York: Center Street, 2007.

Stark, Jayson. "Cardinals Complete Impossible Dream." ESPN. 29 October 29, 2011.

State of Arkansas. Governor's Office. By Governor Mike Beebe. August 15, 2011.

Stephen David Entertainment, prod. "The Men Who Built America." *When One Ends Another Begins*. History Channel. HISTP, Los Angeles, CA, May 25, 2014.

Still, William. *The Underground Rail Road*, Philadelphia: Porter & Coates, 1872. Kindle Edition.

Stjernstrom, Nels. *The Joy of Accomplishment*, LeTourneau University, Longview, TX. 1989.

Story of the Sunday School Life of Henry J. Heinz Covering Sixty-Four Years from 1854 to 1919. Pittsburgh, PA: 1920.

"The Stories of Those Who Lost Their Lives in Chinook Crash." CNN. August 12, 2011.

Stimson, Richard. www.wrightstories.com. March 2001.

Sun, Eryn. "Fallen Navy SEAL Officer Aaron Vaughn Celebrated for His Faith in Jesus." Christian Post. August 9, 2011.

Strauss, Joe. "It Was About The Commitment." STLtoday.com. December 11, 2011.

Sullivan, T. M. *Memorial Service to William McKinley, October 6, 1901.* Washington: Printed Privately, 1902. PDF.

Tarbell, Ida M. *The History of the Standard Oil Company.* Vol. 1. New York, N.Y., U.S.A.: McClure Phillips and, 1904. Google Books.

Tarbell, Ida M. "John D. Rockefeller: A Character Study Part 1." *McClure's Magazine* July 1905: 227-49. Google Books.

Taylor, Alex. *Amazing Mentholatum—And the Commerce of Curing the Common Cold, 1889-1955.* La Cañada, CA: Angeles Crest, 2006.

Taylor, Sean D. "Tragedy Devastates Special Warfare Community." USA Today. August 7, 2011.

Tedlow, Richard S. "Sam Walton: Great From the Start." Harvard Business School. July 23, 2001.

Teems, David. *Tyndale: The Man Who Gave God an English Voice.* Nashville: Thomas Nelson, 2012.

Thigpen, Daniel. "Raid Stirs up Emotions for Ex-polygamist." Recordnet.com Home Page. April 9, 2008.

Thornton, Harrison. *The History of the Quaker Oats Company,.* Chicago, IL: University of Chicago Press, 1933.

Thornton, John Wingate. *The Pulpit of the American Revolution.* Boston: Gould and Lincoln, 1860. Google Books.

Thrasher, Max Bennett, and Booker T. Washington. *Tuskegee—Its Story and Its Work.* Boston: Small, Maynard, 1901. Google Books.

THV11. "Adam Lee Brown: Body Arrives in Hot Springs." March 23, 2010.

Timpson, Thomas. *British Ecclesiastical History.* London: Aylott & Jones, 1849. Google Books.

Tobin, James. *To Conquer the Air: The Wright Brothers and The Great Race for Flight.* New York: Free Press, 2003.

"Tribute to Adam Brown." LIFE OF DUTY. Patriot Profiles. 2011. www.nralife-ofduty.tv

Trimble, Vance H. *Sam Walton: The Inside Story of America's Richest Man.* New York, N.Y., U.S.A.: Penguin, 1990.

"Tuskegee Airman." National Park Service Museum. www.nps.gov.

Tyndale, William, John Frith, and Thomas Russell. *The Works of the English Reformers: William Tyndale and John Frith.* Vol. 1-3. London: Ebenezer Palmer, 1831. Google Books.

Tyndale, William, and David Daniell. *Tyndale's New Testament.* New Haven: Yale University Press, 1989.

United States Cong. House. Committee on Ways and Means. *Tarriff Information 1921: Hearings on General Tarriff Revision.* Vol. III. Washington, D.C.: U.S. Gov. Printing Office, 1921.

United States. Cong. House. Oversight and Government Reform. By Charles B. Rangel. 111 Cong., 2nd sess. HR Res. 81. *Govtrack.* U.S. Government, March 16, 2010. Web.

"United States Secret Service: History." United States Secret Service: History. 2012. www.secretservice.gov.

US Attorney's Office. "Jacqueline Lebaron Sentenced to Prison." FBI. September 8, 2011.

Utah Attorney General's Office. Arizona Attorney General's Office. *Guidebook for Law Enforcement and Human Services Agencies Who Offer Assistance to Fundamentalist Mormon Families.* By Mark Shurtleff and Tome Horne. 2011.

Vare, Ethlie Ann., and Greg Ptacek. *Women Inventors & Their Discoveries.* Minneapolis: Oliver, 1993. 50-65.

Vickers, Rebecca. *The Life of J.L. Kraft.* Oxford: Heinemann Library, 2005.

Vories, Merrell. *A Mustard Seed in Japan*. Self Published. 1948.

Vories, Merrell. *College Memories and Other Rimes*. Colorado Springs: Consolidated Publishing, 1903.

Vories, Merrell. *The Omi Brotherhood in Nippon*, Omi-Hachiman, Japan: Omi Brotherhood Book Dept., 1934.

Washington, Booker T. *The Future of the American Negro*. Boston: Small, Maynard &, 1902. Google Books.

Washington, Booker T. *The Story of the Negro, the Rise of the Race from Slavery, by Booker T. Washington*. Vol. 1-2. London: Doubleday & Page, 1909. Google Books.

Washington, Booker T. *My Larger Education Being Chapters From My Experience*. Toronto: McClelland & Goodchild, 1911. Google Books.

Washington, Booker T. *Tuskegee and Its People: Their Ideals and Achievements*. New York: Appleton, 1906. Kindle Edition.

Washington, Booker T. *Up from Slavery; an Autobiography*. New York: Doubleday, Page &, 1901. Kindle Edition.

Washington, Booker T., Gloria Yvonne. Jackson, and Sarah O'Neal. Rush. *Timeless Treasures: Reflections of God's Word in the Wisdom of Booker T. Washington : Writings, Quotations, and Scriptures Compiled and Arranged by Two of the Great-Granddaughters of Booker T. Washington*. Bloomington, IN: AuthorHouse, 2006. Kindle Edition.

Wilson, Weldon M. *A Light in the Window: A Tribute Paid to James L. Kraft at the Dedication of the Jade Window ... North Shore Baptist Church of Chicago, Illinois, on September 21, 1952*.

Wallace, Archer. *The Religious Faith of Great Men*. Freeport, NY: Books for Libraries Press, 1934.

Walton, Sam, and John Huey. *Sam Walton, Made in America: My Story*. New York: Doubleday, 1992.

Walton, Sam. "10 Rules for Building a Business." Walmart Corporate. 2012. Web.

Watson, Matt. "Albert Pujols Isn't Sure the Fans Learned From Josh Hancock." AOL News. May 7, 2007.

Weathers, Ed. "The Last Tycoon: Is This Man America's Happiest Millionaire?" Kemmons Wilson A Business Legend. September 1985. Orange Lake.

Webb, Mary Griffin, and Edna Lenore Webb. *Famous Living Americans, with Portraits,* Greencastle, IN: C. Webb &, 1915. 403-15. www.openlibrary.org.

Weld, Theodore, Sarah Grimké, and Angelina Grimke. *American Slavery as It Is the Testimony of a Thousand Witnesses.* New York: American Anti-Slavery Society, 1839. Kindle Edition.

Westfall, Sandra S., and Susan Keating. "Tribute to the Fallen SEALs: Complete List Released." People Magazine. August 11, 2011.

Williams, Brian. "Navy SEAL's Widow: 'We Were Blessed to Be Together'." TODAY.com. August 8, 2011.

Wilson, Kemmons, and Robert Kerr. *Half Luck and Half Brains: The Kemmons Wilson, Holiday Inn Story.* Nashville, TN: Hambleton-Hill Pub., 1996.

Wilson, Kemmons. *The Holiday Inn Story.* New York: Newcomen Society in North America, 1968.

Woodbridge, John. *More Than Conquerors,* Chicago, IL, Moody Press, 1992.

Wojciechowski, Gene. "St. Louis, Cardinals Suffer Another Painful Tragedy." ESPN, April 29, 2007.

Worsley, Henry. *The Life of Martin Luther: In Two Volumes.* Vol. 1-2. London: Bell and Daldy, 1856.

"Wright Brothers Aeroplane Company: Virtual Museum of Pioneer Aviation." www.wright-brothers.org.

Wright Brothers' Flying Machine. Directed by David Axlerod and Michael Barnes. PBS: Nova, 2003. DVD.

Wright, Milton. *Diaries, 1857-1917.* Dayton, OH: Wright State University, 1999.

Wright, Orville, and Wilbur Wright. *The Early History of the Airplane.* Dayton, O.: Dayton-Wright Airplane, 1922. Kindle Edition.

Wright, Wilbur, Orville Wright, and Fred C. Kelly. *Miracle at Kitty Hawk: The Letters of Wilbur and Orville Wright.* [New York]: Da Capo Press, 2002.

Wright, Wilbur, Orville Wright, Octave Chanute, and Marvin Wilks McFarland. *The Papers of Wilbur and Orville Wright, including the Chanute-Wright Letters and Other Papers of Octave Chanute.* New York: McGraw-Hill, 1953.

Wright, Wilbur. "The Story of Flight." Compiled by John H. Ledeboer. *Aeronautics* 15, no. 8 (December 1915): 52-63. Original Print Scanned by Google Play.

Wright-Martin Aircraft Corporation. *The Story of the Aeroplane.* New York: Corporation, 1917. Google Books.

Wyckoff, Edwin Brit. *Hair-Care Millionaire: Madam C.J. Walker and Her Amazing Business.* Berkeley Heights, NJ: Enslow Elementary, 2011.

Wyckoff, William H., and Charles A. Buckbee. *Documentary History of the American Bible Union,* New York: American Bible Union, 1857. Google Books.

Young, James C. "Hershey Unique Philanthropist." *NY Times,* November 18, 1923.

Zacharias, Patricia. "Henry Ford and Thomas Edison: A Friendship of Giants." Detnews.com. August 7, 1996.

Zumbrun, Francis. "Famous Travelers: Edison, Ford, Firestone." *Maryland Forest Service History.* Maryland Forest Service, 2012.

Scripture Quotes

NOG

Scripture quotations marked NOG are from the Holy Bible, Names of God Bible. ©2011 by Baker Publishing Group.

TLB

References

1. ^ Demaus and Lovett, *Tyndale*, 130.

2. ^ Tyndale, et al, *Works*, Vol 1. p. 305.

3. ^ Timpson, *British Ecclesiastical History*, 170. Also see Bobrick, *Wide*, 68-70 & Daniell, *Bible*, 108-110.

4. ^ Demaus and Lovett, *Tyndale*, 36.

5. ^ Demaus and Lovett, *Tyndale*, 67 & Tyndale, *Works*, 4.

6. ^ Demaus and Lovett, *Tyndale*, 72.

7. ^ Foxe, *Acts & Monuments*, Vol 5. p. 117.

8. ^ Teems, *Tyndale*, 268-272.

9. ^ Daniell, David. *Tyndale's New Testament*, IX-X & Farris, *From Tyndale to Madison*, 23 & Teems, *Tyndale*, 60-61.

10. ^ Daniell, David. *The Bible in English*, 152.

11. ^ Tyndale, et al, *Works*, 3.

12. ^ Worsley, *Life*, Vol 1. p. 243.

13. ^ Bobrick, *Wide*, 93-95.

14. ^ Ibid.

15. ^ Tyndale, et al, *Works*, Vol 1. p. 5.

16. ^ Bobrick, *Wide*, 106-107.

17. ^ Tyndale, et al, *Works*, Vol 2. p. 21-26

18. ^ Tyndale, et al, *Works*, Vol 2. p. 21-30 & Bobrick, *Wide*, 112-115 & Daniell, *Bible*, 148-149 & Teems, *Tyndale*, 183.

19. ^ Ellis, *Tyndale*, 92 & Fox, *Acts & Monuments*, Vol 5. p. 134.

20. ^ Tyndale, et al, *Works*, Vol 1. p. 196.

21. ^ Ellis, *Tyndale*, 82.

22. ^ Clarke, *Life*, 101-102, & Ellis, *Tyndale*, 94, & Foxe, *Acts & Monuments*, Vol 5. p 132.

23. ^ Ellis, *Tyndale*, 93.

24. ^ Demaus and Lovett, *Tyndale,* 418.

25. ^ Ibid, 428.

26. ^ Tyndale, et al, *Works,* Vol 1. p. 333.

27. ^ Demaus and Lovett, 403.

28. ^ Foxe, *Acts & Monuments,* Vol 5. p. 127.

29. ^ Tyndale, et al, *Works,* Vol 1. p. 185-196.

30. ^ Ellis, *Tyndale,* 66.

31. ^ Ibid.

32. ^ Tyndale, et al, *Works,* Vol 1. p. 305

33. ^ Foxe, *Acts & Monuments,* Vol 5. p. 163.

34. ^ Ibid, 167.

35. ^ Ibid, 168.

36. ^ Bobrick, Benson. *Wide as the Waters,* 160 & Melvyn Bragg. *The Book of Books,* 336.

37. ^ McIlwain, and James. *Political Works,* 315

38. ^ Arber, *Story,* 68 & Bradford, *Of Plymouth,* 22.

39. ^ Bancroft, *History,* Vol 1. p. 196 & Bradford, *Of Plymouth,* 12.

40. ^ Arber, *Story,* 265.

41. ^ Ibid, 409.

42. ^ *Code of 1650,* 92-93 & Shurtleff, *Records,* 203.

43. ^ Pond, *Lives,* Vol 5, p. 96-97.

44. ^ Bancroft, *History,* Vol 1. p. 405-406.

45. ^ Adams, *Letters of John Adams and His Wife Abigail Adams,* Kindle Location 3293 & Hunt, *History of the Seal,* 9-14.

46. ^ Niles, *Principles and Acts,* 198 & Levy, *First Emancipator,* 75.

47. ^ Bancroft, *History,* Vol 6. p. 54-55

48. ^ Paine, Thomas. *Common Sense.*

49. ^ Thornton, *Pulpit of the American Revolution,* 73 & 79.

50. ^ Ibid, 45.

51. ^ Muhlenberg, *Life,* 53.

52. ^ Marshall and Manuel, *Light,* 291 & Muhlenberg, *Life,* 53.

53. ^ Johnson, *Abraham Lincoln the Christian,* 157-158, & Wallace, *Great Men,* 211.

54. ^ Lincoln, *Complete Writings,* Quotes are from the Lincoln/Douglas Debates, *"House Divided"* Speech, Lincoln Speech July 10, 1858 (replying to Douglas), Lincoln's 2nd Inaugural Address, & Johnson, *Abraham Lincoln,* 134-135 + 173-175.

55. ^ Federer, *America's God & Country,* 551.

56.   ^ Washington, *Up from Slavery*, Chapter 1.

57.   ^ Federer, *America's God & Country*, 676.

58.   ^ Tarbell, "Character Study." 391.

59.   ^ Irving, *Master of Money*, 131.

60.   ^ United States Congress House of Representatives. Committee on Ways and Means. *Tariff Information 1921*, Vol 3. P. 2070-2077.

61.   ^ Parks, *Quiet Strength*, 42 & 55.

62.   ^ "Sacred Text: Tyndale New Testament." British Library Online Gallery.

63.   ^ Matthew 7:24-25 (GNT).

64.   ^ Colossians 1:15a (NLT).

65.   ^ Federer, *America's God and Country*, 539.

66.   ^ Tarbell, "Character Study." 391.

67.   ^ Kraft, *Adventure in Jade*, 3.

68.   ^ Ibid.

69.   ^ Kraft, *Pattern for Prosperity & Message of Inspiring Faith & New Guideposts*, 186.

70.   ^ Ibid.

71.   ^ Kraft, *Pattern for Prosperity & Message of Inspiring Faith & New Guideposts*, 187.

72.   ^ Kraft, *Pattern for Prosperity & Message of Inspiring Faith & New Guideposts*, 187.

73.   ^ Kraft, *Pattern for Prosperity & Message of Inspiring Faith & New Guideposts*,

74.   ^ Carey, *American Inventors*, 234 & Ingham, *Biographical Dictionary*, 738.

75.   ^ Criswell, *"Christ and This Crucial Hour."*

76.   ^ Kraft, *Pattern for Prosperity & Message of Inspiring Faith & New Guideposts*, 189.

77.   ^ Kraft, *Pattern for Prosperity & Message of Inspiring Faith, & New Guideposts*, 189.

78.   ^ Exodus 33:11 (GNT).

79.   ^ John 15:15b (GNT).

80.   ^ Revelations 3:20 (NLT).

81.   ^ Jeremiah 2:32 (KJV).

82.   ^ Jeremiah 2:13 (GW).

83.   ^ 1 John 1:3 (GNT).

84.   ^ Bradford, *Moses*, 6 & 56.

85.   ^ Day, *Business*, 63.

86.   ^ LeTourneau, *Mover of Men and Mountains*, 25.

87.   ^ Ibid, 41.

88.   ^ LeTourneau, *Mover of Men and Mountains,* 53 & Lorimer, *God Runs My Business,* 1.

89.   ^ LeTourneau, *Mover of Men and Mountains,* 54.

90.   ^ Ibid, 57.

91.   ^ Lorimer, *God Runs My Business,* 41.

92.   ^ Ibid, 49.

93.   ^ Ibid, 50.

94.   ^ Ibid, 42.

95.   ^ Ibid, 50-51.

96.   ^ Ibid, 52.

97.   ^ Ibid, 80.

98.   ^ LeTourneau, *Mover of Men and Mountains,* 213. & Lorimer, *God Runs My Business,* 80. & Stjernstrom, *Joy of Accomplishment,* 115-116.

99.   ^ Woodbridge, John. "R. G. LeTourneau," 348 & Stjernstrom, *Joy,* Back cover.

100. ^ LeTourneau, Robert. *Mover of Men and Mountains,* 226.

101. ^ Stjernstrom, *Joy,* 19.

102. ^ Isaiah 49:16b (GNT).

103. ^ Luke 12:7 (NCV).

104. ^ Zechariah 2:8 (NCV).

105. ^ Isaiah 49:15b (GNT).

106. ^ Hebrews 2:5 (ERV).

107. ^ Hebrews 2:6 (ERV).

108. ^ 2 Peter 1:3 (NOG).

109. ^ Ephesians 4:27 (ERV).

110. ^ 1 Peter 5:8-10 (GW).

111. ^ James 1:17a (NLV).

112. ^ Hosea 13:9 (AMP).

113. ^ Truman & Howson, *Robert Colgate,* 55.

114. ^ Vories, *Mustard Seed,* 57.

115. ^ Firestone and Crowther, *Rubber,* 17 & Lief, *Harvey Firestone,* 25.

116. ^ Firestone and Crowther, *Rubber,* 17-18.

117. ^ Firestone and Crowther, *Rubber,* 18.

118. ^ Ford and Crowther, *My Life & Work,* Introduction.

119. ^ Ibid, Chapter 1.

120. ^ Ibid.

121. ^ Ibid.

122. ^ Ibid.

123. ^ Ford and Crowther, *Edison As I Know Him,* 8.

124. ^ Lief, *Harvey Firestone,* 51 & Newton, *Uncommon Friends,* 48.

125.   ^ Ford and Crowther, *My Life & Work,* Chapter 2.

126.   ^ Ford and Crowther, *Edison,* 1-5.

127.   ^ Ford and Crowther, *My Life & Work,* Chapter 2.

128.   ^ United States Congress, *Tariff,* Vol 3. P. 2076.

129.   ^ Lief, *Harvey Firestone,* 53.

130.   ^ Firestone and Crowther, *Rubber,* 80.

131.   ^ Ibid, 253.

132.   ^ Edwards, Ethel. *Carver of Tuskegee,* 67 & 112.

133.   ^ Lief, *Harvey Firestone,* 190.

134.   ^ Ibid, 151.

135.   ^ Lief, *Harvey Firestone,* 284 & Newton, *Uncommon Friends,* 82.

136.   ^ Zumbrun, *Famous Travelers,* Part 7.

137.   ^ Newton, *Uncommon Friends,* 99.

138.   ^ Ford and Crowther, *My Life & Work.* Chapter 19.

139.   ^ 2 Corinthians 3:17 (ERV).

140.   ^ Galatians 5:1 (NLV).

141.   ^ Galatians 5:18 (ERV).

142.   ^ Deuteronomy 1:31b (GW).

143.   ^ Lief, *Harvey Firestone,* 297.

144.   ^ Jenness, *Man Who Asked God Questions,* 19.

145.   ^ Edwards, *Carver of Tuskegee,* 76.

146.   ^ United States Congress, *Tariff,* Vol 3. P. 2070-2077.

147.   ^ Federer, *Life & Faith,* 9.

148.   ^ Jenness, *Man Who Asked God Questions,* 12.

149.   ^ Federer, *Life & Faith,* 15.

150.   ^ Edwards, *Carver of Tuskegee,* 159-160 & Federer, *Life & Faith,* 74.

151.   ^ Clark, *Talks with the Flowers,* 21.

152.   ^ Ibid, 33-34.

153.   ^ Ibid, 6.

154.   ^ Jenness, *Man Who Asked God Questions,* 19-20.

155.   ^ Ferrell, *Fruits of Creation,* 50, & Holt, *George Washington Carver,* 227, & Jenness, *Man Who Asked God Questions,* 18-20 & McMillen, *Too Many Farmers,* 172, & McMillen, *Great Creator,* 8, & Manber, *Wizard of Tuskegee,* 119-120.

156.   ^ Edwards, *Carver of Tuskegee,* 143 & Holt, *George Washington Carver,* 266.

157.   ^ Federer, *Life & Faith,* 61-64 & Ferrell, *Fruits of Creation,* 63 & Edwards, *Carver of Tuskegee* 143.

158.   ^ Federer, *Life & Faith,* 9.

159.   ^ Clark, *Talks with the Flowers,* 12-13.

160.   ^ Edwards, *Carver of Tuskegee*, 105.

161.   ^ Hill, *Heard God's Whisper*, 29-36.

162.   ^ Ibid, 65, 68-69.

163.   ^ Federer, *Life & Faith*, 61.

164.   ^ James 1:5 (ERV).

165.   ^ Psalm 68:19b (KJV).

166.   ^ Psalm 84:11b (NLT).

167.   ^ Psalm 37:4 (GNT).

168.   ^ John 16:24 (GW).

169.   ^ Psalm 81:16b (CEV).

170.   ^ Johnson, *Together We Build*, 84.

171.   ^ Vories, *Mustard Seed*, 41.

172.   James 1:5 (ERV).

173.   Psalms 68:19b (KJV).

174.   Psalms 84:11b (NLT).

175.   Psalms 37:4 (GNT).

176.   John 16:24 (GW).

177.   Psalms 81:16b (CEV).

178.   Johnson, *Together We Build*, 84.

179.   Vories, *Mustard Seed*, 41.

180.   ^ Hardin, *Colgate Story*, 24.

181.   ^ Abbe & Howson, *Robert Colgate*, 49-50 & Hardin, *Colgate Story*, 48.

182.   ^ Hardin, *Colgate Story*, 51.

183.   ^ Ibid, 50-51.

184.   ^ Ibid, 25.

185.   ^ Johnson, *Abraham Lincoln the Christian*, 41 & 55 & Johnson, *George Washington*, 147-148.

186.   ^ Everts, *William Colgate*, 121-123.

187.   ^ Ibid, 131-132.

188.   ^ Ibid, 143, 147-148.

189.   ^ Everts, *William Colgate*, 129-130.

190.   ^ Ibid, 110-111.

191.   ^ Ibid, 111.

192.   ^ Everts, *William Colgate*, 115, & Hardin, *Colgate Story*, 37.

193.   ^ Everts, *William Colgate*, 198 & Hardin, *Colgate Story*, 41.

194.   ^ Everts, *William Colgate*, 202-203, 218-219.

195.   ^ Everts, *William Colgate*, 236-237 & Hardin, *Colgate Story*, 44.

196. ^ *The New Testament of Our Lord and Savior Jesus Christ. The Common English Version; Corrected by the Final Committee of the American Bible Union.* New York: American Bible Union, 1866. Archive.org.

Note this edition is called the second edition because the Bible Union revised the original translation of the Bible Society.

197. ^ Everts, *William Colgate,* 189 & Hardin, *Colgate Story,* 127.

198. ^ Abbe & Howson, *Robert Colgate,* 62 & Everts, *William Colgate,* 265.

199. ^ Northrop, *A Cloud of Witnesses,* 93 & Habakkuk 2:14.

200. ^ Hardin, *Colgate Story,* 112.

201. ^ Everts, *William Colgate,* 90.

202. ^ Mark 10:29b-30 (ERV).

203. ^ Deuteronomy 28:6 (NLV).

204. ^ Exodus 33:15 (ERV).

205. ^ Exodus 33:14 (ERV).

206. ^ Ford and Crowther, *My Life and Work,* Chapter 3.

207. ^ Lief, *Harvey Firestone,* 298.

208. ^ Day, *Christian in Big Business,* 54.

209. ^ Day, *Christian in Big Business,* 53.

210. ^ Job 5:19 (KJV)

211. ^ Day, *Christian in Big Business,* 57.

212. ^ Ibid, 51.

213. ^ Ibid, 69.

214. ^ Ibid, 77.

215. ^ Ibid.

216. ^ Ibid, 80.

217. ^ Ibid, 80-81.

218. ^ Day, *Christian in Big Business,* 58, & Musser, *Cereal Tycoon,* 37 & 160, & Moody, *Life of Dwight L. Moody,* 134.

219. ^ Day, *Christian in Big Business,* 59.

220. ^ Ibid.

221. ^ Ibid, 81.

222. ^ Ibid, 57.

223. ^ Thornton, *History of the Quaker Oats,* 84-85.

224. ^ Ibid, 94-95.

225. ^ Day, *Christian in Big Business,* 126.

226. ^ Ibid, 126.

227. ^ Thornton, *History of the Quaker Oats,* 236.

228. ^ Day, *Christian in Big Business,* 184.

229. ^ Ibid, 137.

230.   ^ Ibid, 185.
231.   ^ Ibid, 177.
232.   ^ Ibid, 285.
233.   ^ Ibid, 285.
234.   ^ Ibid, 151.
235.   ^ Ibid, 273. Crowell is referring to John 6:26.
236.   ^ Musser, *Cereal Tycoon*, 2.
237.   ^ The Henry Parsons Crowell and Susan Coleman Crowell Trust. *"Our Funding Priorities."* www.crowelltrust.org.
238.   ^ Day, *Christian in Big Business*, 162 & Musser, *Cereal Tycoon*, 3.
239.   ^ Daniel 2:21a (GNT).
240.   ^ Genesis 8:22 (ERV).
241.   ^ Joshua 3:3-4 (ERV).
242.   ^ James 1:4 (NLV).
243.   ^ Hebrews 10:36 (CEV).
244.   ^ Isaiah 40:30-31 (MSG).
245.   ^ Everts, *William Colgate*, 236-237.
246.   ^ Ash, *Mary Kay*, 175.
247.   ^ Vories, *Omi Brotherhood*, iii.
248.   ^ Vories, *Mustard Seed*, 3.
249.   ^ Vories, *Omi Brotherhood*, 9.
250.   ^ Vories, *Mustard Seed*, 7.
251.   ^ Vories, *Omi Brotherhood*, 54.
252.   ^ Ibid, 59.
253.   ^Vories, *Mustard Seed*, 4.
254.   ^ Ibid, 6, 21.
255.   ^ That businessman could have been either Henry Heinz or A. A. Hyde, both of whom traveled to Japan during that time period and were known to give generously to missionaries.
256.   ^ Vories, *Mustard Seed*, 10.
257.   ^ Ibid, 22.
258.   ^ Fletcher, *Bridge of Love*, 83.
259.   ^ Vories, *Omi Brotherhood*, 170.
260.   ^ Vories, *Mustard Seed*, 59
261.   ^ Vories, *Omi Brotherhood*, 167.
262.   ^ Fletcher, *Bridge of Love*, 192 & Vories, *Mustard Seed*, 63.
263.   ^ Fletcher, *Bridge of Love*, 211 & Lyon, "American in Japan" 57.
264.   ^ Fletcher, *Bridge of Love*, 209.
265.   ^ Vories, *Omi Brotherhood*, 167.

266. ^ James 1:2-4 (MSG).

267. ^ 1 Peter 2:20 (CEV).

268. ^ 1 Peter 4:15-16 (GNT).

269. ^ Romans 8:17 (MSG).

270. ^ Hebrews 5:8 (MSG).

271. ^ Matthew 26:39 (GNT).

272. ^ John 14:21 (ERV).

273. ^ Mark 15:34 (GNT).

274. ^ 1 Peter 2:19 (GNT).

275. ^ 1 Thessalonians 5:18 (GNT).

276. ^ Hebrews 13:15-16 (NLV).

277. ^ 2 Timothy 3:12 (GNT).

278. ^ 1 Peter 2:23 (NLT).

279. ^ 1Thessalonians 2:4 (GNT).

280. ^ 2Timothy 2:12 (NLV).

281. ^ Woodbridge, *More Than Conquerors,* 73.

282. ^ Jim Elliot wrote that before being killed on the mission field of Ecuador in 1956.

283. ^ Penney, *Lines,* 181.

284. ^ Irving, *Master of Money,* 32.

285. ^ Ibid, 33.

286. ^ Ibid, 42.

287. ^ Irving, *Master of Money,* 147-148.

288. ^ Ibid, 61.

289. ^ Layman's, *Speech,* 358-362. (Hyde is quoting Matthew 7:20 & Acts 20:35)

290. ^ Irving, *Master of Money,* 87-89.

291. ^ Vories, *Mustard Seed,* 61.

292. ^ Hyde, A. A. *Modern Man,* 23 & Irving, *Master of Money,* 69.

293. ^ Irving, *Master of Money,* 103 & Taylor, *Amazing Mentholatum,* 129.

294. ^ Irving, *Master of Money,* 70.

295. ^ Taylor, *Amazing Mentholatum,* 125-126.

296. ^ Irving, *Master of Money,* 65-66.

297. ^ Ibid, 75-76.

298. ^ Ibid, 115-119.

299. ^ Allen, "Trying to Get His Debt All Paid Off." 676.

300. ^ Hyde, A. A. *Modern Man,* 21 & Irving, *Master of Money,* 39-40 & 144-145.

301. ^ Irving, *Master of Money,* 84 & Taylor, *Amazing Mentholatum,* XI.

302. ^ Allen, "Trying to Get His Debt All Paid Off," 677.

303. ^ Taylor, *Amazing Mentholatum,* 178.

304. ^ Irving, *Master of Money,* 154-156.

305. ^ Ibid, 145.
306. ^ Ibid, 55.
307. ^ Deuteronomy 15:11 (ERV).
308. ^ Matthew 22:39b (ERV).
309. ^ Isaiah 65:22 (GNT).
310. ^ John 12:3b-6 (ERV) & John 12:7-8 (MSG).
311. ^ Irving, *Master of Money,* 64
312. ^ Irving, *Master of Money,* 144-145.
313. ^ 2 Corinthians 12:14b (ERV).
314. ^ 1 Timothy 5:8b (ERV).
315. ^ Irving, *Master of Money,* 12.
316. ^ Proverbs 13:22a (NLV).
317. ^ Proverbs 19:14a (NLV).
318. ^ Ecclesiastes 3:13 (GNT).
319. ^ Woodbridge, *More Than Conquerors,* 74.
320. ^ Forbes, *Making America,* 301.
321. ^ Heinz, *Henry J. Heinz,* 11 & McCafferty, *Biography,* 56.
322. ^ McCafferty, *Biography,* 101.
323. ^ Ibid, 29.
324. ^ Ibid, 84.
325. ^ Ingham, *Biographical Dictionary,* 567.
326. ^ McCafferty, *Biography,* 147-148.
327. ^ Heinz, *Henry J. Heinz,* 16.
328. ^ McCafferty, *Biography,* 26.
329. ^ Heinz, *Henry J. Heinz,* 18.
330. ^ *Sunday School Life of Henry J. Heinz,* 11.
331. ^ 2Corinthians 3:6 (ERV)
332. ^ Heinz, *Henry J. Heinz,* 18.
333. ^ McCafferty, *Biography,* 32-33.
334. ^ McCafferty, *Biography,* 91.
335. ^ Ibid, 196.
336. ^ Ibid, 201.
337. ^ Ibid, 100.
338. ^ Brown, *Sunday School Tour of the Orient,* 275.
339. ^ Ibid, 346.
340. ^ Heinz, *Henry J. Heinz,* 23.
341. ^ McCafferty, *Biography,* 208.
342. ^ Ibid, 27-29.
343. ^ Ibid, 156.

344. ^ Heinz, *Henry J. Heinz*, 21 & McCafferty, *Biography*, 189-190.

345. ^ James 4:10 (GNT).

346. ^ Philippians 2:8a (ERV).

347. ^ John 5:30 (CEV).

348. ^ Matthew 11:28-30 (ERV).

349. ^ 1 Peter 5:7 (NET).

350. ^ Jeremiah 9:23-24a (CEV).

351. ^ Proverbs 16:18 (ERV).

352. ^ Wright *et al.*, *Papers*, 26.

353. ^ Irving, *Master of Money*, 116-117.

354. ^ Bradford, *Scenes*, 35.

355. ^ Drew, *Northside*, 30.

356. ^ Bradford, *Moses*, 29.

357. ^ Ibid, 30.

358. ^ Smedley, *History*, 250-251.

359. ^ New England Freedman's Aid Society, *Freedmen's Record*, 36.

360. ^ Bradford, *Moses*, 42.

361. ^ Still, *Underground Railroad*, Loc 6166.

362. ^ Bradford, *Scenes*, 5.

363. ^ Bradford, *Moses*, 53-54.

364. ^ Bradford, *Scenes*, 49 & Smedley, *History*, 368 & Still, *Underground Railroad*, Loc 10937.

365. ^ Bradford, *Moses*, 73-74 & *Scenes*, 50-51.

366. ^ Bradford, *Moses*, 8, 90-91.

367. ^ Ibid, 83.

368. ^ U.S. Army, *Spies & Spying*, Kindle Location 593.

369. ^ Siebert, *Underground Railroad*, 189.

370. ^ U.S. Army, *Spies & Spying*, Kindle Location 593.

371. ^ Ibid.

372. ^ Ibid.

373. ^ Bradford, *Moses*, 77.

374. ^ Washington, *Up From Slavery*, Chapter 1.

375. ^ Matthew 4:1 (CEV).

376. ^ Luke 6:12 (GNT).

377. ^ John 14:16-17 (GNT).

378. ^ John 16:13a (CEV).

379. ^ Jeremiah 10:21 (GNT).

380. ^ 1 John 16:13c (CEV).

381. ^ 1 John 2:27 (GNT).

382.   ^ Colossians 3:15a (GNT).

383.   ^ John 16:13b (CEV).

384.   ^ John 16:14-15 (CEV).

385.   ^ Hill, *Heard God's Whisper*, 32.

386.   ^ Kraft, "Pattern For Prosperity." *New Guideposts*, 189 & "Pattern for Prosperity." *St. Petersburg Times*, February, 16, 1951.

387.   ^ Washington, *Up From Slavery*, Chapter 1.

388.   ^ Ibid.

389.   ^ Washington, *Up From Slavery*, Chapter 11 & Washington, *Timeless Treasures*, Kindle Location 769.

390.   ^ Washington, *Up From Slavery*, Chapter 1.

391.   ^ Ibid.

392.   ^ Washington, *Up From Slavery*, Chapter 3.

393.   ^ Perry, *Unshakable Faith*, 67.

394.   ^ Washington, *Timeless Treasures*, Kindle Location 1457.

395.   ^ Ibid, 76.

396.   ^ Washington, *Up From Slavery*, Chapter 9.

397.   ^ Ibid, 77.

398.   ^ Perry, *Unshakable Faith*, 247.

399.   ^ Ibid, 218.

400.   ^ Washington, *Larger Education*, 223.

401.   ^ NY Times, "Mr. McKinley at Tuskegee." 1898.

402.   ^ Washington, *Timeless Treasures*, Kindle Location 1219 & 1233.

403.   ^ Washington, *Up From Slavery*, Chapter 13.

404.   ^ Ibid, Chapter 16.

405.   ^ Ibid.

406.   ^ Fisher, Isaac. "The Funeral of Booker T. Washington."

407.   ^ Ibid.

408.   ^ Roosevelt, President Theodore, "A Tribute to Booker T. Washington."

409.   ^ "Tuskegee Airmen."

410.   ^ Washington, *Timeless Treasures*, Kindle Location 1667.

411.   ^ 1 Corinthians 2:9b (NLV).

412.   ^ 1 Corinthians 2:10 (NLV).

413.   ^ 1 Samuel 13:6 (MSG).

414.   ^ 1 Samuel 14:6 (CEV).

415.   ^ 1 Samuel 14:7b (GNT).

416.   ^ 1 Samuel 14:13-15 (CEV).

417.   ^ 2 Kings 7:2 (ERV).

418.   ^ 2 Kings 7:16b (MSG).

419.   ^ 2 Kings 7:17 (GNT).

420.   ^ Hebrews 3:15b (NLT).

421.   ^ Hebrews 3:19b (ERV).

422.   ^ Psalm 78:19 (ERV).

423.   ^ Psalm 78:21a (MSG).

424.   ^ Psalm 78:41b (GNT).

425.   ^ Hebrews 3:12b (CEV).

426.   ^ Matthew 13:58 (ERV).

427.   ^ Ephesians 3:20b (MSG).

428.   ^ Wright, Wilbur. "Flight's Future," Smithsonian Education - Stories of the Wrights' Flight, March 25, 1909. Web.

429.   ^ Ford and Crowther, *My Life and Work,* Chapter 5 & 19.

430.   ^ Bundles, *On Her Own Ground,* 43 & NY Times, *Wealthiest,* November 4, 1917.

431.   ^ Leslie, *Miss Leslie's Lady's House-Book,* 8-13.

432.   ^ Bundles, *On Her Own Ground,* 48, & Lowry, *Her Dream,* 155 & NY Times, *Wealthiest,* November 4, 1917.

433.   ^ Funk, *Queen,* 76 & Smith, *Madam CJ Walker,* 626 & Brodie, *Created Equal,* 116 & Lowry, *Her Dream,* 179.

434.   ^ NY Times, *Wealthiest,* November 4, 1917.

435.   ^ Bundles, *On Her Own Ground,* 83 & Funk, *Queen,* 76.

436.   ^ Smith, *Madam CJ Walker,* 329.

437.   ^ Ibid, 101.

438.   ^ Bundles, *On Her Own Ground,* 135 & Smith, *Madam CJ Walker,* 629 & Wyckoff, *Hair-Care Millionaire,* 21.

439.   ^ Bundles, *On Her Own Ground,* 153.

440.   ^ NY Times, *Wealthiest,* November 4, 1917.

441.   ^ Ibid.

442.   ^ Bundles, *On Her Own Ground,* 247.

443.   ^ Ibid, 269.

444.   ^ Gates, Henry Louis. *Life upon These Shores,* 244.

445.   ^ U.S. Congress, March 3, 2010.

446.   ^ Brodie, *Created Equal,* 115.

447.   ^ Proverbs 13:11b (GW)

448.   ^ Proverbs 31:16 & 24.

449.   ^ Deuteronomy 28:12b (GNT).

450.   ^ Kraft, "Face Up To Fear," *Guideposts Anthology,* 236 & Spokane Daily Chronicle February 26, 1953.

451.   ^ Newton, Uncommon Friends, 7.

452.   ^ Wright, et al. *Miracle at Kitty Hawk,* 6.

453.   ^ Leech, *Days of McKinley,* 584.

454.   ^ Rasuli, Daryl, *James Parker,* 5.

455.   ^ Leech, *Days of McKinley,* 601 & Miller, *President,* 320.

456.   ^ Deuteronomy 30:19a (NLT).

457.   ^ Psalms 115:16b (MSG).

458.   ^ Deuteronomy 28:1a-2a (NASB).

459.   ^ 2 Chronicles 7:14 (KJV)

460.   ^ Deuteronomy 28:2 (NLV).

461.   ^ Luke 13:34b (ERV).

462.   ^ Ecclesiastes 7:29b (ERV).

463.   ^ Genesis 6:3b (GW).

464.   ^ James 1:13 (CEV).

465.   ^ 1 Chronicles 4:9-10 (GNT).

466.   ^ 2 Timothy 1:7 (NLV).

467.   ^ Romans 8:28 (KJV).

468.   ^ Lorimer, God Runs My Business, 45.

469.   ^ Johnstone, William. *Abraham Lincoln: The Christian,* 89.

470.   ^ Utah Attorney General's Office. Arizona Attorney General's Office. *Guidebook for Law Enforcement.* 7-8.

471.   ^ Spencer, "Secrets of Polygamy Revealed."

472.   ^ Ibid.

473.   ^ Crump, "Passage from Polygamy."

474.   ^ Crump, "Passage from Polygamy." & Schmidt, "From Polygamy to Jesus."

475.   ^ Schmidt, *Favorite Wife,* 340-341.

476.   ^ Crump, "Passage from Polygamy." & Schmidt, "From Polygamy to Jesus." & Schmidt, *Favorite Wife,* 346.

477.   ^ Spencer, "All We Knew Was Polygamy," Part 2.

478.   ^ Gokhman, Jennifer. "A Secret Life" & Savage, Cynthia. "Escaping Four Generations of Polygamy."

479.   ^ Spencer, *Shattered Dreams,* 380-381.

480.   ^ 1Samuel 15:22 (NET).

481.   ^ Psalm 51:16-17 (ERV).

482.   ^ Deuteronomy 12:13-14 (ERV).

483.   ^ John 10:18 (ERV).

484.   ^ 2 Corinthians 9:7 (CEV).

485.   ^ Ecclesiastes 5:1 (MSG).

486.   ^ Hosea 6:6 (GW)

487.   ^ Ellis, *Tyndale,* 63-64.

488.   ^ Everts, *Christian Layman,* 237.

489.   ^ Snavely, *Intimate Story,* 133.

490. ^ Ibid.

491. ^ Ibid, 10.

492. ^ Ibid, 11.

493. ^ Ibid.

494. ^ Ibid, 12.

495. ^ Ibid, 19.

496. ^ Ibid.

497. ^ Ibid, 20.

498. ^ Ibid, 21.

499. ^ D'Antonio, *Hershey*, 46.

500. ^ Snavely, *Intimate Story*, 26.

501. ^ Ibid, 41.

502. ^ Ibid, 45 & 172.

503. ^ Ibid, 84, 168-169.

504. ^ Ibid, 501.

505. ^ Ibid, 385.

506. ^ Ibid, 385.

507. ^ Ibid, 309-310.

508. ^ Ibid, 310 & 477.

509. ^ Ibid, 309-310.

510. ^ D'Antonio, *Hershey*, 235.

511. ^ Snavely, *Intimate Story*, 367.

512. ^ Ibid, 385.

513. ^^ These were the churches in the town of Hershey—at the time that he gave each one the big check—Presbyterian, United Brethren, Reformed Mennonite, Church of the Brethren, Lutheran, and Catholic.

514. ^ Snavely, *Intimate Story*, 351.

515. ^ Ibid, 396-397.

516. ^ 2 Chronicles 25:9 (GW).

517. ^ Genesis 41:51 (GNT).

518. ^ Job 42:10b, 12a (GNT).

519. ^ Job 8:7 (GNT).

520. ^ Stjernstrom, Joy of Accomplishment, 49.

521. ^ Ford and Crowther, *My Life and Work,* Introduction.

522. ^ Penney, *Lines,* 124-125 & 174.

523. ^ Ibid, 178.

524. ^ Ibid, 84.

525. " Penney, *View,* 32.

526. ^ Ibid, 32.

527. ^ Penney, *Lines,* 193.

528. ^ Penney, *Golden Rule,* 59.

529. ^ Ibid, 55-56.
530. ^ Penney, *View,* 78.
531. ^ Penney, *Lines,* 108.
532. ^ Ingham, *Biographical Dictionary,* 1071.
533. ^ Matthew 11:28-29 (KJV).
534. ^ Penney, *Lines,* 104.
535. ^ Penney, *Golden Rule,* 155.
536. ^ Penney, *Lines,* 132.
537. ^ Penney, *Golden Rule,* 154.
538. ^ Penney, *Golden Rule,* 151 & Gammon, *Faith,* 95 & Penney, *Lines,* 123.
539. ^ Penney, *Lines,* 104 & 191.
540. ^ Ibid, 94.
541. ^ 1 Samuel 22:2 (GW).
542. ^ 1 Samuel 25:10b-11a (CEV).
543. ^ 1 Samuel 25:13 (CEV).
544. ^ 1 Samuel 25:14-17a (MSG).
545. ^ 1 Samuel 25:18-19 (MSG).
546. ^ 1 Samuel 25:23-24a (MSG).
547. ^ 1 Samuel 25:34b (GNT).
548. ^ 1 Samuel 25:38-39 (GNT).
549. ^ 1 Corinthians 9:7-10 (GNT).
550. ^ James 5:4 (CEV).
551. ^ Hebrews 6:10 (GNT).
552. ^ Ford and Crowther, *My Life & Work,* Chapter 8.
553. ^ Irving, *Master of Money,* 115.
554. ^ Trimble, *Inside Story,* 35.
555. ^ Walton and Huey, *Made in America,* 18.
556. ^ Ibid, 24.
557. ^ Ibid, 728.
558. ^ Walton and Huey, *Made in America,* 35.
559. ^ Trimble, *Inside Story,* 78.
560. ^ Walton and Huey, *Made in America,* 10.
561. ^ Walton, *Made in America,* 40 & Trimble, *Inside Story,* 75.
562. ^ Klepper, *Wealthy 100,* 66 & Ingham, *Business Leaders,* 732.
563. ^ Walton and Huey, *Made in America,* 171.
564. ^ Luke 5:4b (NLV).
565. ^ Luke 5:5b (NLV).
566. ^ Ecclesiastes 11:1 (ERV).
567. ^ Washington, et al. *Timeless Treasures,* Kindle Location 994.

568.   ^ Wilson and Kerr, *Half Luck and Half Brains,* VI. & O'Halloran, PhD. "Kemmons Wilson: An American Original." & Hogan, "20 Steps for Success."

569.   ^ Wilson and Kerr, *Half Luck and Half Brains,* 9 & 12.

570.   ^ Ibid, 28.

571.   ^ Ibid, 32.

572.   ^ Ibid, 39.

573.   ^ Johnson and Roark, *Together We Build,* 52.

574.   ^ Johnson and Roark, *Together We Build,* 61 & Roland Gammon, *Faith,* 173.

575.   ^ Johnson and Roark, *Together We Build,* 55.

576.   ^ Ibid, 62-63.

577.   ^ Ibid, 76.

578.   ^ Johnson and Roark, *Together We Build,* 152 & Wilson, *Half Luck and Half Brains,* 60.

579.   ^ Wilson and Kerr, *Half Luck and Half Brains,* 67.

580.   ^ Ibid, 70.

581.   ^ Johnson and Roark, *Together We Build,* 102 & Wilson, *Half Luck and Half Brains,* 98.

582.   ^ Johnson and Roark, *Together We Build,* 99 & Wilson, *Half Luck and Half Brains,* 120.

583.   ^ Weathers, Ed. "The Last Tycoon."

584.   ^ Wilson and Kerr, *Half Luck and Half Brains,* VII.

585.   ^ Proverbs 27:17 (CEV).

586.   ^ Ecclesiastes 4:8 (GW).

587.   ^ Psalm 68:6a (GW).

588.   ^ Ecclesiastes 4:10 (CEV).

589.   ^ Proverbs 13:20 (ERV).

590.   ^ Irving, *Master,* 78.

591.   ^ Walton and Huey, *Made in America,* 28-29.

592.   ^ Ingham and Feldman, *American Business Leaders,* 11.

593.   ^ Ash, *Mary Kay,* 26 & Ingham and Feldman, *American Business Leaders,* 11 & Kreydatus, "Enriching Women's Lives," 22.

594.   ^ Gross, *Forbes Greatest,* 240 & Ingham and Feldman, *American Business Leaders,* 11.

595.   ^ Ash, *Mary Kay,* 7 & Shook, *Heart & Soul,* 15.

596.   ^ Ash, *Mary Kay,* 106.

597.   ^ Shook, *Heart & Soul,* 19.

598.   ^ Ash, *Mary Kay,* 51 & Farrel, Pam. *Becoming a Brave New Woman.* Eugene, Or.: Harvest House Publishers, 2012. 116.

599.   ^ Ash, *Mary Kay,* 192.

600.   ^ Exodus 18:22b-23a (GNT).

601.   ^ Proverbs 31:15 (GNT).

602.   ^ Johnson and Roark, *Together We Build*, 109.

603.   ^ Chernow, *Titan*, 177.

604.   ^ Sanders, Harland. *Incredible Colonel*, 9 & Margaret Sanders, *Colonel's Secret*, 5.

605.   ^ Sanders, Harland. *Incredible Colonel*, 37 & Margaret Sanders, *Colonel's Secret*, 25-26 & Pearce, *The Colonel*, 30.

606.   ^ Sanders, Harland. *Incredible Colonel*, 47, & Margaret Sanders, *Colonel's Secret*, 55, & Pearce, *The Colonel*, 40-41.

607.   ^ Sanders, Margaret. *Colonel's Secret*, 55.

608.   ^ Sanders, Harland. *Incredible Colonel*, 55.

609.   ^ Ibid, 91.

610.   ^ Sanders, Margaret. *Colonel's Secret*, 212.

611.   ^ Pearce, *The Colonel*, 107.

612.   ^ Ibid, 100.

613.   ^ Sanders, Margaret. *Colonel's Secret*, 280.

614.   ^ Ibid, 326.

615.   ^ Sanders, Harland. *Incredible Colonel*, 143.

616.   ^ Colossians 3:24b (CEV).

617.   ^ Proverbs 21:25 (ERV).

618.   ^ Wilson and Kerr, *Half Luck and Half Brains*, VI & Hogan, *"20 Steps for Success."* & Robert O'Halloran PhD. *"Kemmons Wilson: American Original,"* 6.

619.   ^ NY Times, *Wealthiest*, November 4, 1917.

620.   ^ Wright, *Early History of the Airplane*, Kindle Location 7.

621.   ^ Kelly, *Wright Brothers*, 25.

622.   ^ Crouch, *Bishop's Boys*, 109 & Wright et al., *Miracle at Kitty Hawk*, 8-9.

623.   ^ Miller, *Reminiscences*, 2-3 & 72.

624.   ^ Miller, *Reminiscences*, 4.

625.   ^ Crouch, *Bishop's Boys*, 125.

626.   ^ "Flight Forebears" & Wright et al., *Papers*, 100 & 103.

627.   ^ "Flight Forbears" & Wilbur Wright, *Story of Flight*, 52

628.   ^ English, Dave. "Quotations on Airplanes, Flying and Being A Pilot." Great Aviation Quotes. www.skygod.com. Web. & Johnny Charles Stark, *From Poverty to Silvered Wings of Flight* ([Heber Springs, AR]: J.C. Stark, 2002), pg. #93. & *Four Miles South of Kitty Hawk...* (New York City: Warren McArthur, 1943), pg. #10.

629.   ^ Wright et al., *Papers*, 313.

630. ^ Kelly, *Wright Brothers,* 84.

631. ^ Wilbur Wright, *Story of Flight,* 62 & Wright, *Story of the Aeroplane,* 6.

632. ^ Wright et al., *Papers,* 148.

633. ^ Ibid, 493.

634. ^ Kelly, *Wright Brothers,* 90.

635. ^ Wright et al., *Papers,* 493 & 495.

636. ^ Renstrom, Chronology, 14.

637. ^ Renstrom, Chronology, 18.

638. ^ Kelly, *Wright Brothers,* 142.

639. ^ 1 John 4:1 (NLT).

640. ^ Acts 17:11b (GNT).

641. ^ Ephesians 4:14b (ERV).

642. ^ Colossians 2:8 (NOG).

643. ^ Proverbs 23:4 (KJV).

644. ^ 2Timothy 3:2b (NLT)

645. ^ Exodus 20:17 (KJV).

646. ^ Hebrews 13:5 (BSB).

647. ^ Exodus 18:21 (KJV).

648. ^ 1 Timothy 3:3 (KJV).

649. ^ Matthew 6:24 (ERV).

650. ^ Luke 12:31 (CEV).

651. ^ Deuteronomy 8:12-14b (MSG).

652. ^ Proverbs 1:32b (KJV).

653. ^ Joshua 24:15b (ERV).

654. ^ John 19:28b (GNT).

655. ^ 1 Timothy 6:17 (GW).

656. ^ Acts 24:26b (ERV).

657. ^ Acts 28:30 (ERV).

658. ^ 2 Timothy 1:13 (CEV).

659. ^ Luke 8:3b (ERV).

660. ^ Mark 10:17b (GNT).

661. ^ Mark 10:18 (GNT).

662. ^ Matthew 19:17b (CEB).

663. ^ Mark 10:21b (ERV).

664. ^ Mark 10:22-23 (GNT).

665. ^ Mark 10:26 (KJV).

666. ^ Mark 10:24b-25 (KJV).

667. ^ Matt 10:26a (KJV).

668. ^ Mark 10:27b (KJV).

669. ^ Mark 10:29b (KJV).

670. ^ Mark 10:30b (KJV).

671. ^ Clarke, *Life*, 102 & Fox, *Acts & Monuments*, 545.

672. ^ Walton and Huey, *Made in America*, 46, 249.

673. ^ Chernow, *Titan*, 54 & Flynn, *God's Gold*, 401 & Klepper, *Wealthy 100*, 4.

674. ^ Chernow, *Titan*, 32 & Tarbell, *History of Standard Oil*, 40.

675. ^ Chernow, *Titan*, Page 33 & Flynn, *God's Gold*, 46.

676. ^ Rockefeller, John. *Random Reminiscences*, 15.

677. ^ Ibid, 19.

678. ^ Ibid, 17.

679. ^ Klepper, *Wealthy 100*, 4.

680. ^ Flynn, *God's Gold*, 201.

681. ^ Rockefeller, John. *Random Reminiscences*, 25.

682. ^ Flynn, *God's Gold*, 152.

683. ^ Ibid, 162.

684. ^ Rockefeller, David. *Memoirs*, 6.

685. ^ Forbes, *Making America*, 299.

686. ^ Forbes, *Making America*, 302.

687. ^ Brown, *Study*, 108 & Chernow, *Titan*, 19, & *NY Times*, 10-20-1907.

688. ^ Tarbell, "Character Study." 391.

689. ^ Chernow, *Titan*, 153 & Flynn, *God's Gold*, 401.

690. ^ Klepper, *Wealthy*, 7.

691. ^ Carey, *American Inventors*, 312 & Chernow, *Titan*, 675 & Klepper, *Wealthy*, 6.

692. ^ Luke 12:15b (BSB).

693. ^ Colossians 3:5b (CEV).

694. ^ Mark 8: 36 (KJV).

695. ^ Proverbs 28:6 (ESV).

696. ^ Mark 4:18-19 (KJV).

697. ^ Proverbs 11:28 (KJV).

698. ^ Mark 16:15b (KJV).

699. ^ Ecclesiastes 9:16b (KJV).

700. ^ Psalm 132:15a (KJV).

701. ^ 2 Corinthians 9:8 (GNT).

702. ^ Matthew 6:31 (GNT) & Matthew 6:32-33 (ESV).

703. ^ Proverbs 10:15b (KJV).

704. ^ Psalm 35:27b (AMP).

705. ^ Luke 12:48 (KJV).

706. ^ Psalm 23:1 (GW).

707. ^ Hebrews 6:12b (GNT).

708. ^ 1John 5:4b (KJV).

709. ^ Deuteronomy 8:2b (CEB).

710.   ^ Deuteronomy 8:7, 9. (CEB).

711.   ^ 2 Corinthians 4:17 (NOG).

712.   ^ Psalms 66:12b (KJV).

713.   ^ 3 John 2 (KJV).

714.   ^ Newton, *Uncommon Friends,* 7.

715.   ^ LeTourneau & Lorimer, *God Runs My Business,* 174.

716.   ^ Rains, *Pujols the Great,* 13-14.

717.   ^ Ibid, 17.

718.   ^ Rains, *Pujols the Great,* 32 and Wojciechowski, *"Cardinals Can't Let Pujols Fly."*

719.   ^ Rains, *Pujols the Great,* 59 & Abrams, *Albert Pujols,* 78.

720.   ^ Lamb, *More Than the Game,* 17, & Watson, *"Pujols Isn't Sure Fans Learned From Josh Hancock, & "Bryan Burwell Article,"* Gateway Redbirds.

721.   ^ Lamb, *More Than The Game,* 179.

722.   ^ Stark, *"Cardinals Complete Impossible Dream."*

723.   ^ Leach, *"Pujol's 3 Home Runs Answer Critics."*

724.   ^ DiGiovanna, *"The Angel As Guardian."* & "60 Minutes Profiles Pujols' Charitable Endeavors." & 60 Minutes Interview with Bob Simon & Pujols, Albert. "Giving Back Means Everything."

725.   ^ Pujols, Albert. *My Testimony,* Web.

726.   ^ Luke 17:21b (GNT).

727.   ^ Philippians 2:13 (NLT).

728.   ^ Galatians 5:16a-17b (NLT).

729.   ^ Romans 12:6-8 (NLT).

730.   ^ 2 Kings 4:2b (ERV).

731.   ^ 2 Peter 1:3b (CEV).

732.   ^ Matthew 7:7 (KJV).

733.   ^ Ecclesiastes 9:10a (NLV).

734.   ^ 2 Timothy 2:3 (KJV).

735.   ^ Luke 19:13b (KJV).

736.   ^ Revelation 3:11 (CEV).

737.   ^ Ash, *Mary Kay,* XV & Ash, *Mary Kay, You Can Have It All,* 9.

738.   ^ Penney, Lines, 107.

739.   ^ Blehm, *Fearless,* 67 & "Tribute to Adam Brown."

740.   ^ "Tribute to Adam Brown."

741.   ^ "Tribute to Adam Brown." & "Overcoming Adversity" 4.

742.   ^ "Dynamic and Destructive." 8.

743.   ^ Ibid.

744.   ^ Blehm, *Fearless,* 74.

745.   ^ Blehm, *Fearless,* 172, & "Kelley Brown." & "Tribute to Adam Brown."

746. ^ Blehm, *Fearless,* 190 & "Tribute to Adam Brown."

747. ^ "Tribute to Adam Brown."

748. ^ Blehm, *Fearless,* 227 & "Tribute to Adam Brown."

749. ^ Blehm, *Fearless,* 222 & "Tribute to Adam Brown."

750. ^ Bronstein, "The Man Who Killed Osama Bin Laden... Is Screwed."

751. ^ Schlesing, "Fallen SEAL Died a Hero, Mourners Told."

752. ^ Isaiah 55:6a (NASB)

753. ^ John 10:28 (GW).

754. ^ Matthew 25:23b (KJV).

755. ^ Kraft, "Pattern For Prosperity," *New Guideposts,* 188.

756. ^ Johnson, *Abraham Lincoln the Christian,* 136-142.

757. ^ Parks, *Quiet Strength,* 18.

758. ^ Ellis, *Tyndale,* 90.

759. ^ Penney, *Lines,* 59.

760. ^ Everts, *William Colgate,* 263.

761. ^ Day, *Christian in Big Business,* 294.

762. ^ Vories, *Mustard Seed,* 41.

763. ^ Holt, *Chautauquan,* 461-462.

764. ^ Clark, *Talks With the Flowers,* 21, 25-26.

765. ^ Heinz, *Henry J. Heinz,* 18.

766. ^ Chernow, *Titan,* 55.

767. ^ "1979 Colonel Sanders Interview."

768. ^ Stjernstrom, *The Joy of Accomplishment,* 94.

769. ^ Firestone, Harvey Samuel, and Samuel Crowther. *Men and Rubber; the Story of Business,* 237.

770. ^ Wyckoff, *Hair-care Millionaire,* 28 & Bundles, *On Her Own Ground,* 153.

771. ^ Walton and Huey, *Made in America,* 249. & www.walmart.com.

772. ^ Wilson and Kerr, *Half Luck and Half Brains,* VI. & O'Halloran, "Kemmons Wilson: An American Original." & Hogan, Dr. John. "20 Steps for Success."

773. ^ Howard, *Wilbur and Orville,* 270 & Wright et al, *Miracle at Kitty Hawk,* 270.

774. ^ Wright, et al. *Miracle at Kitty Hawk,* 92.

775. ^ Johnson and Roark, *Together We Build,* 194.

776. ^ Washington, *Timeless Treasures,* Kindle Location 1557.

777. ^ Snavely, *Intimate Story,* 477.

778. ^ Irving, *Master of Money,* 110.

779. ^ Schmidt, *"Life After Being a Sister Wife."*

780. ^ Spencer, "All We Knew Was Polygamy," Part 2.

781. ^ Federer, *America's God and Country,* 445.

782. ^ Federer, *America's God and Country*, 594. (Note: Mark Twain was not a Christian. This quote is included because its too funny!)

783. ^ Johnson, *Abraham Lincoln the Christian*, 165.

784. ^ Ash, *Mary Kay*, 60 & Shook, *Heart & Soul*, 18.

785. ^ Albert Pujols, "A Message of Faith."

786. ^ "Dynamic and Destructive," 8.

787. ^ Kraft, "Pattern For Prosperity," *New Guideposts*, 188 & "Pattern for Prosperity." *St. Petersburg Times*, February 16, 1951.

788. ^ Scherder, "Memorial Service Honors Navy SEAL in Green Forest."

789. ^ Blehm, *Fearless*, 210, & "The Navy SEALS' Dying Words."

790. ^ Blehm, "The Navy SEALS' Dying Words."

791. ^ Carroll News, "Senior Chief Thomas Arthur Ratzlaff-Special Warfare Operator." & Duke, "I Wouldn't Wish This on Anyone." & Mathews, "Green Forest SEAL" & Reilly and Wiltrout, "Walks of Life."

792. ^ Mathews, "Green Forest SEAL".

About The Author

Rebekah Brewster is a professional writer who loves making words come alive on the page. She is a California girl with a Midwestern heart. Her hobbies are reading lots of books, cooking, and hiking. She loves this country and all those who sacrifice for it. She also cares deeply about her readers. If you enjoyed the book, please leave a good review on the website where purchased.

Rebekah also wrote Christians That Fought Slavery and Troublemakers. If you would like Rebekah to speak at your church, email her at info@quietbeauty.org. Quietbeauty Publishing is a salute to the introverts of the world. The silent professionals who seamlessly get things done behind the scenes with our quiet personalities. We are quiet because we are creative.

www.ingramcontent.com/pod-product-compliance
Lightning Source LLC
Chambersburg PA
CBHW020428130626
46549CB00001B/42